A Walk to the Sea

Ray Moody

Rockumentarypress

Copyright © 2020 Ray Moody

All rights reserved.

ISBN: 9798612448013

CONTENTS

1	A Walk to the Sea	1
2	Stepping Out	5
3	On the Buses	15
4	The Gallows Droop	23
5	London Town	31
6	Outbound to St Bees	41
7	To the Lighthouse	47
8	First Man Out	63
9	Flat Lands	69
10	Walking Upwards, Tilting Backwards	75
11	Walking Downwards, Tilting forwards	85
12	Ennerdale Midge	93
13	Once Bitten	105
14	Calming Waters	111
15	Black Sail	123
16	The Tarn with No Name	127
17	Berthed in Borrowdale	139
18	Talking Italian	153
19	Far from Easy in Easedale	157
20	A Warning for the Hasty	169

21	The Lion and the Lamb	179
22	Why does it always Rain on Me.	191
23	Pouring in Patterdale	199
24	As I walked out one misty morning	211
25	Wondrous Place	227
26	Watching the Detectives	239
27	The Wild man of the Moors	251
28	A Place for Licking wounds	269
29	Nine Standards Jig	279
30	The Witches of Keld	291
31	Down by the River	297
32	The Lead Mines of Swaledale	307
33	We Tea'ed on the Lawn	321
34	Blue Remembered Hills	339
35	The Start of the Trouble	349
36	Our Path is blocked by a Cello	357
37	The Lion on Blakey Ridge	369
38	Glaisdale Rigg is a Joy to Tread	377
39	Deliverance	387
40	Aftermath	399

Dedicated to Graham Santos and the boys of 1971

Nine Standards Rigg

Chapter 1 - A Walk to The Sea

I guess there must have always been something there. That call from the wild. I think I first became aware of it at the age of fourteen, when I discovered that a safe place to hide away from the school bullies at lunchtime was in the library.

Sitting one day aimlessly flicking my way through a gazetteer of Great Britain, I was suddenly struck by a black-and-white photograph of a sinister looking mountainous ridge. Its distinctive shape was dramatically outlined against a dark, foreboding sky. The caption underneath it read, 'Mallerstang Edge, bordering the Yorkshire Dales.'

Apart from day trips to the seaside, I had never left my hometown of Hull. So, had I been asked to point them out on a map, had no real idea where the Yorkshire Dales were, even though I actually lived in East Yorkshire.

But there was something mesmerizing about the photograph. It captured a view of a savage wilderness, a lonely, frighteningly desolate place that existed miles away from anywhere. A place that was rained on, snowed on, and the wind howled around its every crevice and boulder, whilst the rest of the world, living in towns and cities, and seemingly oblivious to it, were busy getting on with their everyday lives.

I was born and bred a city boy, used to the noise

of constant road traffic; bright streetlights shining in through net curtained windows and a regular flow of shouting drunks making their way home from the pub on an evening. So, despite being captivated by the photograph, there was no possibility at the time that I would ever have contemplated exploring the Great Outdoors, especially as it would also have meant sleeping in a tent.

Tents back then didn't come with the luxury of a sewn in groundsheet. So, hikers were more likely than not to have to share their night under canvas with the ubiquitous earwig, a bunch of shiny black rain beetles, or a whole host of other such horn'ned beasts.

Not that I would have been able to afford to buy any, but there was also very little in the way of specially designed, fashionable walking gear. The market for it had yet to be created. Backpacks were haversacks, usually khaki coloured army surplus with brass ends on the straps, leftovers from the Second World War. Cagoules didn't exist, and the whole idea of waterproof and breathable fabrics was only just beginning to be thought of, in that oh, so revolutionary decade, the Swingin' Sixties.

The closest you could get to wearing specialist outdoor clothing back then was to either don a lightweight zip up the front jacket called a windcheater. Or, for the real rambling enthusiast, there was the pull over the head anorak with a pouch pocket across the chest, as worn and sported by British Army Commandos. Neither of these garments were fully waterproof, so you also needed to carry a yellow cycle cape or a black plastic Mac to wear in particularly bad weather.

Walking boots too were prone to letting in the wet, even after giving them several coats of dubbing, and the only design choice you had was whether they came in brown or black leather.

Nevertheless, attired in this lot, with your army surplus haversack slung across your back containing a canvas tent and its wooden poles, a methylated spirit burning stove, a billycan or two, various tins of Campbell's soup and a bottle of Camp Coffee, you could stagger off into the wilderness of the moors and dales whistling 'The Happy Wanderer'. Lightweight, like breathable fabrics, had yet to be invented.

Even Master Fell-Wanderer, Alfred Wainwright, during his sixty years of tramps in the Lakes and Dales, is said to have simply donned one of his old tweed jackets and a pair of heavy-duty shoes for his explorations of the fells.

Perhaps the only real bonus for the hiker wishing to explore the Great Outdoors back then was that it was before the savage Beeching rail cuts of the 1960s. And you could still catch a train to almost anywhere in Britain. Hikers could step out of a dusty railway carriage at some sleepy branch line station in the middle of nowhere and start their walk.

As I moved into my later teenage years, the photograph of Mallerstang Edge was put to the back of my mind as I spent my time in pursuit of rock music and girls, girls and rock music, and not always in that order.

The Walker's statue on the corner of the road down to Moor Row, the place where I once met a friendly Liverpool policeman.

Chapter 2 - Stepping Out

Fast forward a few years. I'm now twenty-three and a student at Teacher Training College. There's a notice on the Common Room wall, the Student's Union is organizing a 40-mile-long trek across the North York Moors. The walk has a sinister name, it's called the Lyke Wake Walk, and the challenge is that it must be completed within 24 hours. The carrot is that, on its completion, all successful participants will receive a small black and silver coffin-shaped badge to enable them to show off their steel. I want to show off my steel, I'm interested, I'm intrigued, and I want one of those badges.

Student gossip has it that the walk follows a rough and sometimes barely discernable path across wild, untamed, bog-ridden parts of the North York Moors. At that time, the last local wilderness.

It's claimed that the trail to be followed was once trodden by cowled monks, who in total silence carried their dead in rough-hewn coffins to some far-off burial ground. The final clincher for me is that the walk will start at midnight. I'm a night person; I never go to bed before dawn. So, I eagerly sign up for the trip.

A few weeks later, I spend the hours before the off sitting in a pair of borrowed boots on a bench in a village pub, drinking intoxicating lager. The likely effect of this on my walking, and on the rest of the party of students walking, is blatantly obvious. Sadly, I realize this fact too late. Several hours later, in the pitch black, as I stumble my way along a rough moorland path through knee-deep heather, I'm beginning to realize that this prelude in the pub is clearly some means of sedating the walk's participants for what lies ahead.

I've belatedly discovered that once out here amidst the vast open spaces of the North York Moors, there is no turning back. Firstly, because there are so few roads crossing the moors that you could escape on. And secondly, because nobody would be able to show you the way back, as very few people actually know it. Equally, hardly anyone, apart from a couple of walk leaders, know the way forward, as few students have bothered to bring along a torch, a compass, and a map. So, we're stuck with these guys for the duration of the walk. But back then, I wasn't just intoxicated by the lager, but by the sheer indestructibility and arrogance of youth.

Unfortunately, by the time we arrive at our first stopping point, my semi-intoxicated state, and even my youthful state, have long since worn off. Like all male students after a few drinks, I want to go to bed. And if not sharing it with someone, then closing my eyes and giving it some seriously big Z's. I really don't feel like walking a step further.

As I lay spent, I console myself by roughly estimating that we must have already completed about two-thirds of the walk. So at least there's not much further to go. Then some Job's comforter in an anorak lets slip that despite my best efforts, we have only just covered five miles.

'Five miles!'

The guy's either deranged or has simply got it wrong. Perhaps I have been a bit optimistic, but surely, we must have completed twenty miles by now.

I query this fact with one of the walk leaders. Finding great difficulty in hiding his amusement, the walk leader claims that the Anorak is correct; we have indeed only just walked five miles.

'Five miles!'

I'm incredulous. If this is so, then I can't even begin to get my head around the figure of the thirty-five miles remaining. How is it humanly possible to cover such a distance when the feet in my borrowed boots tell me that they feel as though they've already done more than enough walking? It's simply ludicrous!

Like a sulky child, I seriously contemplate giving up. But this would mean spending the rest of the day on the backup refreshment coach and having to keep making flaky excuses to fellow students about an ankle or a knee going. It would also entail having to hang about with that group of people who are dishing out the refreshments. Most of whom claim that they would have loved to be doing the walk, but unfortunately, due to this, that, or the other, they can't. And anyway, they've done this or some other similar walk before. Those same people, who as they serve us with food and drink and witness our anxiety, seem to grin at us malevolently.

Then, I remember the badge, that tiny silver and black, coffin-shaped badge. It shines out in my mind like a beacon of hope. Eventually, like Lazarus, I slowly rise from the ground and continue onwards.

Thirty miles later, I'm laid flat-out on the moorland heather, begging for mercy, to be released from this torment. Please forgive me, for whatever it is I've done in my life to deserve this, whatever it was, I promise I will never ever do it again.

I lay staring up at the sky, that vast open sky above me. In the City, I've never seen such a sky as this.

I've walked through the night and watched it turn into day and now the day is slowly turning back into night, but still, we walk on. I've endured the burning heat of a sweltering June sun with nowhere to hide amidst the heather from its blazing rays, and I've felt the clinging damp as I've walked through a wilderness night.

I'm suffering from sleep deprivation and my body is begging me to stop. But the wide-open spaces of the North York Moors won't let me. Like that brook, they just go on and on, seemingly forever.

There's no escape. I'm trapped in a self-imposed nightmare, walking in agony on plates of heel to toe blisters.

Unbeknown to me, my feet have also become creased and corrugated from water that got into my boots many hours before and has had no way to escape. The so-called experts in our party warned us, early on, not to take our boots off. Because of our swelling feet, they claimed we might not be able to get them back on again. I've taken them literally at their word and haven't dared to do so.

What has made the walk even worse for me is that I recently decided to give up smoking. And in a moment of utter madness, thought that the North York Moors would be the ideal place to do it. I've been outdone by my own cunning. Out here amidst the heather, there are no stores where you can buy cigarettes. So, I knew that I would have no option but to endure cold turkey, as I haven't brought any along with me. Well, at least not real ones. As a safeguard, I did visit a local Health Food store and bought a packet of nicotine-free herbal cigarettes. These go by the dubious brand name of Honey Rose. But far from tasting of honey, or smelling like roses, they both smell and taste like a garden bonfire. In attempting to smoke one whilst coming here on the coach, a senior member of staff sternly informed me that on our return, I would be reported to the principal. The guy believed that I was blatantly sitting there smoking a joint. My offer to let him have a draw, as a way of proving that I wasn't, did little to reassure him.

So, for the past fifteen hours, I've been walking on an endless moorland highway, suffering from both sleep deprivation and the effects of nicotine withdrawal. My tongue hangs loose from my mouth as I stagger forward like a bent old man of eighty. I've become a zombie in a timeless state of being. My legs move with no instructions from my brain. I'm on autopilot and the engine could cease at any moment.

Just as I'm about to lose all hope, there on the far horizon, I can see the faintest view of a television antenna glinting in the rays of the setting sun. We've been told to watch out for this as it signals the end of the walk. It uplifts me and, like a wounded hero, I slowly, but more purposely, limp towards it. The nightmare is nearly over. I've been thrown a lifeline.

Closer and closer the television mast comes. Maybe, just maybe, if I continue to stumble my way forward in my zombie-like state, despite the desperate pain in my feet, I might just make it.

But then there is a final sting in the tail as a huge cleft suddenly opens up in the earth before me. I later learn that it's the high and narrow ravine of Jugger Howe. Collapsing down, I lay prostrate on the heather, almost weeping at the sight of it. I really should have read up on this walk. I can't face, or even contemplate, the terrible descent down, and the relatively worse climb back up the other side of the chasm, before the last stretch of moorland leading to the television mast.

I'm almost hysterical at the thought of it. I can't put my body through anymore and lay staring up at the sky, that vast open sky above me. As I gaze up, I can see that the light is beginning to fade from it and know that I can't lie there forever and must at least make it to the road to be picked up. Unfortunately, this too is on the other side of this huge cleft in the earth.

After about twenty minutes, I somehow find the courage to drag my weary frame up. Then, at a pace of half a step at a time, slowly and awkwardly descend to the bottom of the ravine. Then, even more slowly, stagger my way back up the other side.

After this, everything becomes a blur. I cross a road and then totter on what seems like an endless uphill highway of peat towards the television mast.

My eyes no longer focus and look neither right nor left. With my head down, my eyes concentrate on the boggy track beneath me. My body is in total shock and in imminent danger of closing down, as my wobbly legs stagger left and right, left and right.

Then, after what has seemed an eternity, almost unable to look up to believe it, the television mast stands before me like some huge steel giant.

Knowing that there is only the North Sea beyond it, I sink down on the earth below it and lay motionless. A sacrifice at the feet of this iron God.

Forty miles across the North York Moors in one day are at an end, but I don't know if I'll ever be able to stand again. Every part of my body aches and elicits pain. My feet feel pulverized and raw. I lay with the cool evening breeze blowing over me as twilight begins to shroud the moor.

Eventually, seeking relief, I'm able at last to manipulate my legs sufficiently to enable me to slowly and almost surgically remove my boots. The feeling of sheer ecstasy I experience as they fall to the ground is indescribable. Then, I carefully peel away my sagging socks, which have become glued to my feet with the blood and puss that has flowed from so many broken blisters. Puffed up with pain, as they emerge into the daylight, my feet appear raw and swollen to almost twice their size. Skin hangs loose from open wounds where the tops of blisters have been torn away, and they weep with no skin to protect them. Water, which has spent nearly seventeen hours trapped in my boots, has corrugated the soles of my feet.

With my socks off, the evening air cools them and a strange tingling feeling close to ecstasy prevails. I lay there, one over-heated, exhausted mess, watching the darkening sky as night draws on. As I do so, I swear to God, myself and anyone else around me who cares to listen, that never again in my life will I indulge myself in such a ridiculous, masochistic pastime.

A Walk to the Sea

It takes weeks for my feet to recover, for the open wounds to heal and the broken skin to dry and fall off and for new skin to start to re-grow. As the pain and tingling slowly subside, there are flashbacks to the walk. And I often wince for a moment at the thought of them.

But free from the walk, in those dark moments, my brain plays tricks with me, making out that despite the pain, there was actually something out there on those moors that I enjoyed.

I laugh at the notion and shake my head in disbelief. But the thought persists. I have no idea what it was, but eventually have to admit to myself that perhaps on reflection, there was something, in spite of the anguish and the pain, about being out there in the vast open spaces of the North York Moors that I was at one with.

Somewhere remote in my brain they call to me. I once again shake my head, both in disbelief and in an attempt to ignore it. But the thought won't go away. In future days, when in my student flat I play the Pink Floyd album 'Meddle' on my record player and listen to the track 'Echoes', just as though I've been hypnotized, I'm momentarily transported back to those moors. Somehow in that music I can hear the sounds, and sense that strange stillness that was out there. The moors are beckoning, the moors are calling, the moors are waiting.

Leon at the former campsite near Clay Bank Top

Chapter 3 – On the Buses

After leaving Teacher Training College, true to life, I use my new qualifications to gain employment as a conductor on the buses in the Yorkshire city of Leeds. I spend my time working six days a week to a 24-hour clock. The job is almost run along military lines, and management style is quite authoritarian. The strange thing is that the company allows staff to have a walking club. Once a year, it organizes a long-distance walk for charity, and management willingly arranges for staff to change their shifts to enable them to take part.

It has now been several years since my last excursion out there in the Great Outdoors, and my memory has paled a little. So, I submit to, and experience for the first time, the wildness of the Yorkshire Dales in the shape of the Three Peaks of Penyghent, Whernside, and Ingleborough. The walk is tiring and still painful, especially in cheap boots. But I'm beginning to think, that perhaps despite the pain there is something, which I can't quite put my finger on, about these adventures out there in the wide-open spaces of the moors and dales that does attract me.

The club organizes a further walk in the wilds of Yorkshire the following year, and although longer, it seems easier and inspires me. Rather than wait a further twelve months for the next walk, I decide to organize one for myself.

In-between collecting fares on the Roundhay Road, I read a book about one of our National Trails, the Pennine Way, Britain's first officially recognized long-distance walk. It starts from Edale in Derbyshire and finishes at Kirk Yetholm on the Scottish border. It usually takes at least two weeks to complete the whole walk. Unfortunately, due to work commitments; I calculate that I can only manage three days.

So, I select what the book claims are some of the highlights of the walk. The stretch from Middleton-in-Teesdale to the hamlet of Dufton, followed by climbing the highest section of the Pennine Way, the walk up and over Cross Fell to the village of Alston.

Unlike Alfred Wainwright, the greatest lone walker of them all, I'm still very much afraid of the Great Outdoors and wouldn't dream of going out there alone. So, I plan to take with me my future wife Pauline and my long-time friend Santos.

On the surface, Santos appears to be a much fitter and physically well-built specimen than myself. As soon as I mention the walk to him, he regales us with tales of his six months of army training and the endless route marches he endured before his eventual demobilization for continuously going absent without leave. Nevertheless, this does suggest that he's no stranger to the Great Outdoors and should know how to equip himself for our adventure.

When the day of the walk arrives, Santos turns up

A Walk to the Sea

for our three-day trek wearing a pair of bright red shorts and a skimpy tee-shirt. He carries his provisions, a packet of crisps and a couple of chocolate bars, in a flimsy plastic shopping bag.

The plan, which the three of us have discussed for several weeks and agreed to, is to arrive early in the County Durham village of Middleton-in-Teesdale and park the car. We'll then pull on our boots and set off, following the trail of the Pennine Way to the village of Dufton. Here, at the end of our first day's walking, we'll find bed-and-breakfast accommodation. The next day, we'll climb over Cross Fell and after arriving down in the village of Alston, will once again enjoy an overnight stay. The following morning, we'll hitchhike our way back to Middleton-in-Teesdale, where we've left the car. Our itinerary would appear to be foolproof.

Santos, being the only one of us with a licence, drives us to Middleton. We arrive there early and park the car. The first stage of the plan is complete. Now all we have to do is to pull on our boots, tighten our boot laces, get our few things together and begin our walk to Dufton.

Sadly, Santos appears to have other ideas.

"Look, there's no sense in us rushing off, let's stay here and start the walk fresh in the morning!"

It's 10 am, the sun is shining and there's still plenty left of the day. So, I suggest to him that delaying the walk will endanger our already very restricted three-day schedule. But Santos is confident that with luck with the hitching, we can still do it, even if we take today out. I'm not so sure that we can and don't want to alter our plans and hang about Middleton-in-Teesdale all day. Then Santos reminds us that whilst we were resting in the car during our journey here, he has had a strenuous ninety-minute drive. Not wanting to upset the crew after receiving a nod from Pauline, I reluctantly agree to his proposal.

Santos's next suggestion is that we should scour the village looking for suitable bed-and-breakfast accommodation. We're young, we're poor, and Pauline and I have so far lived our life on a budget and have never been able to afford to stay in a bed-and-breakfast establishment. Santos, on the other hand, according to Santos, has lived his life in the fast lane. He's stayed at many and regularly regales us with tales of how he's used to living the high life and how hanging about with us often reverts to slumming.

So, we follow our Man-of-the-World's lead. For Santos, scouring appears to entail knocking on the door of the first house that you come to.

"Thud, thud, thud," he gives the door a good, hefty knock.

From inside the house, we can hear the sound of slow, ponderous footsteps coming down what must be a very long hallway. Eventually, the door is reached, and after the undoing of numerous locks and bolts, it slowly opens, and an old man appears in the doorway. As he does so, the three of us, as one, let out an involuntary gasp and take a step backwards.

We're staring at the sight of a poor fellow, closer to ninety than eighty, whose countenance shows clearly visible signs of him having recently suffered a stroke, the effects of which appear to have pulled his mouth up the side of his face. A silence falls on our party, during which we stare at the man whilst he stares insanely back at us.

Santos breaks the silence.

"We, we want a room." He stammers, in his best 'man of the world' voice.

A further period of silence follows, during which the man, who doesn't appear to have understood, continues to stare blankly at us.

"We want a room!" repeats Santos.

Showing great effort in using his voice, the man echoes what Santos has just said to him.

"You, you want a room?" he says tremulously.

"Yes, we want a room," practically bellows Santos, displaying signs of his growing impatience.

No further words are uttered. The man totters to the side, and using his one good arm, beckons us into his abode. We don't want to go in. But it would be far too embarrassing to turn away. So reluctantly and nervously, we enter.

We're young, naïve, and have never seen or

experienced the effects of a stroke. Therefore, as the door closes behind us, we can be forgiven for wondering whether the man is mad. Has he really understood what we want? I also selfishly give thought to more practical matters, such as how is he going to be able to make our breakfast when he only appears to possess one working arm?

Our fears, however, aren't realized, and that night we're not murdered in our beds. The following morning, we bid the man and his wife, the cook and bed-maker, who had been absent during our arrival, farewell, and set off for the village of Dufton.

A pleasant sunny morning is spent meandering beside the silvery river Tees as we pass by a series of dramatic waterfalls. Eventually, after crossing over an isolated metal bridge, the environment almost immediately becomes much more austere.

Continuing to follow the river as it flows through the silent ravine of Falcon Clints, we climb up alongside the tumultuous waterfall of Cauldron Snout. By now, the sun has gone in; the sky has turned grey, and it's begun to drizzle.

Since the early part of the day, we've felt increasingly isolated. There seems to be nobody else out here. We're three lonely figures walking across a timeless landscape that more and more appears like an unexplored wilderness. With limited map reading and compass skills, each of us is silently keeping our nerve that we're heading towards the next small pocket of civilization, a remote Northumbrian farmstead.

Water pours over rocks in silent streams that most of humankind will never, ever see or experience. This is untamed territory. Surely prehistoric man and woman must have once bent down here to drink that flowing water. The scene can't have changed in thousands of years.

It comes as a great relief to us when we arrive at a farm in the middle of nowhere, where at its gate it advertises that it sells teas. As we stop for refreshments, it feels good to hear another human voice again. The farmer's wife is very welcoming and sits and talks with us while we drink our tea.

Many years later, when we were actually walking on the Pennine Way, we stopped off here at this same farm. During our conversation with the farmer's wife, I vaguely recollected that when they were shooting one of his televised walking series, Alfred Wainwright had visited several farms in the area for refreshments.

"Did Wainwright come here for tea when he was filming his television series?" I enquire.

"Why aye, he did love," the woman recollects, but then her face grows severe.

"But I had to ask him to leave."

I almost gulp on my tea, asked Wainwright to leave. I'm finding this very difficult to believe. That seemingly gentle giant of a man, our hero, getting thrown out.

"Whatever for?" I ask,

"Well, he kept swearing, and I had my children in the house."

Wainwright swearing! This is even more incredulous.

"What on earth did he say?" I ask in total disbelief. The farmer's wife lowers her voice.

"Well, during his conversation, he kept using the word frigging, and when I asked him to stop, he wouldn't. He said, "I've been frigging since 1908 missus, and I'm not going to stop now!"

So, I had to ask him to leave.

The illustrious Santos and Moody

Chapter 4 – The Gallows Droop

With our tea finished, we reluctantly depart from the safety and warmth of the farmhouse. The inclement weather has set in for the day, making it feel cold and dismal.

After finding our way across a narrow, icy flowing stream, we begin to walk over an inhospitable, boggy moorland plateau. In the bleak, wet landscape, we're feeling even more isolated and alone. With no landmarks to guide us, we have to trust to our limited map reading and compass skills that we're heading in the right direction.

It's now late afternoon, and mist floats above the surface of the moor. The gloomy weather has meant that even though it's only four o'clock, the sky is growing dark.

Exhausted, we finally arrive at, and almost fall into, the vast canyon of High Cup Nick. The mist swirls and parts at the very moment we reach its rim, and we only just stop ourselves from tumbling down into its gaping void.

Even under a leaden sky, the scene is spectacular. This is one of those special places that everyone should see, even if just once, in their lifetime. This huge natural amphitheater cut into the earth, stretches off towards the Lakeland fells.

Like three Ancient Britons, we stand on its rocky lip and gaze in at it in awe. The silent chasm falls dramatically away at our feet, and in the swirling mist, it seems as though we're the only souls left alive in the world.

There has been a chill in the air since the drizzle began several hours ago, and the mist cloaks everything around us even more thickly. Santos now sports bright red lobster legs, which almost match his, often complained about chaffing shorts. His plastic shopping bag has become limp and droops down at his side. Despite its awesomeness, we daren't therefore linger here for too long, and after five minutes, set off again. After a further hour of hobbling along the side of the huge chasm, a farm road brings us out into the village of Dufton.

Having walked for twenty miles, we're all tired, and Santos, being so scantily clad, has particularly felt the effects of the day. His thoughts have also turned elsewhere, and he has an ache in his loins for his latest girlfriend back in Leeds. For him, another day of feeling cold, wet and weary, holds no attraction whatsoever. And the idea of further walking has paled a little, if not a lot. Combined with this, the possibility of a night of passion weighs heavy.

As we pass through the village of Dufton under a rapidly darkening sky, we catch glimpses of tomorrow's walk, including the distinctively pointed Dufton Pike and the rise of Knock Fell, both of which look high and spectacular.

Even though we don't have to climb Dufton Pike,

this appears to provide the final decider for Santos. He attempts to convince us of the fruitlessness of carrying on. And suggests that he doesn't want to spoil the rest of the walk for us. So if we want to continue, he might just return to Middleton-in-Teesdale on his own.

Despite his noble gesture, this would leave us having to hitch a ride all the way back to Leeds, as he will be taking his car with him. Not wanting abandoning, and with us also feeling wet, tired and weary, Pauline and I are tempted into retirement, and we curtail the walk.

Rather than search for bed-and-breakfast accommodation in Dufton, we now have the problem of getting back to Middleton-in-Teesdale where we started out from this morning and where we've left the car. The village is twenty miles away, the same distance we've just walked today, and we can hardly go back the way we came.

Even if we had the cab fare, which we don't, out here in the Sticks, there's no way we could catch a taxi. We therefore have no alternative but to follow the country lanes all the way back to Middleton, and hope, rather than believe, Santos's optimistic view about the possibility of us being able to hitch a lift somewhere along the way.

The problem is that we'll be walking on narrow B roads, little used by anyone other than local farmers. It's also growing dark, and so we're unlikely to be seen.

Along with the thought of walking a further twenty miles, we have the added worry of having to pass the 'Trees.'

During our time in Middleton-in-Teesdale and in various conversations throughout the walk, Santos, who has read a whole library of pulp fiction on witchcraft and the occult, has never stopped telling us about a certain wooded copse. It's believed to stand on the site of an old burial mound alongside the road, about a mile out of Middleton. The trees bear some dire name, like the 'Gallows Droop', and it's claimed, in the literature that Santos has read, that if you pass them at exactly the witching hour of midnight, then the Devil will appear to claim your soul. What this amounts to, roughly speaking, is that your end will be nigh. Which, according to the legend, will take the form of being found hanging from one of the trees in the morning. Several travellers have apparently been discovered in this way over the centuries.

When this information had become a topic of conversation in broad daylight, we had all laughed about it and I had made a mental note never to pass these particular trees at midnight. I mean, who in their right mind would.

But circumstances change and here we are, beginning a twenty-mile journey back to Middleton-in-Teesdale. We'll be walking down empty, narrow country lanes, which will culminate in us having to pass the dreaded trees.

Worst of all, making a rough calculation on my watch, it suggests that unless we're able to get a lift, we'll have an estimated arrival time at the trees sometime around the witching hour.

Our return journey begins. After road walking a few miles from Dufton, we stop off at a fish and chip shop, which luckily, we find open in the nearby village of Brough. This appears to be the last outpost of civilization before Middleton. After this, despite Santos's optimism, not one car passes by us, and not another human soul do we meet along the way. As we stroll down the back roads to Middleton, night draws on, growing blacker and blacker.

Being born a natural coward, something I've found I'm particularly good at, I slip easily into my role. Having a very vivid imagination, I begin to count the miles left to passing the dreaded trees. Our journey back began at five-thirty, so I roughly estimate that with easy walking on country lanes at, say, three miles per hour, we're more than likely to pass the trees sometime around midnight. We've already walked 20 miles today and so can't go any faster and can only go slower.

I consider the possibility that perhaps Santos's literature has got it wrong. The trees probably don't even exist and the tale is likely to be a load of old nonsense that some local 'Woolly backs' have thought up. Sadly, this does little to appease my fertile imagination. Santos is a true believer in such things and is clearly worried. Pauline is more grounded but open to the possibility.

Mile after mile we tramp, each one adding to the twenty we've already covered during the day. Closer and closer, we're getting to Middleton and the place by the road where the trees are claimed to stand. With just over a mile to go, I'm constantly checking my watch and can see that it's nearly midnight.

A full moon looms up high above us, owls hoot and the scene is set. Silence has now fallen on our party. In each of our heads, we're planning our strategies. Should we take to our heels as we approach the trees? Or, if something does manifest itself, should we try to barter our way out of the situation? By, in my case, offering Santos as a sacrifice. After all, he's the one who got us into this mess.

Less than a mile to go, all three of us are completely exhausted. Having now walked for nearly forty miles, should the worst happen, there will be little chance of us being able to run for it.

Not a word has been spoken for many minutes. Despite no one mentioning it, we're all inwardly quaking, and had been talking gibberish, desperately trying to speak about anything but the trees.

Suddenly, an arc of bright white light illuminates the total darkness all around us. I grow faint. Is this it, the prelude to the Devil's appearance? Santos's face quivers. His jaw looks like it's moving, but no words are coming out. For a moment, he takes up a stance, as though he's opting for the running option. But his legs won't allow him to move.

An instantly recognizable sound now reaches our ears. Instinctively, through years of experience of standing on motorway slip roads, up go our thumbs. A car brakes and comes to a halt beside us.

'Middleton?' says a boy racer from the open window of his vehicle.

He could have said Timbuktu; we would still have clambered in. The car doors slam shut behind us, and the young dude whisks us away. Sanctuary, sanctuary, we're safe.

A few moments later, the car catches a very distinctive-looking clump of trees in its headlights. Standing on a raised, ancient burial mound, they tower high above us. As we pass beneath them, the shadows of the trees' wide, outstretched, sinister looking branches reach down towards us, like the legs of a huge spider. As they do so, the three of us, as one, cower down in our seats.

The tower of Shap Abbey

Chapter 5 - London Town

Then it all goes quiet for a while. Pauline and I are now thirty-something's living in the big city of London. We've almost forgotten about walking, unless it's on the sometimes-baking hot streets of the capital. But one night I read in the TV section of the Evening Standard that the Lakeland author, Alfred Wainwright, has created a walk across England. The latter part of which passes through Lyke Wake Walk country, the 40-mile-long trek over the North York moors I did back in my student days.

I'm now quite nostalgic about it. The memories have dimmed, the wounds have healed, and it has become a defining moment in time capturing my youth.

The four-part televised weekly series begins this evening, and even though the section of the walk I want to see won't be shown until the final week, I decide to give it a look.

So, I sit and reluctantly half-watch the programme, wishing that this was already week four, as I'm sure that the rest of the walk will mean absolutely nothing to me. But after only a few minutes viewing, I'm drawn in, as Wainwright enthralls me.

Thereafter, week by week, I watch the remaining episodes. Finally, on week four, there it is, views of the walking trails I followed all those years ago on the North York Moors.

The scenes cover almost half of the Lyke Wake Walk, and there on the screen is the instigator of that walk, of that instrument of torture from my youth, Bill Cowley, and he's meeting Alfred Wainwright, two giants of moor and fell walking brought together. What an insight some television producer must have had.

As the program ends, I'm enthused. The call from the wild is beckoning me once more.

Not really expecting a positive response, I casually say to Pauline, who has also been enjoying the programs.

"Why don't we do this end section of the Coast-to-Coast walk, it'll rekindle memories of my student days when I tramped across the North York Moors on the Lyke Wake Walk."

Pauline understands how that walk affected me, as I've mentioned it often over the years. It's now late evening, and she's enjoyed a bottle of wine. Suitably happy, she utters the fateful words.

"Why don't we do it all?"

With those words, our great adventure begins.

The very next day, before she has had time to reflect, I take the Tube from Hendon Central down into London and visit a bookshop on the Tottenham Court Road. There I purchase a copy of the coffee-table sized book, 'Wainwright's Coast-to-Coast walk', and begin to plan our journey.

A Walk to the Sea

I devour the book, and Pauline, with little prompting, devours it after me. We live and breathe every word, purr at every photograph, and then set about preparing for our walk to the sea.

Apart from those few walking excursions earlier in our lives, we're both still relatively new to the Great Outdoors. I've never walked in the Lakes and have only had a couple of limited treks in the Dales and that one walk on the North York Moors. Also, as there is no way we can afford to spend more than a night in emergency bed-and-breakfast accommodation, we'll have to backpack the walk, carrying our tent and belongings all the way.

We're new to backpacking and so will have to purchase all of the necessary equipment, including a backpack and everything that goes in it.

Wainwright suggests that the Coast-to-Coast walk will take a fortnight to complete, so we must prepare for it.

I realize that the first and most important item we require is a backpack. Getting the right one for the rest of our stuff to go into would appear to be essential.

There is an Outdoor Sports store on the Kilburn High Road, close to where I work, and I go there every lunchtime to view the vast range of tents, sleeping bags and backpacks for sale. After saving money from my salary for a couple of months, I finally visit the place to actually buy something.

Naively, I'm looking for the biggest backpack I can get. The bigger the better as the more I can carry. So, I head straight for the stand displaying the 85 Litre backpacks or 'sacks' as I've discovered that the walking fraternity calls them.

Unfortunately, when I check the price tags and count my money, I can't afford one. I'm ten pounds short. The biggest and best-looking backpack I can afford is a 65-Litre Karrimor, and I did so much want to look professional. But keen to get our equipment together, I buy it.

Months later, I would appreciate that being five foot, six inches tall, I had bought exactly the right size of sack and would soon discover the bigger your backpack, the more you're likely to cram into it.

During the next few months, Pauline and I continue to read and reread our Coast-to-Coast book. We hang on Wainwright's words and his classic expressions and immerse ourselves in each of the book's dramatic photographs.

We've decided to undertake the walk in August, during my college vacation. As the date nears, I return to the bookshop and purchase a copy of Wainwright's pocket-sized walking guide, 'A Coast-to-Coast Walk'. We both then read this from cover to cover and do so many times. It makes for such good reading, even better than the larger book.

A few years later, we would trek the Pennine Way just to be able to read and use another walking guide

A Walk to the Sea

written by Alfred Wainwright.

When reading through our guidebook, I try to identify places where Wainwright suggests that the going might get tough and consider possible escape routes. Pauline picks up on Wainwright's thoughts such as those referring to Haystacks, the Lakeland fell where he suggests that if you get lost on it, you should kneel down and pray for deliverance. Pauline takes this quite literally.

Personally, I seek out the word 'bog'. Having sunk up to my waist in one all those years ago on the North York Moors, I've been affected by it ever since. So much so that I insist on taking a 'bog rope' along with us on the Coast-to-Coast walk. Wainwright's guide suggests that peat bogs will feature in a couple of places on the route. We're likely to come across them in the Lakes when climbing over to Far Easedale and when crossing over the Pennines. There would therefore appear to be at least two locations where it might be required.

Beyond his descriptions of the trek, Wainwright's writing at times read almost like poetry. I memorize several of his thought-provoking phrases and sayings so that I can repeat them again on route. One of my favourites is, "Glaisdale Rigg is a joy to tread!" and I can't wait to utter the words in situ whilst out there on our adventure.

The weeks pass and the summer vacation looms. By now we've also bought a brightly coloured 25

Litre backpack for Pauline, a two-man ridge tent and a couple of very thin and cheap sleep mats.

Living in a one room rented flat in London and paying for our son to attend a private school back in Hull means that we're continually on a budget.

I purchase a pair of 'Trekking' boots for twenty-five-pounds. These sport luminous yellow laces and are being marketed as a must for Boy Scouts. They come with the bonus of having a range of animal footprints carved on their soles. Should a Pine Marten pass our way, I'll be able to identify its tracks. Pauline buys an even cheaper pair of thin brown fell boots.

Not having sufficient funds to afford to purchase Cagoules, we hunt in our home for any kind of waterproof garments and find a couple of ancient plastic jackets.

As an emergency backup, I'm also taking along two large, black bin liners. If the weather turns treacherous, and it becomes necessary, the plan is to quickly cut out some head and arm holes into these and to don them. They're only to be worn in a heavy downpour and hopefully, when no one else is around to see it.

Pauline's backpack doesn't seem to have much padding under the straps. I come up with the brilliant idea of taking two small square washing-up sponges along with us so that she can put them under the shoulder straps to help to ease the weight of her sack.

The idea is so ingenious and so cheap that I'm surprised nobody else has thought of it.

We've searched our house for thick socks and found about five pairs between us. Most of these have been inherited from Pauline's father and are extra-large.

In terms of sleeping, I've checked the weight of both single and double sleeping bags and I'm contemplating whether carrying a double might weigh less than us both carrying a single. It would also mean that I can be responsible for it, taking some of the load off Pauline.

A double sleeping bag does appear to weigh marginally less than two singles in the price range we can afford, so I purchase one. I also naively believe that the two of us sharing might make us warmer and cosier on an evening.

With just a week to go, we suddenly discover that we can't get our twelve-year-old son looked after while we're away, so he'll have to come with us. Frantically searching around for some gear for him, we purchase a single sleeping bag. But he'll have to do the walk wearing trainers, and his stuff will need to be shared between our two backpacks.

The start of the walk is nearly upon us, just another couple of days, and we'll be setting off. We're both getting excited, and when we buy our rail tickets to St Bees in advance, our adventure is becoming more and more of a reality.

Unfortunately, the day before we're due to set off, Pauline walks into a lamppost and is concussed, as she nearly fractures her skull. We're on tenterhooks. After months of planning, we may have to call the whole walk off. But Pauline is stoic as usual, and despite an aching head, we spend the evening filling our backpacks.

Even though I have Wainwright's walking guide, I'm also taking along our large pictorial Coast-to-Coast book. I believe that it will be exciting to look at photographs of the places we'll be visiting the night before we actually see them.

Pauline has packed plenty of smart clothes to wear on an evening in the village pubs. She's also carrying several pairs of her favourite stiletto heeled shoes. I'm taking along a pair of binoculars, so that we can view the way ahead when we're in the 'High Places', that terrific name given to the Lakeland fells. We'll also be able to use them to look from fell to fell for other walkers, to confirm that we're still on route.

After long remembering sinking into a peat bog on the Lyke Wake Walk, I've found a lengthy piece of cord that can be used as a bog rope if either of us sinks into the mire.

Having got my hands on a guide to packing our backpacks from a walking magazine, I follow the instructions; Tent stood upright with the sleeping bag wedged beside it, next the dry clothes bag, then the food bag, followed by the plates and pans. In a nutshell, the heaviest stuff at the top of the sack, lighter stuff at the bottom. I cram the plastic plates down the front of the sack and put the gas canisters in one side pocket and the plastic cups, a jar of coffee, and the tent pegs in the other.

With our sacks packed and our boots on, we do circuits of the living room, parading one after the other. On our front room carpet, it doesn't seem at all bad and I'm convinced that the long flat metal rods built into the back of my sack will be taking most of the weight.

Apart from one or two places on route, we don't know where we'll be able to buy gas for our stove, so I'm carrying three canisters. I'm also taking along fourteen clean tee-shirts, one for each day of the walk.

The night is like Christmas. Our bloated sacks stand side by side like two sentries waiting for the dawn, and we can hardly sleep.

The start of Ennerdale Water

Room for one more inside. the dreaded Tent

Chapter 6 - Outbound to St Bees

The day of the walk dawns at last, and after boarding three different trains, we finally arrive at the quaint Cumbrian seaside village of St Bees.

On the way, we've visited the shops in Carlisle city centre to purchase a hat to keep the sun off my head during the walk. Despite my overflowing backpack, I've discovered that I've left mine at home. Ideally, I'm looking for something in white with a wide brim, like the floppy hat I wore back in my youth. This is my chance to become that pseudo-hippie again. To be the free spirit that I once was.

The only wide-brimmed white hat I can find has a jaunty coloured headband around its crown, which has a large feather stuck in it. Admiring myself in the mirror, I try to project the carefree image of the long-haired youth that once attended Britain's Woodstock, the infamous 1970 Isle of Wight Rock Festival, aka Jimi Hendrix's Last Stand. In reality, I look like some kind of dealer at a horse fair. But hey, what the hell, I buy it.

Our final train departs, leaving us standing with our backpacks on the platform of the sleepy railway station at St Bees. Looking around, we might have just stepped back in time and arrived by steam engine at this maroon painted, 19th century station. Red, sand-filled fire buckets hang off the wall in exactly the same position they would have hung a hundred years ago.

This is it then, after months of preparation, we're on the cusp of starting our Great Adventure. Standing on the empty platform taking in our surroundings, only the sound of summer birds and distant voices can be heard amidst this unchanging scene.

Our plan, or to be more honest, my plan, is to experience everything we've read about in Wainwright's coffee-table book of the walk.

We begin by visiting the ruddy-coloured sandstone church of St Bega. Inside, amongst the dark shadows of this ancient building, we view an interesting display of historical artifacts.

Leaving the church, we cross the road to see the buildings of St Bees public school and its playing fields. Walking down the high street, we look in at each of the village's quaint pubs. There seems to have been only a limited attempt at cashing in on the walk. One pub proclaims a Wainwright Bar and displays a picture of the great man himself smoking his pipe. But this would appear to be about as good as it gets.

The village lies peaceful in the afternoon sunshine. There is a quietness about the place, a stillness. St Bees looks as though it closed down on the outbreak of World War II, and nobody bothered to tell it to reopen.

After a fruitless search for camping at Stonehouse Farm, where we'd planned to stay, we leave the main street and follow the road around to the seafront, where we've read there is another campsite. As we walk down a sleepy country lane, seabirds wail in the sky high above us and we can see St Bees Head gradually appearing in the distance. I'm heartened that it looks exactly as it does in the photograph in our coffee-table Wainwright. Our feet move on quickly towards it.

Just then, driving along the lane appears a boy racer with a carload of young dudes. As they pass by, they stare out from their vehicle. Seeing us laden down by our backpacks, the sight of my brand new gleaming white sun hat, with its jaunty headband containing a large feather, is too much for them, and they can't resist.

In unison, they shout, "Gipsy!"

As their car speeds off down the lane, I guess that my plumage must have excited them. But this incident tells me that it doesn't matter where you are, in town or country, city or village; there are always 'New Shits to be found on every block', almost everywhere.

We find the other campsite on the seafront. It's not the one we were intending to stay at, but an old-fashioned commercial site, featuring a field of jaded green-coloured caravans which are parked inside a wire-fenced perimeter.

After searching in vain for the owner to tell us where to put our tent and to fix the price, we unshackle ourselves from our backpacks and begin to empty them.

As I pull our sleeping bag out of my sack and other items emerge, everything is clean and dry and smells of home. How long it will stay this way, I can only guess.

Being on a tight budget, I'm keen to get the financial side of the business out of the way. I want to know how much it costs to camp here so that I can keep a check on what we'll have left to spend.

When calculating the expenses for the trip, I've gone for the worst-case scenario and budgeted for a maximum charge of ten pounds per person, per night for camping. This means that every time we find a cheaper campsite, it will leave spare money in our pot.

Being born a Yorkshire man from Hull, I've already made a rough judgement of what we should be charged for our pitch based on the state of the campsite and its facilities.

Visiting the shower block, we discover it to be awash and most of the toilets dirty. All the signs point to the place being cleaned in the morning. This is of little use to people like us, walkers just spending the night here, who will be moving off soon after first light, probably before any cleaning takes place.

The site owner continues not to show, and so we pitch the tent. After cooking our evening meal, we relax, enjoying the experience of being camped so close to St Bees Head.

Sitting on one of our cheap sleep mats outside the tent, the three of us watch as the foaming waves of the Irish Sea flow in and out. Whatever the cost of camping, the situation of the campsite provides an excellent prelude to the walk. As the sun slowly sets, we continue to stare out across the promenade, over the sand and the breakwaters as it gradually drops down behind St Bees Head.

Deciding at last to turn in, we're about to experience living in our tent for the first time. Leon quickly settles into his sleeping bag, and I unroll ours beside him. Pauline climbs in first and I rather awkwardly join her, having the job of pulling up the zip. There isn't much room, and fastening the bag fully is impossible. We'll have to sleep with the zip halfway down.

As the sky darkens, the three of us, wedged together like sardines, and surrounded by the contents of our backpacks, lay listening to the surging of the sea as it rolls lazily in and out. Despite Pauline and I being cramped back-to-back, the sound of the waves washing the shoreline is soothing. It excites and promises good things to come.

High above the Grisedale Valley on St Sunday Crag

Chapter 7 - To the Lighthouse

The sound of coughing outside our tent awakens us to a bright Cumbrian morning. Pauline pops her head out to deal with the campsite owner, who stands there and demands far too excessive camping fees for what we've received on his pitch.

We telephoned a few campsites before setting off and most seem to charge between five and ten pounds for each person, sharing a tent. Yet here is a man requesting eleven pounds each for camping on a worn-out piece of grass and for using an ablutions block, which last night left a lot to be desired. That he has now come to clean the place is of little use to us.

Pauline pays the man, but I'm hoping that I've budgeted accurately for the trip. If the camping fees across England are as expensive as this, then we'll be on a tight budget.

Fortunately, we discover later that the fees charged here were at the time the costliest along the whole route.

Despite its spectacular position so close to the sea, we wouldn't use this site again for many years. Eventually, new ownership took over. The place was much improved and the welcome a lot more friendly. The camping field also changed, and because of its raised location, now has wonderful views on an evening over the lit-up village of St Bees.

Having spent just one night under canvas, we're already belatedly realizing that buying a ridge tent wasn't such a good idea. The tent is too narrow, especially for three of us, and with the sloping roof there's little headroom unless we sit exactly in the middle. It also means that throughout the walk, if we're not all laying down flat, two of us will always have to sit behind the other, blocking out any views. Such as when we're cooking.

On future walks, we would stay at Stonehouse Farm in the centre of the village. Looking back, I find it difficult to imagine how on that first walk we missed it. Stonehouse Farm always provides a nice, clean, calm, and comfortable start to the walk. Camping on a landscaped lawn surrounded by the trappings of a working farm with dogs, cats, and horses moving about spoils you for the rest of the journey.

One of the friendly old farm dogs, Moss, once joined us on the Coast-to-Coast walk. He followed us one morning as we left the yard. We got the impression that being a wise old dog, he must have wondered where all the walkers who stayed there disappeared off to and followed a couple to see. He came with us as far as the village of Sandwith. And he would have gone further had we not telephoned the farmer to come and collect him. Whenever we camped at the farm after this, and Moss saw us, he always had a wistful look in his eyes, as though

A Walk to the Sea

remembering the day he accompanied us on the Coast-to-Coast walk.

The moment has finally arrived. After all the weeks and months of preparation and expectation, the Irish Sea now lies within touching distance, awaiting our baptism.

We breakfast on tinned beans and rubbery vegetarian sausages, a luxury we bought in Carlisle. Putting on our walking gear, the tent's taken down, our sacks are packed, and we're ready for the off.

Just like we did back at home, I've once again filled my sack according to the instructions gleaned from a walking magazine.

It explained how you should always fill your backpack with the heaviest stuff at the top and the lighter stuff at the bottom. The tent and the poles went in first and stood upright. Then, with difficulty, I wedged the double-sleeping bag alongside it, followed by the clothes bag on top of it, then the food bag and finally the plastic plates and the pans. I've stretched a side pocket to fit in the gas stove with the canister attached to it. Until it's empty, the canister can't be removed. This makes it a very awkward item to pack. I can already see that the stretching is causing the stitching around the zip to pull away from the pocket.

Twenty years later, the standard backpacking stove is tiny and the gas canister screws on and off as you need it. So, now the two things can be packed away separately. The stove attachment folds up like a tripod into a tiny plastic box and will sit anywhere in your backpack, allowing the canister to fit neatly into your side-pocket.

Sadly, today, once the gas canister has been pierced, it needs to remain attached to the stove. This makes it a difficult shape to fit into the backpack. As the trip progresses, I'll also find it a challenge to fit a new canister without losing half the gas.

With our sacks packed, we heave them up onto our shoulders. Both of us stagger forward for a moment with the momentum of having this sudden weight on our backs. Once steadied, we leave the confines of the campsite and reach the promenade. After walking along it for a few yards, we find a concrete slipway and follow it down onto the beach.

In the far distance, the sea looks wild and a long way out. Bending down, the three of us each pick up a pebble off the seashore. Tradition says that we should carry it with us cross England to Robin Hood's Bay, where we will hopefully throw it into the North Sea. Continuing our journey across the sand to dip our feet in the Irish Sea, its waves can only just be seen on the horizon, about half a mile away.

On and on we walk, leaving our footprints forever etched into the wet St Bees sand. We're now well-beyond the promontory of St Bees Head, and the sand is becoming softer and wetter, and we're

A Walk to the Sea

beginning to get that sinking feeling. The sea looks angry and is roaring at us. Is it an omen to turn back? The first waves finally lap over our boots, nearly filling them. We've had our baptism and been christened; our initiation is complete, and our walk to the North Sea has begun.

Turning our backs on the frothing foam, I once again tighten the straps of my backpack. Our sacks are already ominously weighing heavy, and I hitch mine up as high as it will go. I'm hoping that this technique will help to lift some of the weight off my shoulders.

I'm slowly beginning to realize that the backpack doesn't take all the weight. It's a misapprehension I've been under even before purchasing it.

Pauline's soft fell boots have let in seawater, and from bitter experience I advise her to take them off to get rid of it.

Retracing our footprints, we reach the promenade. Leaving the sand behind, we set off down it towards the high rounded cliff top of St Bees Head.

It's now nine-thirty in the morning, and small clusters of hesitant people are gathered along the promenade. Some are following in our footsteps and making their way down onto the sand to initiate themselves into the walk.

Sounds of jocular laughter and confident voices fill the air as final farewells are said to family and friends.

Most of the individuals here are about to start the Coast-to-Coast walk. But seem keen to linger, to savour and prolong these first moments that they've planned for, for so long.

For some of them, it might have all begun with a copy of Alfred Wainwright's classic guidebook, 'A Coast-to-Coast Walk', given to them last Christmas. Perhaps others, like us, became hooked after seeing his television series.

For a few, it's possibly the culmination of a working life, a coda to their existence, something that they'd always planned to do once time allowed. Now that time has come.

Spread out along the crowded promenade are young students, groups of twenty/thirty-something males, groups of older males, pensioners, males on their own, females on their own, couples made up of a boy and a girl, two girls or two boys, whole families of mum, dad, and the kids, and they all seem geared up for the walk.

Dutch, German and North American voices can be heard amongst the English.

The one thing all these people have in common is that they've come to this remote village on the edge of Cumbria to start this walk.

Today, it seems to be particularly busy, possibly because it's the weekend, the height of summer and the schools have just closed. Several of these small groups, like us, are looking around them, perhaps puzzled or even shocked that so many others have had the same idea as themselves in deciding to undertake this walk across England. I muse that if all these people were to set off at once, there would be an absolute stampede up St Bees Head.

At the end of the promenade, a wooden fingerpost points to the cliff side and a dry muddy path etches its way up it. This is our first climb, our initial test. I'm excited. Will we be up to it, especially with all the weight we're carrying on our backs?

Several of the walkers we've passed along the promenade are also sporting brand-new, spotless backpacks. This suggests that there are perhaps others who are beginners to backpacking and the concept of long-distance walking. I wonder just how many of them, like me, are still suffering from the delusion that their backpack will be doing most of the carrying for them, taking the weight off their bodies.

Up the sloping, rutted path ascending St Bees Head, we climb. Twisting and turning several times, we arrive breathless at a rounded hillock which, for a moment, breaks the ascent. Standing with our hands on our hips, we greedily gulp in the air. Despite only being about halfway up the cliff side, we've already gained significant height and now look down on St Bees.

The village and the caravan site are spread out below us like the picture in our coffee table Coast-to-Coast book. In the far distance, we can see the smoking chimneys of the Nuclear Power station at Sellafield.

As we stand waiting for our breath to return, I can feel that the middle of my back is already wet with perspiration from my exertions. Pulling on my backpack straps, I once again hitch up my sack. It really is weighing heavy.

Two German girls, who are both carrying identical bright orange backpacks, arrive breathless at the hillock and rest a short distance away from us. They also have their hands on their hips. Their packs are enormous and look as heavy as ours. Despite this being the only path up St Bees Head, the girls have their maps out, as though they're already wishing to confirm the route.

With our breath back, we continue on up the cliff and finally reach the top of the initial climb. The views below us are now even more dramatic. After another short rest, we begin to follow a steadily rising path along the crest of the cliff.

Walkers are spread out in front and behind us like in some race. One walker appears to still have his wife and children with him. Perhaps they'll come along for the first few miles of the journey, giving him support and encouragement. Maybe they wish they could be doing it with him, but because of family commitments, can't.

Seagulls wail high above our heads, and far below us, the Irish Sea now looks almost tranquil as a fishing boat chugs slowly by. The path continues to rise and I'm fast starting to believe that there's no longer such a thing as flat earth.

The effect of a warm morning sun, and continually ascending with the weight of our sacks on our backs, means that we're already feeling exhausted. Our faces are red, and mine is covered in perspiration. Despite the path being easy to follow, this is hard work.

After what has seemed like an eternity of traversing the cliff top, a white-painted Coast Guard Lookout station appears on the horizon. This is a longed for landmark we've been hoping to see.

A hundred yards further on, the magnificent sight of St Bees lighthouse also comes into view. Arriving there will be the first real sign that we've completed at least a tiny part of the Coast-to-Coast walk.

Alfred Wainwright famously once stood in front of the lighthouse and looked out to sea. We'll soon be standing in the footsteps of the Master Fell-Wanderer.

The path is finally levelling out and even beginning to descend. As it drops further and further down, I'm coming to the awful realization that before we can reach the lighthouse, we must lose all of the height we've just spent the last hour sweating and straining to gain. Even more alarmingly, it means that we'll have to win it all back again. As the path descends ever more steeply down towards Fleswick

Bay, I feel as though we've wasted all the effort we've so far made.

I want to experience every inch of this walk and poor loyal Pauline and Leon follow me. Rather than continuing along it, we must leave the main path and visit Fleswick Bay, not because it looks an exciting place to explore, a cutting between the cliff sides, but because Alfred Wainwright once came here.

At the bottom of the path, we arrive at a great gash in St Bees Head. Leaving behind the main route, we make our way down through a narrow, high-sided ravine and follow it to the sea.

As we get closer to the shoreline, the smell of decaying seaweed fills the air. We're walking over a pavement of slime-covered rocks.

On reaching a strip of sandy beach, the reek of the rotting vegetation is almost overpowering. But we can see that someone has pitched a small tent on a nearby green coated slab of rock. It looks as though they wild camped here last night. I wonder how they could have possibly stood that awful, nauseating stench.

Despite the unbearable smell, as Walt Disney might have once said, 'We've found ourselves a cove!' An enchanting place where the surf gently laps up against a tiny stretch of golden sand. Just as we did back on the beach at St Bees, we once again dip our feet in the Irish Sea as though further confirming that we've started the walk.

A Walk to the Sea

With spectacular high cliffs behind us, the scene could be the sandy beach of a desert island, where the waves roll lazily in and out all day as they wash the shoreline smooth. The smell of the seaweed, however, is too much and there's still a lot of walking ahead of us. We leave the sand and climb back up the ravine.

On returning to the main path, we pass through a kissing gate and begin a long, steep, diagonal climb up the cliff side as we attempt to regain all of the height we've just lost.

As the path slopes its way up towards the cliff top, the weight of my backpack drags me backwards, the steeper it becomes. Sweat begins to pour even more profusely down my spine. With the sheer physical effort involved, we're forced to stop and rest for a moment every twenty yards or so and stand and enjoy the views down into Fleswick Bay.

Eventually, we arrive back on the top of the cliff at the same height we were at previously. Looking behind us, we can see walkers on the other side of the ravine, slowly making their way down towards Fleswick Bay.

Resuming our journey, the cliff continues to rise, but the lighthouse and the lookout station are getting closer and are now only about a quarter of a mile away. We follow the trail as it steadily climbs towards them.

Thoroughly exhausted, we finally arrive at the

white-painted St Bees lighthouse. The walking has taken its toll, the climb over the cliff-top and the descent into Fleswick Bay have drained us. We've completed just two miles of the Coast-to-Coast walk, and yet I feel all in. My backpack has betrayed me. I seem to have been doing all the carrying.

I thought that the modern backpack was designed to lift the weight off your body. If so, then mine has failed spectacularly, and I feel disillusioned.

Standing once again with our hands on our hips, the three of us deeply draw in the air. Then, as though freeing myself from a parachute, I unclip my backpack. It falls off me at speed, rushing towards the earth like a meteorite from outer space.

My tee-shirt's soaked with sweat all the way down my spine and has stuck to my back. I stare across at Pauline. She looks all in.

Despite her sack being smaller than mine, she has also overfilled it and now, like me, is paying the price. It's far too heavy, and her face is pale from the effort of carrying it.

It has slowly dawned on me that perhaps bringing along Wainwright's coffee table sized Coast-to-Coast book, the binoculars and fourteen changes of tee-shirt, might not have been such a good idea. But it's too late now to do anything about it.

I can see that Pauline is also having doubts about lugging her stiletto-heeled shoes for the pub on an evening. Something that she insisted on bringing.

Even Leon, who is carrying nothing, looks red from his exertions.

Each of us greedily gulps down water from our drinks bottles to try to stem the heat coming from our bodies.

Then, for the first of many times, I unstick my wet tee-shirt from my back to let the air flow freely around it.

I'm also feeling guilty about carrying several other extra items, including the tins of spaghetti and rice pudding, which I bought from the village store in St Bees. They too might possibly have been a mistake.

Just two miles of the walk have been completed and yet we're absolutely exhausted, almost out on our feet. Surely, the cliff top can't carry on rising.

Pauline and I both need to jettison some weight from our backpacks. Should we throw our excess baggage down into the Irish Sea? I know that if the terrain for the rest of the walk continues like this, then with the loads we're both carrying, we can't possibly keep going and might even have to give up.

I feel like an overloaded packhorse and I'm sure that Pauline does, too. We've done no training for the walk and considered that we should be able to ease ourselves into it. We're at a moment of crisis.

I imagine what Santos would say if he were here with us right now.

"Look guys, I'll tell you what, why don't you wait

here with the backpacks while I nip back into St Bees and get the car. I'm sure there must be a road to the lighthouse, and I can pick you up from there."

His face fades from my thoughts as a party of Coast-to-Coast walkers, who are hardly breaking a sweat, pass by. We try to hide our sheer fatigue by smiling fixedly at them.

"Yes, we're really enjoying it, just taking a breather, trying to establish whether that's Ireland or the Isle of Man over there."

A walker in his mid-fifties passes by us. He stops a little way off and stands and waits for the rest of his party to catch up. They appear to be already dropping behind. We find out later that his group are rumoured to be four senior detectives from Scotland Yard who have been brought together on some kind of team building exercise.

Another couple of walkers come into view, a middle-aged man, and his spouse. The man's sack is so large and distended that he appears to be wearing a wardrobe on his back. Alongside him, his wife, who is carrying nothing, practically beams at him.

"Look how strong my lovely husband is!" her face seems to say.

He smiles back at her. His sack is enormous, it's a well-stretched 85-Litre. Either the weight is killing him, or he's been pumping iron for the past year. Perhaps it's the price he has to pay for getting her to come with him on such a strenuous holiday.

A Walk to the Sea

Later we discover that the couple are Toast-to-Toasting, the name envious backpackers give to their richer walking cousins who can afford the luxury of a hot shower, soft beds and cooked meals waiting for them at the end of a day's march. But if they're 'Toasting', then just what on earth is in that backpack? They aren't carrying a tent, sleeping bags, cooking equipment and food like us, so it must all be clothing and personal effects.

As we stand looking across at the walled grounds of the lighthouse, we slowly get our breath back. For a while, I didn't think I'd ever recover from the exertion of climbing up St Bees Head. But life is at last returning to my limbs.

Not a word has passed between Pauline and myself about giving up, but for a split second, I've certainly thought about it. If not actually finishing, then at least finding some way of rearranging the walk. How on earth are we going to get through the next 188 miles with this weight on our backs? I'm sure that had a certain persuasive Mr. Santos been with us in our moment of weakness, then we may well have considered, and possibly succumbed, to some slight alteration to the plan.

Ray Moody

You must expect some wet days on the walk, better here on the way to the North York Moors than in the Lakes

Chapter 8 – First Man Out

I turn and once again stare out over the Irish Sea. This time in a real attempt to spot the Isle of Man. This is the place where the British Government interned my German grandfather during both the First and Second World Wars. Classed as an enemy alien, he was ferried across to a camp over there and must have looked back at this coastline during his journey.

When we first ground to a halt at the lighthouse, I couldn't have gone a step further and knew that Pauline was feeling the same. Both of us being absolutely spent, I doubted whether our bodies would ever get their strength back. But, after about ten minutes, with the weight of our backpacks off our shoulders, energy, like a recharging battery, is slowly returning to our limbs. After a few more minutes' rest, we hitch up our sacks and resume our journey.

As we urge our feet forward to get them going again, I'm hoping that we've passed the apex of St Bees Head and that things will ease up for a while, especially for Pauline. A bad first day could put her off the rest of the walk.

My prayers are being answered, there's now only a slight rise to the ground. We appear at last to be at the top of the cliff as the walking is beginning to ease. We must have reached the pinnacle of St Bees Head, as the rough path we're on is definitely plateauing.

We're encouraged and now follow a much

narrower and wilder path along the eroded cliff edge.

At times, there are sudden dramatic views down the cliff-side to the sea many feet below us.

As the walking eases, we're beginning to get our strength back. The path, however, is becoming rougher and isn't as well trodden. There are also fewer people following us, and the trail seems quieter. This suggests that we must be leaving day-trip country behind. The track isn't as distinct as it was on the earlier part of the cliff, so maybe we're at last heading off into the wild.

The walk supporters who were accompanying and encouraging their spouses up St Bees Head must have surely stopped at the lighthouse, that's if they haven't already turned back before the drop down into Fleswick Bay.

Walkers are spread out at a distance in front of us. Their heads keep appearing and disappearing amongst the high undergrowth alongside the path. Sometimes the path goes to the very edge of the cliff and a sheer drop falls dramatically away at our feet, all the way down to the Irish Sea.

A cornfield appears on our right and a lone walker, wearing a bright yellow fleece jacket and carrying a full backpack, suddenly makes a beeline across it. We stop for a moment to consult our guidebook. Does this guy know something we don't? Other walkers further along the path have also stopped and are consulting their guidebooks and maps.

Pauline and I confer. As much as we're keen to leave St Bees Head and turn inland, that's definitely not the way, and like the rest of the walkers up ahead of us, we continue on over the cliff top. Nobody bothers shouting to the man to tell him he's gone amiss.

We don't come across anyone that evening in Ennerdale Bridge wearing his distinctive yellow fleece jacket. Nor do we see him again on the trail. Pauline feels guilty about it.

"We should have shouted to let him know he was going the wrong way. Or at least tried to encourage him not to give up."

Perhaps he's the first casualty of the walk, but the two German girls, with the bright orange backpacks, who we saw at the start of the climb up St Bees Head, also seem to be dropping further and further back.

Later, we discover that they gave up on the second day of the trail. This was strange, because one of them had already asked me where they could buy their Coast-to-Coast badges, usually bought on completion of the walk. Had they got hold of some and decided to finish?

Trudging on along the narrow path, faster paced walkers want to get by, and we have to keep moving to the side to let them pass. Sometimes walkers tailgate us, practically treading on our heels, but not passing. This forces us to quicken our pace and to walk at theirs, which doesn't feel either natural or comfortable.

When walkers overtake us, it makes Pauline and I appear like complete beginners. So, when we hear voices on the path behind, we start to increase our pace, but eventually, unable to maintain the speed, have to admit defeat and step to one side. To cover our shame, as the walkers pass by us, we adopt the ploy of pretending to be admiring the view.

Apart from couples and the occasional lone walker, most of the people who have passed us so far seem to have been groups of young men, who full of bravado, laugh and joke as they make their way along the trail.

St Bees Head is beginning at last to curve inland, a sign that we're close to the end of it. Soon, a wide bay opens up in front of us, and we have clear views of the Irish Sea with the jetty at Whitehaven jutting out into it.

Our pace slackens. As much as we want the cliff top to finish, it seems sad now, knowing that we're nearing the end of the beginning of the walk. This is the last time we'll see the sea until the finish at Robin Hood's Bay, and we'll soon be turning our backs on it.

It reminds me of when I was a child at school and started a brand-new exercise book. Opening it up for the first time, I always wrote so neatly on that first fresh, clean page. But somehow, once it was turned, it never did seem quite the same. Will our walk be like this, I wonder?

Arriving at a wall of red sandstone, we can see that travellers over the centuries have carved their initials into it. Pauline finds a space and scratches our three names onto the rock, leaving them there for posterity. Sadly, we would never be able to find them again.

The full extent of the town of Whitehaven appears on the other side of the bay. Passing by a deep quarry where sandstone is being blasted from the earth, we finally leave the cliff top and the Irish Sea behind us.

The start of the trouble, the trig point on Beacon Hill

The Dutch Girls at the Lion, nearly 30 years later we would still be receiving a Xmas Card from them

Chapter 9 - Flatlands

On reaching the rear of a cottage, a narrow strip of tarmac appears. A flat surface at last, a chance to get our breath back. We're relieved, it looks like the walking for a while will be done down quiet country lanes.

Sauntering along on a smooth road again, after the constant undulation of the path over the cliff top, feels good. Our batteries are slowly recharging, and step-by-step, energy is returning to our legs. Santos's face fades from my mind.

In the far distance, a green spreading hill can be seen. It signals our first real sighting of Lakeland. Naively, we don't realize it yet, but we're staring at Dent, a 'small hill' that we've read about so often in our coffee table Wainwright and will soon have to climb.

The road leads us gently through the quiet settlement of Sandwith. One of its pubs appears to have closed. So too has its Post Office, but another pub is still open.

Leaving the village, we follow a long straight country lane and pass by the metal sign that declares you are about to enter Sandwith. On the reverse of it, someone has stenciled in black paint the words,

'Robin Hood's Bay, 188 miles.'

Surely this can't have been a Coast-to-Coast walker carrying a spray can and a stencil? We see no more of these the whole length of the walk, so it suggests that somebody must have taken the time to come all the way out here to do it.

The road seems to be making a beeline for the distant hill of Dent. At a bend, we leave it and follow a green lane, an ancient grassy byway, once used by horses and carts. It goes through several farmyards. As we pass Bell House farm, dogs start barking.

"Wouldn't that be a great name for a band," says Pauline, "Bella and the Barking Dogs!"

The farmer appears in the doorway of his cottage.

"Looks like rain," he says confidently, with the knowledge acquired from years of working on the land.

"Do you think so?" Pauline asks anxiously, having an innate fear of thunder and lightning.

"Yes, definitely."

Then, with reference to our walking boots and backpacks,

"Sooner you than me, I'm off indoors." and with that he goes inside.

Leaving the farmyard, a path takes us down to a gate and onto the relatively flat bottom of a valley. Passing under a railway line through a short narrow tunnel, we find plenty of evidence that a herd of cattle have recently trod this way.

Beyond the railway line we're walking on the marshy floor of a wide shallow valley. Slowly, we begin to climb out of it. Passing by a dried-up pond, we hear later that this is the place where some Coast-to-Coast walkers wild camped on their first night.

Keen to get the walk started, rather than spend a last evening enjoying the relative comforts of St Bees, they spent it here. The land is marshy and waterlogged, and looks far from being an attractive location to camp for the night.

Beyond the pond, the path becomes hazy, and the route is unclear. For a moment, we flounder about and end up near an enclosed wood. Consulting our guidebook, I wonder whether we should take what would be a wrong turn through an entrance into it.

But Pauline finds faint evidence on the ground of the correct path which leads straight on. Following it, we begin the final climb out of the valley via another green lane.

Judging by the sound of traffic in the distance, it's leading us towards a major road. The lane is long and steep, and it's taking an age to reach the end of it. The weight of my backpack and the continuous rise in the lane causes the sweat to flow freely down my spine. Once again, the back of my tee-shirt is soaking wet. A car passes by up ahead. On seeing this, our pace quickens, and we at last emerge out onto the Whitehaven to St Bees Road.

Nearly three hours of walking have taken place, but according to a sign, we're still only a matter of miles away from St Bees. Waiting for a gap in the traffic, we cross over the road at a T Junction and start to walk down into the village of Moor Row.

Several years later, on the corner of this road, a sandstone sculpture of a hiker on the Coast-to-Coast Walk would be erected. It would pay homage to Alfred Wainwright and the benefits that the walk and the people doing it, have brought to the local economy. The figure is only about four-foot tall. Why couldn't they have made it life-size? Didn't they have enough sandstone? The walker wears an old-style anorak complete with drawstrings and a pouch pocket across his chest, just like the ones I mentioned earlier in the book. But didn't Wainwright simply don one of his old tweed jackets to walk the fells?

Like thousands of other Coast-to-Coast walkers, we've often stood by the statue and posed as we've photographed each other.

This is also the place, where, on a later walk, we would meet a solo Coast-to-Coast walker who we got on particularly well with. We spent the next few days walking and talking together along the trail. Sadly, he had to cut his walk short in Patterdale. But just before he left, he told us that he was a police officer from Liverpool. It's a strange thing, but I wonder if I would have been quite so open had I known this at the beginning.

Our bodies are slowly recovering from our early exertions over St Bees Head and the climb out of the valley. We now also have the luxury of a pavement to walk on all the way into Moor Row. Easy mileage, we meander down the road. It feels good to have solid ground beneath our feet again, even if there are the beginnings of an ominous rise to the footpath.

Moor Row gives the impression of being a commuter village, where everyone is out at work for the day. It's probably the home of many of the workers from the Nuclear Power Station at Sellafield. Passing through its empty streets, the place is quiet, and we soon leave it following a country lane.

A stile appears in the hedgerow. Climbing over it, we follow a path through fields before walking over a disused railway line.

After half a mile, we enter the village of Cleator via a thoroughfare bearing our mentor's name, Wainwright Passage.

On the village's main street, we arrive at the last grocery store we'll come across for several days. The next one will be deep in Lakeland at Grasmere.

After today, finding shops will be rare, which is why I'm carrying lots of packets of dehydrated pasta. If a shop sells something else I can buy to top up our evening meal, it will be a bonus.

A sign advertises that the establishment bakes its own pies. Entering the tiny store, we join a queue. On reaching the front, I order three steaming hot cheese and onion pies. The shopkeeper brings them straight from an oven at the rear of the premises. By the time we leave the shop, there is a long queue behind us waiting to buy pies.

And no wonder, devouring ours in the grounds of a nearby church, we discover that they taste so gorgeous that I leave Pauline and Leon sitting on a bench and rush back to the shop. Luckily, I'm able to purchase the last remaining pies. These will add splendour to our evening meal.

Whether it was because they'd just come out of the oven that they tasted so good, but I've never again eaten any that were as nice.

The proprietor tells us that we've been lucky today because normally the pies sell out within an hour of them being baked. We're not surprised, as not only are they so tasty but are also reasonably priced.

I discover that the shop sells bottles of Dandelion and Burdock, a beverage I last enjoyed as a child. I buy a bottle to relive a few memories.

We've passed by this store many times over the years. But have never again timed it right to be able to buy any pies. And no wonder, a customer in the queue that day brought along a box, which she filled up with an order of two dozen for her workmates.

On the Grisedale Pass

Chapter 10 - Walking Upwards, Tilting Backwards

Strapping on our backpacks outside the shop, we cross the road and go down the street directly opposite. A sign informs us that it leads to Blackhow Bridge. Arriving there, we stand for a moment, looking down at the stream while I finish my drink.

The small hill of Dent has suddenly become much larger and now looms up high above the village. Leaving the bridge, we ascen an upward path towards it. A track turns off the path, and we follow it as it passes by the ruined buildings of what looks like an ancient derelict farm. What there is of a wide, muddy, pot-holed track is covered in slurry. Gingerly picking our way through the decaying liquid, we leap across one stagnant pool only to find another. A few chickens scurry about amongst the muck, and the whole farm looks as though a bomb has hit it. However, on closer inspection, I can see a light on in one of the buildings. It seems unbelievable, but someone might actually be living here.

We leave the farm at a small road and immediately cross it to arrive at a forest gate. The gate signals the start of the climb up Dent, which will provide the biggest challenge of the day. Closing it behind us, we rest for a moment and then begin to ascend the wide forest road. The surface of it is made up of limestone chippings, which shine white in the sun. The road slowly twists and turns its way upwards around Dent.

It's two-thirty in the afternoon and very warm. The sun is beating down on the blinding forest track and the heat is reflecting back up at us. The climb is relentless, and my overfull backpack weighs heavy again. I feel as though I'm in some kind of ridiculous strongman challenge and have been given the task of carrying a sack of coal all the way up to the top of Dent.

As I did so many times on St Bees Head, I once again regret carrying too much. I curse my stupidity for bringing along the coffee table volume of Wainwright's Coast-to-Coast Walk and the heavy pair of binoculars, just two items I would willingly dump right now.

The forest road is steep, and we can only manage it in twenty-yard spurts. As we climb higher, it's getting steeper, and we have to drop down to even shorter distances. I take the lead, walk on about ten yards, and then wait for Pauline and Leon to catch up. Each time I stop, I don my familiar St Bees Head pose, standing with my hands on my hips, red-faced and sweating profusely while Pauline and Leon slowly limp towards me. On arrival, they immediately adopt my demeanour.

For some time now, I've taken to inserting my thumbs under my shoulder straps in a vain attempt to lift the weight of my backpack off my shoulders. Its heaviness is forcing the straps to cut into my flesh. I'm feeling groovy, but it's nothing to do with the Swingin' Sixties.

There's no one else about, and the quiet chalky road just goes on and on, twisting and turning, as it slowly contours its way around Dent. We can see nothing except for the trees and bushes on either side of us.

As I take my ten-yard break, I look back at Pauline and the effort she's putting into climbing the hill. Her backpack is also far too heavy, and her face shows distinct signs that she's feeling it.

Just like at St Bees lighthouse, this seems to be another good place to call a halt to the walk.

Santos's face returns to taunt me.

"Give it up, man!"

"What on earth are you torturing yourself for?"

The sun beats mercilessly down on us, and the white, stony forest road continues to reflect the heat. The back of my tee-shirt has become a river of sweat, a torrent flowing freely down my spine. If this is just a hill, then what will it be like tomorrow when we're walking on the real Lakeland fells?

Pauline looks all in, and Santos's voice again enters my ears.

"Look, you're supposed to be on vacation, is this what you call taking a break?"

"You're torturing that poor girl, give it up!"

After yet another bend in the road, and what has

felt like an eternity of walking uphill, Pauline spots a clearing in the trees up ahead. At last, there is something for us to aim for.

Plodding on, we arrive at the clearing. Looking up it, we can see where the tree line runs out and the start of the upper, open, grassy slope of Dent begins.

So far, we've been contouring, now we can at last head directly towards the top of the hill.

As we slowly climb up through the clearing, the path is steep. Halfway up it, underneath a tree, someone has pitched a tent, and we can hear snoring coming from within.

We discover later that the tent belongs to a Coast-to-Coast walker who felt that he'd already done quite sufficient climbing for the day and so decided to take a well-earned rest. We'll meet up with him in a few days' time in Patterdale.

Contouring Dent was hard enough. But as we make our way up through the clearing, the path at times is close to vertical. It's difficult to move forward as the weight of our packs are pulling us backwards. We're having to make a real effort to progress and are reduced to advancing in ever-shorter spurts.

What is disheartening is that we're still on the track amidst the trees and not yet on the open hillside. The walking is even more grueling than it was on the forest road, and I only hope that once we're out of the trees, we'll begin to feel as though we're actually getting somewhere.

The doubts that entered my head on the clifftop at St Bees have returned. Perhaps this walk isn't what we thought it would be. If this is only the small hill of Dent, as Wainwright so casually puts it, then what will it be like tomorrow when we're walking on the real fells of Lakeland?

I hate putting Pauline and Leon through it and wonder whether I'm indulging myself in some masochistic pastime and forcing them to suffer it with me.

Resting in-between what are now even shorter spurts of walking, we're at last leaving the lower tree-covered part of Dent behind us. Climbing over a stile, we're finally on its upper open grassy slopes.

Stopping for a moment to pause for breath, I can see that we've already gained significant height. Setting off again, we follow alongside a broken-down wall and slowly grind our way up the hillside. With the heaviness of my backpack, I'm continuing to feel like a coal deliveryman, and we have to stop and rest often.

What is keeping us going is that we can now see the summit of Dent. And seated high up there on a pile of rocks are two Coast-to-Coast walkers who have paid their dues and are sitting, resting, as they slowly get their strength to return.

We have an audience and are being watched. Even though they're still at a distance, I imagine that they can hear our every grunt and groan. As we continue to move tentatively forward like tired old snails, we try to hide our anguish.

At times, with the weight on my back, I'm almost considering screaming for mercy at the relentless climb. As Leon walks on, Pauline and I keep making a ploy of turning around to look at the world spread out far below us. We're both pretending to be admiring what is indeed a spectacular view. Already at this height, we can see the Cumbrian coastline and the Solway Firth.

Dent has turned into a succession of small slopes. Each one needs to be picked off in turn. The summit still looks to be at some distance and the closer we move towards it, the more we're finding that it's so steep in places we're barely able to progress. Gravity is pulling us backwards. Gradually, however, the broken-down wall we've been following runs out, and we begin to leave it behind.

The Intake wall is something I was totally ignorant of until discovering in my Wainwright dictionary that it means we're leaving the last signs of cultivated fell. Beyond it, we're entering the death zone, the uppermost-untamed part of Dent. Now the land belongs to nature. As the wall ran out, it also signalled that we're finally on the upper reaches of this side of the hill.

The figures sitting on the rocks grow larger, and we can now hear their comments. I'm drenched in sweat and my backpack feels as though I've entered the next phase of the Strongest Man challenge. A huge boulder has replaced the sack of coal on my back.

We are, however, at last on the final section of the hill and the going underfoot appears to be easing. Sadly, we're far too drained to appreciate it. The walkers sitting on the well-spread pile of rocks making up the cairn on the top of Dent continue to stare down at us, as though disdainfully viewing our limited progress. Our energy is spent, our tanks are empty, and we're now down to five yards spurts. To attempt to move forward, I'm having to adopt a zigzag pattern to my walking.

A makeshift ragged flag flies from a stick stuck into the rocks on the summit of Dent, as though acknowledging that this is our Everest.

Wainwright's suggestion that Dent is just a 'small hill', causes me to worry. If this is so, then what will the rest of the walk be like? I once again question how we'll manage it. We're now barely ten yards away from the summit and it's embarrassing to stop, but all three of us are so exhausted that we simply have to, if only to avoid having a heart attack. Red faced, we stand and once more view the world laid out far below us.

Despite having little strength left in our bodies to appreciate them, the views are sensational, and we can trace the whole of the journey we've just made.

Whilst it might not be classed as a mountain, this hill is certainly high, there's no disputing that.

Digging deep for breath, we gird up our loins for one final push and then forcing our feet forward, with our backpacks hanging heavy on our hips, totter towards the summit rocks.

I stagger in at the cairn first, with Pauline and Leon trailing in behind me. At last, we're finally here.

Unable to speak, with a fixed smile, I grin innately at the cairn's occupants. We've made it, our first Lakeland top, our first 'mountain'.

Standing beside the cairn, I slowly and awkwardly jettison my backpack. It rolls off me like a huge boulder, and I sway with the sudden loss of weight. Reeling around, I feel quite faint.

Almost collapsing down, I find secure seating on some of the larger lower rocks making up the cairn. With the weight off my back, I experience pleasure I didn't know existed. The grooves in the flesh on my shoulders, caused by the straps of my backpack digging into my skin, have become pleasure zones. I lift my tee-shirt out of each of the furrows and gently rub each of the reddened channels. Then, to get the air to flow to it and begin the drying process, I unstick my sodden tee-shirt from my back.

Pauline and Leon join me on the rocks, and from our lofty position, we sit and stare out at the way we've come. The Irish Sea shines innocently away in

A Walk to the Sea

the distance under a huge sky. The chimneys of Sellafield nonchalantly exhale smoke on the far horizon. Somewhere out there are the paths we've just followed to arrive here. St Bees must be at least ten miles away, and yet it appears as though we could almost throw a stone at it from up here.

We pass a few breathless pleasantries with our fellow walkers, with whom we're sharing the well-spread pile of rocks. Eventually, having had their allocation of time resting at the cairn, they leave us to it.

Thoroughly exhausted, we can at last drop-our-guard and sag down. I wonder if we'll ever be able to move from here again. As we rest, we continue to stare out at the world spread out far below us. The makeshift ragged flag on the summit cairn waves in the light breeze, as though acknowledging our small victory.

A few years after this, on another Coast-to-Coast Walk, we would meet a North American couple here. The man's wife had fallen as she'd climbed Dent and had fractured her arm. She was taken by ambulance to Carlisle Hospital where, with no fuss, she was treated and discharged. As Americans, it amazed them that there was no discussion of payment for her treatment or requests for insurance details. How different it was from when my father-in-law collapsed for a moment in New York with heat exhaustion. When he came to his senses in hospital, he had run up a medical bill of several thousand pounds.

After about ten minutes' rest, life does at last appear to be slowly returning to our bodies again when I thought that it never would. This is something we're learning. Turning our heads, we now look not at the way we've come, but towards the Lakeland Fells. This is the end of the beginning, and tomorrow, as Wainwright has promised, we'll be entering Lakeland proper.

Below us, walkers are slowly climbing up the hill. Most are using the same methodology as ourselves. Short spurts of walking are followed by them standing with their hands on their hips as they deeply gulp in the air and pretend to be admiring the view.

There is also the occasional maverick walker who seems to be able to grind their way up the hill without stopping. Their legs go like pistons, and they refuse to halt until they reach the summit. I'd love to know how they do it.

The cairn on Helvelyn

Chapter 11 – Walking Downwards, Tilting Forwards

A man approaches from the direction of the Lakeland fells, the Ennerdale side of Dent. He joins us at the cairn. Judging by his demeanour, he looks as though he's an ex-army officer. Greeting him, he asks if we're on the Coast-to-Coast walk and then explains that he's also doing it, but in reverse, and this is his final day.

How lucky it's downhill for him now, all the way back to St Bees. He must feel confident that he'll soon reach the finish and will have successfully completed the walk. The man tells us that he's already done the Coast-to-Coast walk the proper way.

How we envy him. I explain the difficulty we're having carrying our backpacks, and confess that we're not sure that we'll be able to complete the walk. Especially, if as Wainwright suggests, that this is just the 'small hill' of Dent and the trouble we've had climbing both it and St Bees Head.

Glancing at our sacks, the man offers us some advice.

"Your problem is you're carrying too much. You need to lessen the weight in your backpacks."

Then, holding his own sack in one hand, to show us how light it is, he leans forward and confides.

"To keep the weight down in my backpack, I'm

even wearing throwaway paper underpants!"

With my vivid imagination, I visualize a trail of his discarded underwear stretching all the way from here to Robin Hood's Bay. At least if we get lost and spot a pair of these, then we'll know that we're back on route.

With this thought in my head, I rise on still shaky legs. Feeling very much like an ancient donkey, I harness myself into my backpack. Once again, I have to endure the very unpleasant sensation of the cold wet sweat on my tee-shirt being pressed firmly against my spine. Staggering forward for a moment with the sudden weight, I look around for a small rock to add to the cairn.

Wainwright suggests that we've done the bulk of the walking for the day, and there's little left in terms of climbing. The rest of the journey looks like it's mostly downhill. So, despite there still being a few miles remaining of today's walk, we should be able to go on autopilot all the way to Ennerdale Bridge.

Taking on board the man's words of wisdom, we bid him farewell. Setting off somewhat unsteadily, we find it difficult at first to make our ceased legs work. We're discovering that the longer you stop for, the harder it is to get going again.

Our legs gradually get back into gear, and we begin to cross the marshy top of Dent. The wide grassy hill is plateauing out, but the walking is not as simple as it first seemed. The ground we're on is submerged in places under several inches of water. We have to scan the surface for occasional rocks to jump from to make our way across it. It feels as though we're wading through a no-man's-land.

Wainwright has said that there is a watershed on Dent. In my complete ignorance, my eyes scour the hilltop for it, believing it to be something provided by the local Water Authorities. I'm expecting to see a small building which I imagine houses some form of pump inside it, which, humming merrily away, drains the water off the fell. I can't spot anything. Perhaps it's hidden amongst the trees, but we look for it in vain on Dent. Have we gone off route, I wonder?

Having now passed over the brow of the hill, we enter the tree line on the other side of Dent. Coming to a forest road, it looks as though it winds its way down into a narrow valley. But Wainwright has told us to watch out for another landmark, a water tank, from which to get our directions. Once again, I misinterpret the information, and look amongst the trees for another facility provided by the Water Authorities. I can't see anything, except for a large dirty plastic container which has a few inches of rainwater at its bottom. Surely this can't be the water tank?

Passing by it, we enter the trees on the other side of the forest road and soon arrive at a high fence. Following it along, we come to a huge, wooden stile.

Spanning the fence, it's so tall that it looks like a scene from the classic movie the Great Escape. I'm half expecting at any moment to see Steve McQueen come riding up on his motorcycle in a bid to gain his freedom by jumping over it and fleeing across the border.

The stile must be ten feet high, and our legs are weary. Taking it in turns to cling onto the sloping structure, we climb up to the top and then over it.

On the other side of the fence, a clear path snakes its way precariously down Dent Fell into the valley of Nanny Catch. Along the bottom of it we can see a fast-flowing beck. We begin the long precipitous journey downhill, following the rough path as it descends into the narrow valley.

This is yet another time on the walk when it once again dawns on me that what goes up must always eventually come back down again. Therefore, if we climb a fell, we will always have to descend to leave it. This seems to me that all the effort we put into climbing the fell is given away so cheaply.

Slowly making our way down the high rounded green hillside, we dig our heels into the earth and tilt our bodies backwards as gravity now tries to pull us forwards. One slip on the grass, and we're likely to slide all the way down into the valley of Nannycatch. Concentration is required every step of the way.

Despite my intense efforts, I still slip, falling over backwards and hitting the ground with a resounding bump. Fortunately, this is where carrying a full backpack pays dividends. As I fall, luckily my pack takes most of the blow from the earth. In places, the path still has last night's rain on it, and as the ground slopes dramatically downhill, it's difficult at times for us to stay on our feet. Occasionally, the path contours left and right, and on these short straight side excursions, it's not as dangerous. However, once the path turns to resume its journey downhill, each step is filled with the expectancy of acquainting ourselves once again with the good earth.

On finally arriving down at the bottom of Dent, we stand in the shallow valley of Nannycatch under the rocky outcrop of Raven Crag. Just as Wainwright promised, this is indeed a tranquil place. A sylvan glade, hidden away from the world.

A narrow, turbulent beck flows swiftly along through the centre of the slender gorge. The scene is only spoilt by the presence of some dead sheep, which lie beside the flowing water amongst some noticeably withered vegetation.

Sitting on a wooden plank bridge a short distance away from them, our packs are off as we dangle our feet above the beck. Gulping down water, we eat the last of our provisions bought from the store in Cleator.

While we're resting, a local farmer passes by with his dog. Seeing the three of us sitting there, he glances nonchalantly at the dead sheep.

"We've had a lot of those!" he says, gesturing towards the sheep.

"And we've had a lot of men in white suits coming to pick them up!" he adds mysteriously, before going on his way.

Enjoying the luxury of having our backpacks off, we continue to relax in the golden rays of the afternoon sun as we sit and watch the water flowing in the beck.

Our guidebook tells us we're only a few miles away from Ennerdale Bridge, our destination for today. And despite the heaviness of our sacks and our sore feet, we now feel confident that we're going to get there.

After half an hour's rest, we reluctantly harness ourselves into our backpacks and move on. Having stopped for so long, we once again find it difficult at first to walk and get back into our stride. Our bodies have seized up.

As the walk progresses, we'll discover that this is the danger of stopping for too long, it's difficult to get going again, and we have to work our way back into the walk.

At a crossroads of fell-sides, our route turns off down a narrow pass and the fast-flowing beck follows it. This pass reminds me of the ones I used to see as a child at the Saturday morning, children's matinee, where we sat watching cowboy and adventure movies. If we're going to get ambushed by red Indians, or ferocious desert tribesmen, this is the place where it will happen.

There are high rocky fells on either side of us, and to our right, Telegraph poles are spaced out at equal distances along the ridge.

Walking alongside the widening beck, a further line of telegraph poles appears on the horizon in front of us. These must follow the main road. Excited, despite feeling weary, we pick up our pace and continue making our way down the pass towards them. As we do so, we keep scanning the horizon for signs of passing cars, which will signal for certain that this is the road leading to Ennerdale Bridge.

In-between the distant telegraph poles, we spot the first glint of the sun shining off a passing vehicle. The path widens, and a sign says that there is a stone circle somewhere up there on the ridge. But we're far too exhausted to even consider going to look for it. Trundling on along the path as it swings left, we eventually arrive at the road.

Despite feeling tired, we're growing excited at the prospect of there only being about a mile left of today's journey. We've nearly completed the first day of the Coast-to-Coast walk, and therefore, have almost achieved something tangible.

Now, walking along a gloriously flat country lane, we're slowly limping our way towards Ennerdale Bridge. Back on terra firma, the stresses and strains of the day are fast being forgotten. The closer we're getting to our destination, the more we're growing in confidence.

The views ahead are spectacular, as shapely green fells begin to appear in the distance. Despite our weary state, we're confident that we're nearing journey's end. Our speed drops down to a meandering pace as our feet are nearly spent.

More and more views of Lakeland are opening up to us. We realize from our surroundings that just as Wainwright has promised, we're now entering Lakeland proper. With our legs akimbo and our backpacks sagging low on our hips, in glorious late afternoon sunshine, we crawl our way into the village of Ennerdale Bridge.

Arriving at the Lighthouse is the first sign that you're getting somewhere!

Chapter 12 - Ennerdale Midge

The village is quiet. The daily commuters haven't returned home from their work at Sellafield or one of the nearby towns, such as Carlisle. Just up ahead of us, we can see some of the more affluent, travel-stained, so-called Toast-to-Toast walkers greeting their hosts as they eagerly book themselves into their bed-and-breakfast accommodation.

They'll soon have a refreshing shower to wash away all of the toils of the day, and a soft bed to lie on to ease all of their aches and pains. After changing into fresh clothes, they'll come down to a prepared evening meal with the prospect of a tempting pudding to follow.

Continuing on through Ennerdale Bridge, we search for the campsite. After passing a Primary School, soon afterwards we find it on the edge of the village. This has meant that after what has already been a long hard day, we've had an extra half mile of walking to endure. Never mind, looking on the bright side, our journey tomorrow will be slightly shorter.

A sign welcomes us to the campsite, and we enter through an open gateway. As we make our way down a gravel drive, dismantled cars and derelict farm machinery lie abandoned on either side of us.

Arriving at a cottage, Pauline knocks on the door, but no one appears to be home. Opposite the cottage stands a faded green painted toilet and shower block.

Continuing onto the camping ground, the scene is much better. It looks almost idyllic and takes our minds off the discarded machinery lying piled up around the place.

The camping ground is practically a small island, surrounded on all sides but one, by the river Ehen. There are already other backpackers here with their tents up. We identify a romantic spot by the gently flowing water where we'll pitch ours.

On arriving there, like releasing a parachute, I unclip my backpack straps and my sack falls off me like a huge boulder. As it slowly rolls down my back, it seems to take an age before it crash-lands on the earth. As it does, there is the sound of a massive thud, and the ground shakes. Such relief, the feeling is one of utter ecstasy.

Staggering around for a moment with the sudden loss of weight, I feel as though I've just thrown the fabled old man of the sea off my back. No wonder that with such a heavy load, my shoulders remain bowed from carrying it. I seem to have had an impossible weight to bear. There were times today, when shouldering my heavy burden, I thought that we would never get here. Removing my sweat soaked tee-shirt, I find that I have inch-wide, red strap marks cut deep into the flesh on each of my shoulders. Surely, something must be wrong. None of the other walkers we've seen along the trail today looked like they were having the same trouble as us carrying their backpacks.

The man on the top of Dent's words fill my ears. "You need to limit what you carry!"

I once again curse my stupidity for bringing along the large hardback copy of Wainwright's Coast-to-Coast walk, the heavy pair of binoculars, the tinned food, too many changes of clothing, etc., etc., etc.

Worse still is that I've planned for us to take the High Stile range ridge route tomorrow, climbing nearly three thousand feet up a fell side. How on earth will we be able to manage it with the heaviness of our backpacks?

Unrolling our cheap sleep mats onto the grass, the three of us collapse down on them and Pauline and I enjoy the sheer pleasure of no longer having an excessive weight on our backs.

The sun still radiates warmth in the late afternoon sky, and we relax in its soothing rays. For a long while, we lay, hardly able to move. Our bodies are spent and in shock. They've closed down and given up for the day. There'll be no further torture.

Thoroughly exhausted, we lie, trying to get our energy to return. My feet feel sore and blistered, and second only to the joy of having jettisoned my backpack is the sheer pleasure of removing my boots and socks.

A warm breeze blows over my bare feet, and I gently rub them on the cool green grass. The feeling is indescribable. We continue to bask in the glorious late afternoon sunshine, enjoying the relief of not having massive burdens on our backs and the absolute joy of air flowing around our feet.

It's almost thirty minutes before I'm able at last to rise and stagger with Leon down to the river to immerse our feet in its flowing waters in an attempt to cool down. Balancing on a slimy rock, the ice-cold water coming off the surrounding fells gushes over them. It feels as though it has healing powers. The steady flow eases my swollen feet and helps to take the heat of the day away from my body. As I return with my feet tingling from the coldness of the river, the grass massages them and I feel strong enough to help Pauline to put the tent up.

With it pitched and my back and feet slowly recovering, for the first time, I stand and view the tents of our fellow walkers. Most of the people assembled here will be accompanying us on our journey across England. These are the comparative strangers who we're likely to keep meeting up with throughout the next thirteen days of our walk. Some of them we've already briefly met today along the trail, most of them passed by us at a pace.

One group of men, all in their late twenties, appears to have a guy with long, flowing hair as their leader. Camping in a semi-circle of tents, his party sits around him, listening to their warrior chief, who clutches a wooden staff as he holds court.

We'll keep meeting up with this bunch of guys

many times during the days to come. Because of their fast-single file walking style, and their long-haired leader always marching at the front of his troops carrying his staff, we will begin to refer to them as the Romans.

Another tent contains a mother and her teenage daughter who are very friendly and from the Netherlands. Out on the trail, it's easy to spot them, as the girl wears a very distinctive pair of blue and white striped shorts. These can be seen for miles, and in the days to come they will prove useful in the mist, as we use them as pathfinders.

A further group of walkers consists of a family with a boy, a girl, and a dog. Each member of their team carries a walking pole, and so we'll name them the Sticks.

There is also a middle-class mother with her eleven-year-old son. He sits outside his tent with a fading look of anguish on his face. The boy looks all in, and even our inexperienced eyes tell us that he's carrying far too heavy a backpack for his age.

Another large party of walkers are on an organized trip. Their tents and belongings are being ferried for them to the various campsites on the Coast-to-Coast route in a van. Even so, several of the walkers are still carrying full backpacks. Their ages range from late teens to early sixties, and the group comprises of twelve individuals. They're a mixture of males and females who have never met before, complete strangers getting to know each other's idiosyncrasies along the trail.

There are also two pensioners, closer to seventy than sixty, who are intending to backpack most of the way. They both carry one of those typical pensioner's walking sticks, which are adorned with a display of metal badges showing off the various places they've visited.

Several other tents pitched here belong to walkers doing the Coast-to-Coast walk, and we'll keep meeting up with them on the trail. Sometimes they'll stagger their journey, getting out-of-sync with us, and then rejoin us further on along the route. There are also many walkers down in the village bed-and-breakfasting, or Toast-to-Toasting.

We discover from various conversations that most of the backpacking parties here have planned walking itineraries similar to that of our own. Just one lone backpacker is aiming to do the long day from Rosthwaite to Patterdale. This will make his walk a day shorter.

Life at last appears to have returned to most of my limbs. Leaving Pauline sitting in the tent catching up on her reading and Leon playing with a boy from one of the other parties, I explore the campsite.

The situation of the tents beside the river is glorious, but when I look at the actual facilities, a toilet, a shower and a kitchen sink housed in an old green painted ablutions block, I can see that they're far from clean. I guess that this is a case of a farmer allowing camping on his land, rather than us pitching on a commercial site where you would expect better. I therefore grow accustomed to there being 'a spot of muck' at such places.

Returning to the tent, I start work on our evening meal. As vegetarians, not eating meat or fish means that our diet for the next thirteen days is likely to be even more restricted than usual. I'm carrying a mountain of packets of dehydrated pasta, and a vegetarian mince called Beanfeast. Between them, these only really amount to two different flavours, tomato and cheese.

My task is to attempt to improve our meals by supplementing them with whatever extras I can get my hands on along the trail. I'm also carrying dried mashed potato powder and packets of crisps, which can act as a side serving with our meals. When we come across the rarity of a village store; I'll look for something else to go with our evening meal. Today we have the luxury of the cheese and onion pies we got back in Cleator, and a large tin of rice pudding I bought in St Bees and have regretted carrying ever since.

If there aren't any meat free pasties available in a village store, I'll look for some other possible treats to add to our meal. I don't really like pasta and it's only for purposes of weight, convenience and a restricted diet that I'm carrying so many packets of it. Not liking pasta, I always try to cook it so that it ameliorates into a soft mass. If we come across a rare shop during the day, then I'll allow myself to buy a tin of something to carry in the side pocket of my backpack. This will usually be tinned rice pudding as a treat.

For some unaccountable reason, the few village stores we'll come across always seem to sell tinned potatoes, tinned peas or other types of tinned vegetables. I'll learn to turn the pasta into a kind of stew by adding potatoes and peas to it. During the walk, I'll also develop a taste for Eccles cakes and Malt loaf. I never drink soft drinks but find that after walking on a hot day, a cold bottle of Lucosade hits the spot, even though normally I think it tastes awful.

Pauline leaves the tent to go for a wash. On her return, she tells me that she's been talking to the Dutch Girls and explained to them about the trouble we've been having with the weight of our backpacks.

They've told her about a service called 'The Packhorse', which will pick up your sack and deliver it to the next place on route for what seems like a very reasonable fee. It sounds too good to be true, so I'm not raising my hopes. But the Dutch Girls have given Pauline a telephone number to ring.

Even though our walk is on a budget, getting one of our sacks carried in the morning, and on any other occasion when we might need to, would be unbelievable. Especially tomorrow, as my plan is for us to climb nearly three thousand feet up to the summit of Red Pike and then traverse the tops of the High Stile range of fells. This will hopefully culminate in us visiting Wainwright's last resting place on the top of Haystacks. The Lakeland fell where we've read that his ashes have recently been scattered.

While I finish making our evening meal, Pauline dashes off into Ennerdale village to find a phone box to telephone the Packhorse Service.

She returns smiling about twenty minutes later and, unbelievably, has arranged for one of our sacks to be picked-up and carried tomorrow. All we apparently have to do is to leave our sack near the farm cottage when we depart in the morning. The Packhorse will then pick it up and transport it to our next campsite in Borrowdale. We've been asked to put the fees in an envelope attached to our backpack.

What a service, I pinch myself, as I still can't quite believe that it exists. If it works, then it could prove to be the best money we'll spend throughout the walk.

Getting my heavy backpack transported will mean that I'll be able to carry Pauline's relatively lighter sack, freeing her up from the weight.

After our meal, I sort out a clean tee-shirt, and we get ready for a well-earned drink in the village pub. As we change our clothes and Pauline selects a pair of stiletto-heeled shoes from the range she's brought along, the sun is setting, and clouds of midges begin to hover in the air outside our tent.

Because of our inexperience, unlike the other backpackers' tents, our ridge tent doesn't have a 'No See Um' facility, a mosquito net that can be zipped up at the entrance.

We're soon to discover that this is a serious mistake. The only way we can attempt to keep the midges out is to close the front flaps. But no matter how we tie them together, they're still getting in, and we're being bitten. Abandoning the tent, we make for the pub.

Hordes of midges hang in the air, and we have to walk through them. They follow us all the way to the campsite entrance. Arriving there, we meet the jolly farmer, who stands dabbing his face with what looks like a bar of soap. I casually mention to him that we've been driven out by the midges.

"Here you are, lad!" he says, thrusting his bar of soap towards me.

Having just seen him dabbing his own face with it, I politely decline, but he insists.

It turns out to be a midge repellent stick, similar in shape to that used for freshening up under your arms. Having witnessed the farmer applying it generously to his own weather-beaten countenance, as kind as his offer is, I'm reluctant to rub it into my face. So, I lightly touch one or two areas on my brow.

The farmer looks at me dubiously.

A Walk to the Sea

"Nay lad, rub it in!" he says, as he applies force to my hand with his own.

I've no choice but to grasp the nettle as he helps me to liberally smear the repellent all over my face.

"Aye, that's better," he says, putting the lid back on his magic portion.

Down at the pub, the Toast-to-Toasters are already gathered and looking serene in their smart clothes. Fresh and clean, with a pint of beer or a glass of wine in their hand, they positively beam with the satisfaction of having got the first day of the walk over with. They've had a shower, a rest, and have a prepared evening meal inside them.

A hotchpotch of backpackers from the campsite trail in after us. Most have changed their clothes, but some still bear traces of today's walk. The inn has pretensions of being 'posh', a place for the well-heeled. We're all expected to be on our best behaviour.

The Romans and several other campers stand around the wide, log-filled fireplace discussing today's journey. Gradually, the various Toast-to-Toasters, hearing snippets of their conversation, join in.

"Yeah, it nearly killed us climbing up Dent!"
"I thought it was harder coming down!"
"I can't wait to experience the real fells tomorrow."
"It'll be a lot tougher in the Lakes."
"Are you going over Haystacks?"

"No, we're taking the valley route."

"Did you know that you can drop in for a coffee at the Black Sail Youth Hostel?"

"Can you?"

With all the effort of the first day's walking behind them, tales and exaggerations are eagerly being swopped between kindred spirits, and a merry time is being had by all.

When we return in the twilight from the pub and arrive back at the campsite, the midges are swarming in even greater hordes and hang like dark clouds in the air. They have a bloodlust and are looking for victims.

Walking through them, they make unrelenting attacks on our flesh. We try to outwit them by running to our tent, but they chase after us and by the time we've undone the flaps, our faces and heads have been well-bitten. Once inside, we tie the flaps together and pile spare clothes and our sacks up against the entrance.

What I wouldn't give for a zip, and a sheet of 'No-See-um' at this moment!

Grisedale Tarn

Chapter 13 – Once Bitten

We awake to the warmth of a fresh sunny morning with the sound of water flowing gently down the river Ehen. I can feel that there is something wrong with my face and borrow Pauline's makeup mirror to take a look. Despite the farmer's magic potion, my face is swollen in several places. It's not just from the midge bites received returning from the pub, but from where they've got in through our tent flaps during the night.

We've learnt yet another very important lesson, never buy a tent that doesn't have a 'No See Um' mesh sewn into it if you want to deter the midges. Having no midge net, no zip on the flaps and only straps to tie them together, we've been at their mercy all night. I make a mental note to ditch the tent as soon as we get home and, in the future, to only buy one that includes zips and a sheet of No-See-Um.

We'll also discover that you need to ensure that the tiny squares of the midge net are small enough not to let the midges through. A tent we bought later did precisely that.

A few weeks after we returned home, we heard about a walker who had also camped at this site after completing the first day of the Coast-to-Coast walk. He'd decided that because of the humid heat, he would sleep with his tent flap open. As he slept, he apparently inhaled so many midges into his lungs that the next morning an ambulance had to be called, and he spent the rest of his vacation in hospital and had to abandon the walk altogether.

Despite the midge bites, the reality of spending a tranquil summer evening camped by flowing water has still not yet fully dawned on us.

Before we leave the site, we pay the farmer our camping fees. He tells us that he often has to telephone a local taxi service to take disillusioned walkers back to St Bees to catch a train home. He thinks it's because the reality of the walk has begun to kick in.

Even the first day of the Coast-to-Coast can apparently prove too much for some. They might have spent the last year diligently planning it, but the promises of the coffee table Wainwright, read in the comfort of their living room, with lush photographs of verdant pastures, can for a few, soon become soured with the sweat and toil of a hard day's walking.

It seems a shame, because there were times yesterday when feeling utterly exhausted, we too, for a fleeting moment, felt like giving up. Had a certain persuasive Mr. Santos been with us, then I'm sure that we might well have given it much more serious consideration, especially if we'd been offered a plausible alternative.

But when the reality that the world isn't a flat place kicks in and you experience the fact that your backpack weighs a lot heavier than it did when you

A Walk to the Sea

were walking around your living room carpet. Then you could be forgiven if you waver a little. This would be even more understandable if you were also worn out and covered in sweat and suddenly remembered that this is supposed to be your summer holiday. The time when you're meant to be taking a break from hard work and could be relaxing on some golden beach.

I guess it must be a case of, "If this is the first day of the walk and I'm already having trouble, then what will it be like in Lakeland proper?" I suppose these walkers consider it's better to turn back now before they experience the relative wildness and remoteness of the Lakeland fells.

Apparently, not all of yesterday's Coast-to-Coast walkers stopped at Ennerdale Bridge. We've heard on the grapevine that two backpackers pushed on, determined to reach the Black Sail Youth Hostel, a further eight miles away.

After their already relatively long first day, they would have had to traverse the afforested side of Ennerdale Water. Then, at the end of the lake, endure the seemingly endless six-mile trudge along the tedious forest road under the High Stile range. Before eventually arriving at the Black Sail Youth Hostel.

They must have reached there thoroughly spent, probably at eight or even nine o'clock at night, too late for the evening meal. They would have turned what was a reasonable day's walking into a nightmare.

We meet up with this couple of walkers a few days later. They tell us that not only did they carry on, but somehow got lost and ended up in the wrong valley.

Finding themselves off route in the village of Buttermere, they never made it to the Black Sail hut and were so tired that they wild camped the night beside the lake. This threw their walk out-of-sync and meant that the following day they had another long trek, as they had to get from there to Grasmere.

Several years later, Pauline and I returned to the campsite at Ennerdale Bridge. We'd heard on the grapevine that the farmer's wife had died, and in recent times he'd been coping on his own. On arrival at the site, we knocked on the door of the cottage, but there was no reply. Thinking that he must be out, we decided to pitch our tent with the idea of paying him his camping fees in the morning.

Arriving at the actual camping ground, it was empty. There wasn't a tent pitched, and the grass was long and hadn't been cut for quite a while. There were also even more piles of rubbish stacked up everywhere. Visiting the toilets, we discovered them to be practically cesspools. They looked as though they hadn't been cleaned in months. So bad was the overpowering smell and the state of the toilet bowls that we thought it healthier to urinate in some nearby bushes. Going to fill our water bottles, we also found that the tap wasn't working and had to get our water

A Walk to the Sea

from a pipe in the playground of the village school.

Judging by the condition of the campsite, the owner must have been too ill or frail to look after it any longer, and he clearly wasn't getting any help. On closer examination, as we passed by the farm cottage, it too seemed almost derelict. Despite passing his door again, we didn't see the farmer that day.

The following morning, we discovered that several more tents had been pitched late the previous night. They belonged to a party of Duke of Edinburgh Award students.

Speaking to their expedition leader, who had turned up to check on them, he thought that with there being no water to drink or wash with, no showers, no toilets, and an unkempt field of grass, he considered that conditions were so bad he was going to tell his party to leave without paying. He also claimed that he would be advising his local education authority not to use this site again for any future outward-bound expeditions.

We too weren't pleased with the state of the place, but not wanting to hit a man when he's down and bilk him, as we left, we knocked extra loudly on the door of the farm cottage. This time there was a faint stirring in the building, and the campsite owner eventually made his way to the front door and opened it.

He stood there, looking pale and gaunt. When

Pauline told him that we had camped the night at the site, he seemed thoughtful. We both imagined that he was mulling over the state of the place, which he must have known was so run down. He then explained that he hadn't been well, and that things had gotten on top of him, and he did indeed look ill.

Nodding in empathy, we thought that perhaps being embarrassed about conditions at the campsite; he was probably considering requesting some smaller token camping fees from us, or even none at all.

We were therefore shocked and completely taken aback when not only did he demand the full camping fees, but they appeared to have gone up.

He asked for two pounds more than what he'd charged us the last time we'd stayed there.

Stunned into silence and wishing that we too had followed the lead of the Duke of Edinburgh Award students and left without paying, we paid up, vowing never to return.

It was, however, to be the final season for the site, as word soon spread amongst the walking fraternity about the state of the place. But we couldn't help thinking as we left the campsite that in trying not to bilk the farmer, we had ourselves been bilked.

Chapter 14 – Calming Waters

Leaving my burgeoning backpack standing near the farm cottage, ready for the Packhorse to collect, I gleefully strap on Pauline's relatively lighter sack.

While we're out walking today, mine should be transported from here to tonight's campsite in Borrowdale. I still can't quite believe that such a fantastic service as this exists. I just hope that my backpack is waiting for us at the end of the day.

Turning out of the campsite, we follow the main road, but soon leave it to turn off down a quiet lane which leads towards the lake of Ennerdale Water.

The silence is profound and only broken by birdsong coming from the nearby trees. The early morning sun shines down on us, and we grow excited as the first huge fells surrounding the lake begin to appear above the tree line. Crossing over a bridge, we pass through a car park and Ennerdale Water suddenly springs dramatically into view.

The sight is breath-taking, and we stand for a moment and stare at the vast extent of its silvery surface. Surrounded by mountains, their reflections disappear deep into its waters.

As we take our first steps along a narrow path by the side of the lake, the sad figure of a man in his mid-thirties carrying a heavy backpack comes limping towards us. He looks somewhat dishevelled, showing signs that he wild camped last night beside Ennerdale water. Pauline, who will speak to anyone, greets him. The man staggers to a halt, and, clearly wishing to talk, pours out his heart to us.

It seems that he too began the Coast-to-Coast walk yesterday but has developed a blister so big on one of his feet that he's decided that there's nothing for it but for him to give up. The poor man is clearly distressed about it. Like us, he has spent last winter planning and preparing for the walk, gorging himself on Wainwright's guidebook. Completing the Coast-to-Coast walk has become his whole raison d'être.

The guy is single, unemployed and has put together his bit of kit using the money he's saved from his Job Seekers allowance. He has bought what gear he's been able to afford from his limited budget. After paying for his train ticket to St Bees, he only has a small amount of cash left to cover the costs on his journey.

Despite not having done any backpacking before, to limit expenses, he'd planned to reduce the number of days the Coast-to-Coast walk would take him, committing himself to a high daily mileage. He also intended to wild camp most of the way, with only occasional stops at established campsites to freshen up. This was the reason why he hadn't spent last night at Ennerdale Bridge and had walked on in his new and very solid-looking boots. The extra miles, together with his recently purchased footwear, probably accounted for his blister. He admits to having no experience of wild camping. But yesterday he had met up with a well-practiced wild camper who had given him a few tips, but who had now left him beside the lake.

The poor guy was also relying on the next payment of his Job Seekers Allowance being paid into his bank account during the walk to fund the second part of his journey. He's clearly heartbroken about having to give up and makes a pathetic sight as he limps off back to St Bees, where he'll have to face the problem of getting home after having only bought a one-way ticket. He leaves us with the words,

"Never mind, I'll try again next year." Our hearts go out to him.

He's not the only person who we'll meet attempting the Coast-to-Coast in-between jobs. These guys must sense a window of opportunity. They have the time available to undertake the walk, but will have to do it with extremely limited finances.

Two backpackers we met on a later walk were also doing it on a budget. They were planning to wild camp all the way, with just occasional nights slipping surreptitiously into a commercial campsite for a quick wash and a shower. Once again, they were having to fast track their journey, both to keep expenses down and to get back in time for their next appointment at the Job Centre.

When we quite by chance met up with one of these guys some months later, he told us that their walk had been horrendous.

They'd experienced several days of rain, during which all of their camping gear had got wet, and they had nowhere to dry it. Their lack of planning in terms of carrying food and the few shops they came across during their trek meant that they'd been at the mercy of pub meals. They were having to dine out in establishments used to catering for the comfortable pockets of well-heeled visitors to Lakeland, rather than backpackers on a budget.

This soon drained their limited resources of cash. But not wanting to give up, the pair continued on their journey. The final days of their walk became longer and longer in a desperate attempt to finish. It had all become a nightmare, and they hobbled into Robin Hood's Bay, two limping, starving, spent wrecks.

The full extent of the first half of Ennerdale Water is opening up to us. Its surface gleams like a mirror in the morning sunlight, as it must have done for thousands of years. The path by the lake is initially flat and makes for easy walking. We're heading towards a rocky outcrop known as Robin Hood's Chair. It's the centre point of the lake, jutting out into its tranquil waters. As we meander along the lake's edge, small waves continuously lap the shoreline at our feet.

Up ahead in the distance, a mist hangs over what we're soon to discover is Red Pike and the start of the High Stile range of fells, the place to which we're heading.

Staring across at the opposite side of the lake, we try to identify the spot where there was once a hotel. It's claimed that the hotel's residents could one fish out of its windows straight into Ennerdale Water.

As we near Robin Hood's chair, the initially easygoing path is becoming rock-strewn, and the ground underfoot is far more serious.

On reaching the rocky outcrop, we commence the climb up it. We're having to use our hands to clamber about amongst the rocks, but soon find ourselves standing high above the lake.

Resting for a moment, we stare out at the vast expanse of Ennerdale Water. For the first time, we can see both ends of the lake. Red Pike, and the start of the High Style range of fells now also look much closer.

Descending back down to the water's edge, we leave behind the early part of Ennerdale Water as it disappears from view. We're walking towards the other end of the lake, which can now be seen in the distance. The path is rock-strewn, and the side of the shore has become tree lined.

Entering the compacted foliage, small inlets block our path, and we make our way around them, dodging about amongst the trees covering the fell-side. Numerous narrow streams drain the water off the fells into the lake. Sometimes we're able to cross over them using stepping-stones and submerged rocks, at other times, we simply have to jump the gap.

After what has seemed like an eternity of hopping, skipping, and jumping, we finally leave the trees behind. The end of the Lake is now in full view. Looking back at the way we've come, Ennerdale water continues to shimmer splendidly in the morning sunlight, but up ahead mist still hangs around the tops of the High Stile range of fells.

Beyond the lake, we pass through a gate into open pasture. Making our way past a herd of grazing cattle, we come to a narrow lane and follow it down to a pontoon bridge. The bridge provides a crossing point over to the other side of the valley. The three of us sit on the side of it and dangle our feet above a flowing beck, which drains its waters into Ennerdale Lake.

Since leaving the campsite this morning, I've been getting a strange sensation on the reverse of my knee. It feels as though something has bitten me. Pauline has already looked at it and given the general area a squeeze. But she couldn't find any puncture marks.

As we sit watching the water flowing into the lake, I notice that the skin on the back of my leg is turning an opaque yellow and this colourful hue is spreading its way down my leg. Perturbed, I ask Pauline to take another look at it.

She does so reluctantly, poking the general area

and pressing it with her thumbs. But once again, she claims there's nothing to be seen.

Sensing that she's about to give up, I demand a second opinion and suggest that she should give the flesh at the back of my knee a really hard squeeze.

Perhaps trying to encourage me not to ask her to do it again, she presses her thumbs firmly on the top of my calf. Then, using her full force, crushes the flesh in one almighty painful squeeze.

As she does so, a jet of yellow puss shoots out of my leg and all over her, providing ample evidence that I have indeed been bitten by something, possibly a horse fly.

My leg almost immediately feels better, and I'm glad that I insisted on further treatment. Retaining the poison is only likely to have spread it further down my leg and could have led to me being unable to continue the walk.

Leaving the bridge, we arrive at a forest road. If followed, this eventually leads to the Black Sail Youth Hostel. But our plan today is to take Wainwright's suggestion and climb the fell-side to reach Red Pike. We'll then walk along the ridge over the High Stile Range of fells before dropping down to the corridor of Scarth Gap. From there we intend to climb back up onto the final fell of Haystacks and pay homage to Wainwright, whose ashes, we've read, were recently scattered up there alongside the small mountain lake of Innominate tarn.

Although I was initially sceptical about it, leaving my backpack behind at the campsite for the Packhorse Service to pick up has already proved to be such a good idea. Apart from wearing a pouch around her waist, Pauline doesn't have to carry anything. And even though her backpack, which I'm now carrying, is still heavy, it's so much lighter than my own, and we've been able to move along a lot more quickly.

When Pauline first told me about the Packhorse Service, I had doubts that such a facility existed. If it did, then what was the catch? It was only when she rang them from the telephone box in Ennerdale Bridge and booked in our backpack that I dared to believe. Paying a few pounds to have your heavy sack carried, ridding yourself of all that weight when you need to, is a 'no-brainer'.

Carrying Pauline's backpack, after yesterday's mammoth load, I feel almost like a spring lamb. Leaving my own sack behind makes it possible for us to undertake today's climb up Red Pike. Bearing in mind our struggle over Dent, it would have been impossible if Pauline and I were hauling our own overfilled backpacks.

Having joined the forest road at the end of the lake, we're still on the main route and are walking towards the distant Black Sail youth hostel. But we soon need to leave it and keep looking for signs of a clearing amongst the trees on the fell-side. This will signal the start of the climb up to Red Pike.

Eventually, a gap appears between the trees, but we hesitate. The Pike looks an awful long way up. But if we don't go for it now, our only chance to climb the fell will have gone.

I take the lead and, turning off the road, start the long, nearly three thousand feet climb up over the rough, undulating, grassy terrain. Apart from the 'small hill' of Dent, this is the first real fell we've ever climbed. So, we are naturally nervous.

We have a long day in front of us before we'll get to Rosthwaite and our campsite this evening. Now, instead of going in a straight line down the Ennerdale Valley, we're turning off it and will have to get to the top of the ridge before we'll make any further progress on our journey. The detour will take extra time, so the rest of the Coast-to-Coast walkers are likely to get ahead of us.

As we tenaciously attempt to make our way up the grassy fell-side, the going is difficult, and we lurch about amongst the foothills of the fell. Gradually, however, we begin to gain height.

As we approach the halfway point of the fell, two day-walkers appear up ahead of us. They stand arguing about the climb. He wants to continue up, and she wants to go back down.

It's the first of many times that I'll realize climbing mountains can be bad for relationships.

One of you is keen to get to the top, the other

would like to get there, but is perhaps more nervous about doing so.

The couple appear to have reached an impasse and as we pass by them, they stand there silent, and we soon leave them behind.

The path up the fell-side steepens. Just like on Dent, we're attempting to walk forward, but don't seem to be getting anywhere. Sweat pours off me and the back of my tee-shirt has once again become wringing wet. This time it's caused by Pauline's backpack, which claims to have a special airflow system that should help to prevent it from happening.

I'm so thankful, however, that I'm not carrying my own overfull backpack and, remembering the couple we saw on the way up, am even more grateful that Pauline isn't carrying hers.

The final climb up to the Pike is becoming so steep that as enthusiastic as I am, even I'm having doubts about it. We keep stopping and stand gulping in the air as we stare back at the full extent of Ennerdale water, which now lies a long way below us.

"Perhaps we should have kept on along the forest road, there might not be anyone else up here, and we could be all on our own," suggests Pauline, when for the umpteenth time we stand with our hands on our hips gulping in the air.

I'm once again so relieved that the Packhorse Service is transporting my sack, and that Pauline isn't having to carry hers.

After almost an hour of ascent, we finally arrive at the summit of Red Pike. It's a feeling of both relief and elation. We've done it, climbed our first real fell and bagged our first Wainwright.

I stagger towards the trig point and throw my backpack disdainfully down on the rocky floor. Then, in time-honoured fashion, the three of us stand once again with our hands on our hips and even more deeply gulp in the air.

From our lofty height, we stare out over the mile after mile of fell tops which make up the skyline of Lakeland. With my breath slowly returning, I feel exhilarated and shout at the sky.

"Top of the World, Ma!" in my best Jimmy Cagney voice.

The views all around us are stunning, not least with Ennerdale Water down below us on one side and Buttermere Lake on the other.

The additional bonus for reaching the Pike is that ahead now lies a ridge walk across the tops of the fells of the High Stile Range. Apart from the occasional short up and down, it should both smoothly and spectacularly take us all the way along to the mountain pass of Scarth Gap.

The short-term pain of climbing the fell means that we've avoided the longer-term drudgery of a five mile, relatively mundane trudge along the forest road. Up here on the ridge, the walking is varied, and the views are second to none. Any worries Pauline had about us being isolated on the fell-top have also proved ill-founded. Hordes of day walkers are roaming around the fell, having climbed up from the Buttermere valley.

With our strength returned, I pull on my backpack and we start our journey along the ridge. As we make our way over it, we experience occasional short drops down and then climbs back up. On negotiating a scary slide down a scree run, Leon, who is behind me, starts a mini avalanche and loose rocks fly by my head.

But being up here seems so much more preferable to taking the long drag along the valley bottom. We're walking on the top of the world, and the views all around us are phenomenal. We're Kings of all we survey. The short-term pain of climbing the fell has proved to be well worth it.

Journey's End

Chapter 15 – Black Sail

Climbing down off the ridge, we arrive at the junction of Scarth Gap, a mountain pass situated between the High Stile range and the bulk of Haystacks. It's also the corridor between the Buttermere and the Ennerdale valleys. The sun has gone behind the clouds, and it has become quite dull. After the relatively busy fell tops, we seem to be on our own again. A chill wind blows through the gap, and the rocky fell of Haystacks looks more and more foreboding under a greying sky.

Should we go back down and rejoin the main Coast-to-Coast route beyond the Black Sail Youth Hostel, where there might still be walkers going that way. Or should we continue?

The problem is that we wish to pay homage to Alfred Wainwright, who died only a few months ago. We would like to see Innominate Tarn, the place where we've read that his ashes have been scattered on his favorite fell of Haystacks. But we also want to visit the Black Sail Hut, which he must have so often passed and even relatively recently visited.

Believing that no one out here in the 'wild' is likely to steal them, we leave Leon and my backpack perched on a large rock. Freed from the weight, Pauline and I literally run down Scarth Gap and don't stop until we arrive at the Black Sail hostel.

The hut stands silent and looks closed to youth hostelers. Sitting on a bench outside, we take in the phenomenal views surrounding us. These include the giant fells of Pillar and Great Gable, which one day we will climb. And directly opposite is the high lip of rock leading out of the valley over to Wasdale Head.

As we sit there, a seemingly optimistic North American walker and his party arrive at the hut. They've come out of some nearby small green hillocks, which we've learnt from our Wainwright dictionary, are called drumlins.

Their leader initially ignores us and bangs loudly on the locked door of the hostel. The sound echoes around the empty building. Receiving no reply, the man turns to me and asks politely.

"Gee Buddy, can you get coffee here?"

In my head, I laugh at the thought, as the hostel is obviously shut. But I discover later that the man is correct. You can usually call in and make yourself a mug of tea or coffee, leaving a small payment for your drink. Today, it appears that the hostel staff have gone off to restock their provisions.

Some years later, we would stay at the Black Sail hut, camping outside and having all our meals, washing, and entertainment inside. Unfortunately, we did get off to a bad start.

Coming over from Wasdale Head on a glorious summer's day, we arrived at the hut during the early afternoon. Once again, there didn't appear to be anyone at home. Desperate for the loo, and the hostel's toilets being locked, so that we wouldn't be on show to anyone out walking on the surrounding fells, we went around to the rear of the hostel to relieve ourselves.

As I urinated close to the back wall of the hut and Pauline squatted on the ground, the curtains of a room at the rear of the building suddenly shot open. There, staring directly out at both of us in full flow, was the hostel warden. He must have been taking an afternoon nap, and the sound of water splashing up against the hut had disturbed him. Embarrassed, we both immediately stopped proceedings, and like two naughty schoolchildren, went sheepishly around to the front of the hostel to face him. The warden greeted us quite diplomatically, and acting as though nothing had happened, never mentioned it once during our stay.

The hut had a lovely warm stove, and many old photographs showing its history covered the walls. These displayed the building as Alfred Wainwright would have seen it when he first roamed the Ennerdale Valley during the nineteen twenties and thirties. We played board games with the rest of the guests, and the warden was a great host. It was a truly magical experience.

That night we slept in our tent, close by the hut in the pitch-black valley. Only tiny stars high above us provided any light. We were the only souls out there, just the two of us surrounded by the silent mountains of Great Gable, Haystacks, and Pillar. The profound silence was only broken by the sound of water flowing in the nearby beck. I remember thinking about Wainwright and his occasional nighttime sojourns on the fell tops, keeping a lonely vigil with just a blanket around his shoulders for company as he paced up and down, waiting for the dawn.

A young unemployed youth we met that night at the hostel told us how the previous year he had enjoyed his first short visit to Lakeland so much that he had gone back there with his tent soon afterwards. He wild camped all through the late summer, only returning home to sign on once a fortnight at the Job Centre. But as September turned to October, and the days became shorter and darker, he found that he had to turn into his sleeping bag earlier and earlier. With nothing to do but lie in the darkness throughout the long autumn and early winter nights, he eventually had to give up and go home.

Crackpot Hall

Chapter 16 - The Tarn with No Name

Retracing our footsteps back up Scarth Gap, it seemed a lot easier coming down than it is climbing back up. But we soon arrive at the place where we've safely left Leon and my backpack.

We're at the apex of the gap and the three of us sit side-by-side on a large boulder getting our breath back. As we rest at the foot of the climb up Haystacks, we stare at a distinct path which climbs its way up the fell.

As we do so, a small party of refined, middle-aged ladies approach us. Judging by their conversation and their attire, they're on a hiking tour of the Lakes. Standing grasping their walking poles, they join us in staring up at the path ascending Haystacks.

There is then some serious shaking of the head by the member of the party, who appears to be their leader, as she takes the decision for the group.

"We're not going up there, it's all teeth and claw!" With that, they're gone, heading off down Scarth Gap towards Buttermere.

It's growing colder. A chill wind once again blows through the gap, and now there is no one else around. We feel isolated, and I once again wonder if we should just have continued on down the valley, past the Youth Hostel, and followed the normal Loft Beck route, where there's likely to be the company of other walkers.

On a later walk, we would take this route, passing the Black Sail Youth Hostel on the way to climbing out of the valley via Loft Beck.

There had been several days of rain, and the beck was overflowing. Beyond a series of drumlins, we met a party of Coast-to-Coast walkers, who we'd earlier given the name the Green Shorts. When we caught up with them, the various members of the group were earnestly looking at their maps and considering the best way to get over the eddying water. Having always taken the High Stile Ridge path, or walked down to Scarth Gap and then climbed over Haystacks, we were ourselves new to the Loft Beck route.

Crossing a beck would normally involve looking for a narrow place to jump over it, or finding a few submerged rocks to stand on to get across. Unfortunately, due to a period of heavy rain, the beck was flowing quite rapidly and had become a tumult of water, which was both deep and wide.

So, when one of the Green Shorts' party suggested that for safety reasons, we should all link hands and form a human chain to cross the beck, this we did.

Boots and socks were removed and hung around necks. Strangers' hands were tightly grasped. Then, like a daisy chain, we all took the plunge and entered the water. It was flowing strongly, but we stood steadfast as it splashed up well above our knees.

Then, a member of the party slipped and fell over backwards and began floating downstream, his backpack behaving like a raft. Somehow, somebody managed to grab hold of him, and not breaking the chain, we made our way to the other bank. Here we attempted to dry our feet before putting our socks and boots back on. Eventually, with damp socks, we set off again to continue the climb out of the valley. But we had only gone a few yards further, when we could now clearly see a higher-level track, which we should all have been on. We'd taken a lower path, which had led to us all being on the wrong side of the beck. If we'd been on the correct route, there would have been no need to cross the water, and no need for the wet socks.

"What if there's nobody up there?" Pauline asks plaintively.

I try to reassure her, but I'm also feeling apprehensive. After all, this is Haystacks, the mountain Alfred Wainwright suggested that if you get lost on it, you should kneel down and pray for deliverance. Whether he said this tongue-in-cheek or not, I don't know, but the rapidly chilling air is forcing us to take a decision. Do we ascend Haystacks, or head back down to the Black Sail Hut and follow the normal Loft Beck route? Taking the plunge, I clip on my backpack, and we begin the climb.

The stony track is initially easy. It begins by going

straight up the fell before zigzagging its way across it. But as we arrive at the end of the track, just as the woman remarked, some hands-on rock climbing is required. Popping our heads up as we ascend, we appear to be nearing the top of the fell. But as the rock-climbing finishes, we discover that it's a false summit. This isn't the crest of Haystacks, and we clamber up onto a rocky plateau. Crossing it, we continue once more to climb upwards before eventually arriving at a pool of water.

I remember from our guidebook that this is just a small unnamed body of water. It's not Innominate Tarn, the place where Wainwright's ashes are reported to have been scattered. It is, however, the first tarn we've ever seen.

Sitting on the tumble of rocks surrounding it, from our lofty position we can look back down on the Ennerdale valley and enjoy tremendous views of the lake and the nearby fells.

But we're still not on the top of Haystacks. Facing us is a further wall of rock. Leaving the tarn, we climb up it, and finally arrive on the highest part of the fell.

Following tracks hither and thither, we eventually find ourselves staring down at a pool of water which has two small islands in it. This is it, the promised land. The photograph from our coffee table Wainwright has come to life, we've found Innominate Tarn.

A Walk to the Sea

As we make our way down towards it, rain begins to fall. Arriving at the tarn's edge, we watch the water splashing the shoreline at our feet. Apart from the sound of the gently lapping waves, the tarn lies silent under a darkening sky. And as Pauline suggested, there doesn't seem to be anyone else around. We're all alone and have the pool of water to ourselves.

Pauline seems to read my thoughts and comments, "There's only us and Wainwright!"

As the water softly washes the sides of the tarn, being here all by ourselves, it seems even more of a magical place. Standing there contemplating, I think back to a televised film of Wainwright's last visit to Haystacks. It had also rained that day, and he'd sheltered under a large outcrop of rock beside the pool. We decide to explore the area surrounding the tarn to look for it. Pauline quickly identifies the spot, and we make our way around the water towards it.

Mist now hangs in the air above the gently lapping waves, and the rain continues to come down. Just as Wainwright had done, we take shelter beneath the same rocky shelf.

As we stand under the outcrop, Pauline spies a fissure in the rock. Looking inside, she discovers a red rose with a small handwritten card attached to it. Reading the message. it's a thankyou note to Wainwright from two walkers, for enabling them to explore the beauty of the Lakeland fells.

Then close by us, on the ground next to the tarn, Leon spots a small, sculptured cairn. It's made up of tiny stones and is only about a foot high. It looks as though it has only recently been built.

So, we're not the only ones who have thought of paying homage to Wainwright. Adding our own small stones to the cairn, we stand in silent contemplation by the side of the tarn and watch as the mist continues to hover in steam-like clouds above it.

As it slowly swirls over the water, the tarn has an ethereal look. It could be a scene from Alfred Lord Tennyson's poem, Mort D'Arthur. I'm half-expecting at any moment to see the armour-clad knight, Sir Bedivere, standing by the pool, contemplating whether to throw King Arthur's precious sword, Excalibur, into it.

Climbing over Haystacks less than a year later, the tiny cairn had gone, kicked into the tarn by someone not wishing a shrine to be created to Alfred Wainwright.

A chill enters our bodies, we've stayed here for too long, it's time to go. There's still some distance to travel on today's journey, and the climb over the High Stile range has meant that we're already a couple of hours behind those walkers who have taken the normal valley route.

I remember again Wainwright's warning that anyone finding themselves lost on Haystacks should kneel down and pray for deliverance. We're novices to fell walking, and the fear of getting lost up here on top of a mountain fills Pauline and I with dread. I'm also discovering that when you're out on the fells, the higher you climb, the colder it gets, so the quicker we lose height on today's journey, the better.

Some years later, we heard about a lone walker who had become lost on Haystacks in bad weather. He claimed that he'd strayed off the main path and was floundering about on the mist filled fell-top and didn't know which way to go. It was late in the year; he was cold, and all alone up there and beginning to get worried.

Then, apparently, he suddenly smelt tobacco smoke and felt a hand being placed on the arm of his wet Cagoule. The man alleged that he was then directed back onto the main path, from where he was able to find his way off the fell. Well, that's how the story goes.

Finding our way off Haystacks and the way down to the Honister Pass was always going to be the trickiest part of today's walk. To follow the route from Innominate Tarn to the Honister Quarry, our guidebook suggests that there will be a lot of twisting and turning.

Saying goodbye to Wainwright, we leave the tarn. The whole fell top is now shrouded in mist, making our route finding even more difficult. Our next landmark, confirming that we're still on track, should be a glimpse of another pool of water, Bleaberry Tarn.

In blind faith, we plod along a rocky path. We're now feeling the effects of the weather and the amount of climbing we've already done today. The mist is growing denser, and the path we're following is narrow. There's nothing but a thick blanket of grey off to our left.

Then, as the mist for a moment swirls and parts, a dramatic view of the Buttermere valley suddenly opens up down below us. There is a precipitous drop just inches away from our feet. The mist closes in again but continues to swirl, like a curtain opening and closing. We catch glimpses of the lakes of Buttermere and Crummock Water in the far distance. Closer at hand, we can see the conically shaped Fleetwith Pike. We're walking high above an abyss and having become aware of it, now even more carefully make our way along the path.

Safely beyond it, staring through the mist, we can make out another pool of water, which we believe is Bleaberry Tarn. Quickly passing by it, we face a wilderness of a misty fell top that needs crossing as we make our way towards Honister Quarry.

Leon and I follow Pauline, who, like the frontiersman Hawkeye, confidently twists and turns this way and that as she attempts to trace the barely discernible track on the rock-strewn ground.

Leading us first left and then right, eventually the

environs open-up, and we find ourselves in a shallow mist filled valley. At its centre, we cross over a beck via a stone slab bridge and there, high up in front of us, beyond a boulder field, we can make out a small stone building. According to our guidebook, it must be the Honister Quarry workers' hut, our next landmark. Climbing up through the boulders, we make our way to it.

Entering the stone shelter, it's even colder inside than it is out. But at least it's keeping the rain off us, which is now coming down much more heavily. The quarry workers have built the hut with a stone fireplace, and there's evidence that somebody recently spent the night here as half-burnt newspapers fill the grate. Once again, after only a few minutes of standing still, we're feeling a chill in our bones. It's a sign we're quickly learning means that we've got to get moving again before the cold permanently enters our bodies.

Leaving the shelter, we're surrounded by piles of rocks and spoil from the quarry. But the route off the fell is clear. We begin to make our way down a stone-built tramway that looks like an extremely long, rocky staircase. At first, it only descends slightly, but as we progress, it begins to drop down much more steeply.

Soon after the start of our descent, a path joins the tramway from the main Coast-to-Coast route. Even though the fells are misty, we can see that there is nobody on it and so must assume that the rest of the walkers are all be well-ahead of us. This is the price we pay for traversing the fells of the High Stile range. But it was worth it.

The tramway drops further and further down. After our long day, the descent to the bottom seems endless. About halfway, we pass pleasantries with an older couple who are making their way up. They're walking the Coast-to-Coast in reverse and are looking for the turnoff for Loft Beck. When we point it out to them, they're relieved, and it feels good that as novices we've been able to help. Heading for Ennerdale Bridge, the couple still have a big part of their day ahead of them, albeit it will be a lot easier once they've arrived down at the Black Sail Hut.

The rain has continued, and mist still floats over the fells. The wet weather appears to be set in for the day. At the bottom of this giant staircase lies the road through Honister Pass, and the Borrowdale valley. Thankfully, we're heading down towards it and civilization. We don't envy the couple as they disappear off along the path and vanish in the mist. Will they reach Ennerdale? They'll have to negotiate their way over the fell to Loft Beck before their route will become foolproof again.

They do get there. We come across them a few days later, sitting on the Packhorse bus in Patterdale. They bang on the coach windows to thank us once again for helping them with their directions. Despite their age, they had already done the Coast-to-Coast walk the proper way and had enjoyed it so much that they'd decided to do it in reverse.

The tramway is becoming quite tedious. As we jerk our way down the scree filled giant steps, each one of them jars our weary bodies.

At last, we finally arrive at the foot of the tramway and can enjoy the sheer pleasure of standing once again on relatively flat earth. It feels good to have got down safely off the fells and even better to have a tarmac road under our feet. From here, it's only a short distance to the deserted buildings of the now closed Honister slate quarry.

Wainwright considered that the derelict quarry was such a sad place to the one he remembered from his younger days. When he'd passed by it then, men could be seen working high up on the fell-side mining slate from the rock. Today, under a darkened sky, as the rain pours down over the old cutting sheds, it reminds me so much of a scene from a ghost town in the mid-west of America. The gold rush is over, and everyone has left 'them thar hills.'

A few years after this, like a phoenix from the ashes, the mine and its buildings would reopen as a tourism attraction. The bonus for Coast-to-Coast walkers would be that they could now stop off here for a coffee and a toilet break. Later there would also be climbing activities and even a zip wire high up on Honister Crag. This would certainly make the way down a lot quicker.

Despite its commercialization, I'm sure that Wainwright would have been glad to see the quarry buildings in use again. Today, though, just as he himself once said, in the pouring rain, as we wander about the old cutting sheds, it really does seem such a sad and dismal place.

The Stencilled sign at Sandwith

Chapter 17 – Berthed in Borrowdale

Leaving the quarry workshops, we look for the start of the old toll road. The rain is now lashing down. How thankful we are to be back on a semi-flat surface again. All three of us are feeling tired, but at least for the rest of the day we won't have to scramble over scree and loose rock.

The former toll road begins well. Running parallel to the main road, a short distance away, it carries traffic through the Lakeland valley towards Keswick. But as the toll road climbs higher, it's steadily moving away from the main road and becoming muddier and rock strewn.

The track leads us into a dark, dank, decaying old wood which, according to our guidebook, bears the name Johnny's Wood. As we trip over fallen branches and pass under constantly dripping wet trees, we think that he's welcome to it.

Perhaps because of our tiredness and the inclement weather, it seems such a cold, miserable place. But with hindsight, it would have been better if we'd simply joined the Keswick Road and followed it straight down into Rosthwaite.

The path through the wood is taking us further and further away from the main road. We keep catching glimpses of it through the trees, but there's no way off our current route which would enable us to rejoin it. We're beginning to look down on it with envy.

Another worry we have is that whilst we're definitely in some wood, we don't really know whether it belongs to Johnny. But now committed, we continue to make our way through it, climbing over fallen tree trunks and jumping over water filled ruts in the path. This is a weary way to end the day. Soaking wet and dishevelled, we've had enough.

Arriving at a fast-flowing beck which blocks our way, on the other bank we can see a building that looks like it could be the Borrowdale Youth Hostel. This is our last landmark of the day. But how do we cross the water to get to it?

The path stops abruptly at a rocky wall as the beck flows dramatically away. Looking closely at the wall, Pauline spots a series of chains attached to it. This suggests that we're meant to hold on to them, to make our way over the water to the other side.

I take the lead and clinging onto the chains, sway perilously close to the flowing beck. Despite their flimsy appearance, the chains are effective, and I make it across. Leon comes next and then Pauline gingerly follows him. All safely landed, we continue along a path on this side of the water. After a few yards, we arrive at the Youth Hostel.

Since leaving Haystacks, the rain has continued to pour down and our cheap plastic jackets have proved far from waterproof. We're tired and our bodies feel chilled and damp. Johnnie's wood has been a sore trial at the end of a very long day.

Cheery voices can be heard coming from inside the youth hostel, and we've already decided to check it out. There's the possibility of sustenance. But more importantly, there might be access to some toilets where we can attempt to dry ourselves.

Leaving my soaking wet backpack on a bench on the hostel's veranda, we enter the building. Will we stand out like sore thumbs amongst all the youth hostellers and be embarrassed by some zealous spotty 'just out of University' member of the hostel staff who might ask what our business is in being in there?

Looking around us, we needn't have worried, they're not all young dudes. There seem to be quite a few middle-aged hostellers about the place, particularly Americans. Making our way through a busy reception area, we mingle with the throng of clean, dry hostellers, who are waiting for their evening meal. How envious we are of them.

Pauline spots a corridor down which she can see a row of toilet cubicles. Acting quickly, we each slip into one and can immediately feel the warmth.

Sitting on the toilet seat, I use paper towels to try to dry as many parts of my sodden body as possible. Undoing my boots, I take off my drenched socks and wring them out into the washbasin.

I've belatedly discovered that my cheap tracker boots aren't waterproof, and I attempt to dry my feet by using reams of paper towels. I then stuff my boots with screwed up paper to try to draw out as much wet and damp as I can. In a further effort to dry my socks, I use the heat from an electric hand dryer.

In the next cubicles, Pauline and Leon are doing exactly the same, except that Pauline is also bothering to smarten herself up and rearranging her hair. I've long since given up on all of that, going instead for the guy who's been out on the fells all day look.

Twenty minutes later, we emerge slightly dryer from the snug and warm security of our cubicles and rejoin the throning mob of youth hostellers in the reception area.

It's still very busy, as the desk there also serves as a tuck shop. Will we be spotted as interlopers and be embarrassed as we're ordered off the premises?

My working-class roots emerge, bringing with them a lack of middle-class confidence that sometimes gets the better of me. Luckily, the hostel staff are far too occupied answering questions to have even noticed us.

"Is there a vegetarian option on this evening?" a North American voice asks.

"Yes, there's a veggie bake!"

"And what's for pudding?"

"Chef's done a lovely pineapple crumble."

Our mouth's water at the sound of this glorious hot food. We're going back to our tent to enjoy a packet of dehydrated tomato and herb pasta shells, with a side serving of crisps. For dessert, I've got a few slices of malt loaf.

A few years later, when we stayed at the legendary Black Sail Youth Hostel, we sampled the aforementioned veggie bake and tasted that glorious crumble. The food did indeed live up to its mouth-watering expectations.

Pauline confidently buys a postcard at the reception counter. Following her lead, Leon gets some sweets and I purchase a carton of milk and a tin of expensive rice pudding. We do seriously consider staying here as we have bought YHA membership as backup for the walk. Unfortunately, the hostel is full, but anyway we'd be separated, and I don't fancy spending the night in a dormitory packed with guys high on testosterone.

After making our purchases, we leave the place feeling a lot warmer and drier and continue on down a lane into the village. Passing by a woman standing in the doorway of a cottage, Pauline asks directions to the campsite, and she points it out to us.

I do hope our backpack will be there, and that the Packhorse has understood my instructions and delivered it, or tonight we'll be without a tent.

I still can't quite believe this incredible service. It seems too good to be true, and you have to put your complete faith in it. Leaving your backpack behind at one place and whilst you're out there getting on with the business of walking, they're delivering it to the next destination on your journey. I'm paying just a few pounds not to have to carry forty pounds on my back for 14 miles. It's an easy decision, but does it work? Is it possible that our sack will be there waiting for us, or will we be tentless tonight?

The rain has stopped, and now glorious evening sunshine pervades a steaming Borrowdale valley. Walking along its flat bottom down tranquil country lanes, high-afforested fells surround us on all sides as we enjoy the comfort of this sudden warmth.

At a crossroads, we follow the main Keswick Road and can soon see the campsite. Near its entrance stands a cottage, to which we report. This is it, the moment of truth. We've arrived at the place where we hope they've delivered my backpack. But is it here?

"Hurray!"

Standing inside the front porch of the cottage is our solitary blue Karrimor backpack. So, the service works! Knocking on the door, a woman with a very strong Cumbrian accent appears and allows us to take our backpack. She then explains that she doesn't want the camping fees now as she collects them in the morning.

Heaving the heavy sack up onto my shoulders, I return Pauline's to her. Leaving the cottage, a short distance down the road, we find the entrance to the campsite.

A Walk to the Sea

Entering the camping ground, we discover that it's a large unkempt grassy field with an aging toilet block at its rear. The grass appears to rely on the services of a sheep to keep it down, and it looks as though it has recently been a bit lazy and hasn't been doing its job.

The site is old-fashioned, and has probably been in operation since before the war. Despite this, it must be a magnet for campers in the area, being situated in the heart of Lakeland and surrounded by so many glorious fells. Customers, I would therefore imagine, are guaranteed, no matter how high the grass is. And there appear to be plenty of large family tents here to prove it.

Looking at my watch, it's nearly eight o'clock in the evening. It's been a long, hard day. Despite the rain stopping and it now being relatively warm, the grass is still wet. We scour the campsite to try to spot the shortest grass available but have to settle for the best we can find. Feeling exhausted, we slowly set up the tent.

Leaving our boots outside, we all climb into it, and with Pauline and I sitting back-to-back, manipulate ourselves sufficiently to enable us to take off our wet clothing. Putting it into one of the few bin liners we've brought along, we manage to keep the wet out of the tent. Taking a lucky dip into my clothes bag, I find a dry tee-shirt and fresh briefs. Free of my waterlogged jogging bottoms and my sodden underwear, I stretch out and lounge gloriously in my clean dry garments. For the last few hours, I've felt as though I've been wearing a wet nappy. It feels like heaven to no longer have drenched material flapping around my legs.

To give Pauline a break from her routine chores at home, I've freely volunteered to cook all our evening meals for the duration of the walk. She isn't at all convinced by my gesture, believing it to be a ploy for me to get my hands on a larger portion of the packet pasta. If it is a ploy, then it's actually to get less. Splitting the chores, Pauline has been designated the duties of boiling the water for our cups of coffee and washing the pots. I think it's a very fair trade off.

Commencing work on our meal. I've noticed during the first few days of the walk that the gas is wasted if you cook outside the tent. Things seem to take an age to heat up, especially if a breeze is blowing. So, I'm now risking every health and safety rule by cooking just inside the doorway of the tent with the flaps tied back. Should the portable gas cooker go up in flames, the plan is to throw it out onto the grass, so I need a clear exit. Cooking inside the tent, as dangerous as it seems, also means that heat from the stove, even if only in a small way, helps to warm us.

Cooking the packet pasta, I boil it to such a softness that I practically ameliorate it. I then serve it with a side portion of cheese and onion crisps.

Whether this is to supplement the meal or to hide the taste of the pasta, I'm not sure. But it's hot food and doesn't actually taste too bad. We also desperately need it to rebuild our energy levels ready for tomorrow.

Pauline is easily pleased and always seems thankful for whatever I cook her. Today I produce my coup de grace, the tin of rice pudding I acquired at the Youth Hostel. She fairly beams at her glistening plateful.

Afterwards, Leon goes out to look for friends on the camping ground and I stack the pan and the dirty plates outside the tent. I'm about to turn off the gas stove when I have a brainwave. The evening air and grass are still damp from the rain, and I've come up with an idea to make our tent warm and cosy.

Closing a tent flap, I keep the other one open. This is in case I need to jettison the stove and to let out any dangerous fumes, such as carbon monoxide. Leaving the stove lit on a low light, I trap it between our sleep mats. Pauline is apprehensive, after all, it's breaking every health and safety rule going. "I'll be careful!" I reassure her and demonstrate how I have the stove wedged so that it can't fall over. Lying back after our feast, we've discovered that in our ridge tent, the best way to do this, to give us maximum room, is for the three of us to lie like sardines, head to toe. Pauline reads whilst I try to get a station on my pocket radio. Within minutes, the whole tent is snug and warm, and it almost feels as though we're sitting in front of the gas fire back at home. To think that we nearly didn't keep faith with our tent and might have wasted money on accommodation at the Youth Hostel.

Half an hour later, feeling restored, I turn off the gas stove and, leaving Pauline to her book, emerge from our warm abode to survey the campsite. I can see that the Romans are here with their familiar semi-circle of tents, so too are the Sticks and the Dutch girls. The boy and his mother are also here. Once again, he looks all in as he sits outside his tent, looking dejected. We've seen him out there on the trail and despite him being a big ten-year-old; he's still carrying a full backpack, which is far too heavy for his age.

On a later Coast-to-Coast walk, we would meet another woman with a similarly aged boy. Whenever we saw them on route, they were always practically running rather than walking, and they did some long days. Judging by her speed, she must have been a regular jogger. At the campsite on an evening, she would ignore the boy's bleating about the distance and how fast they'd travelled. Several times on the walk, they would set off at least an hour after us and scurry by sometime during the day. The woman invariably led, with the poor boy being virtually towed behind in her slipstream. By the time we reached the Pennines, they sped on, and it was the last we saw of them.

I noticed on our arrival here that there are quite a few family-sized tents on the site. It's the summer holidays and people have turned up for a break. Some have lit campfires and are sitting outside their tents sipping cans of beer, which they must have brought along with them in their cars. Most are playing music.

Pauline and Leon join me to visit the quaint old-fashioned toilet block for a final time before turning in. If we need the loos again, we'll have to indulge ourselves in our new nocturnal activity of standing in our bare feet in the moonlight, staring up at the stars while we relieve ourselves. As we do so, we're praying that no insects are crawling between our toes and that we don't take any back to the tent.

The ablutions are housed in some rickety old outbuildings that look as though they've been here since the 1940s. They remind me of the outdoor toilets to be found in the northern terraced houses I grew up in, back in Hull. To match the toilets, there are some big old-fashioned, square porcelain sinks, cold water only for washing pots.

A small grassy hillock slopes its way down to the toilet block. It has a stony path and our bare feet have soon become gritty and wet from using it. I noticed yesterday that most of the European walkers are carrying flip-flops. All we have with us are our boots. Because at the end of a day's walking we're so desperate to take them off, we've no alternative but to walk around the site in our bare feet. Our socks are also still wet from today's trek, and I've hung them from the roof of the tent, hoping that the warmth from our temporary heating system will have helped to dry them.

Turning in, we lay head to toe in our sleeping bags like sardines. I have my small portable radio stuck to my ear and try to find a station, which I'm learning is very difficult when you're surrounded by fells.

Leon quickly falls off to sleep while Pauline attempts to read by capturing the last of the daylight. But eventually she has to admit defeat and give up.

We still can't close our double sleeping bag, which, despite what the description said, was never meant for two people. Once again, I have to leave the side half-unzipped. Nevertheless, tired from today's exertions, we attempt to sleep.

All the aches and pains of the day bring a soothing feeling to our legs. My stinging feet throb where my wet socks have caused blisters and broken skin. It's a strange but nice sensation. Will they have recovered by the morning? They certainly took a hammering today as we climbed the High Stile range and over Haystacks down to the Honister Pass. Then there was all of that 'frigging about' in Johnny's Wood, as Wainwright might have perhaps so quaintly put it.

The light fades from the August sky, and it finally

darkens. The eleven o'clock news comes quietly out of my radio, which I have pressed to my ear so as not to disturb fellow campers. Silence falls on the campsite; the Borrowdale valley is at rest.

In the semi-gloom, the fells directly opposite look like dozing elephants crouching on their knees, as though they too are falling into slumber. All is still, all is at peace.

Suddenly, in my drowsy state, I can hear faint voices in the distance. At first, they're barely audible, but as they get closer, they're becoming louder. It must be some of the large tent dwellers, here on holiday, returning from the village pub. These guys sound wide-awake and full of vigor. They can't have climbed the fells and walked fourteen miles today as we have.

In small parties, they arrive back at their tents and sit at their entrances, shouting to each other. Clearly, their bodies don't ache and need rest like ours.

Music is now coming out of a plethora of portable devices and the volume is slowly being turned up. Parties are taking place as people congregate around some of the larger tents. Continuous cackling laugher and raised voices reach us from all four corners of the campsite.

Whilst the Coast-to-Coast walkers are trying to sleep, the rest of the site wants to party. We lay listening to their tales, their shouts, and their raucous laughter. If it was just one tent, then perhaps somebody would be brave enough to tell them to shut up, but large tents cover most of the camping ground.

Despite the music and the loudness of the voices, the campsite proprietor is nowhere to be seen, and the racket continues well into the early hours of the morning.

"Never mind," I say to Pauline. "It's our bodies that need to rest, not our brains."

In spite of the noise, sheer fatigue means that we eventually fall off to sleep and leave them to it.

The climb up back onto the Moors from Clay Bank Top

Chapter 18 – Talking Italian

At exactly fifteen minutes past six in the morning, the sound of coughing outside our tent awakens us, and a large German shepherd dog sticks its nose through the tent flap.

"Camping fees, five pounds each please!" says the woman with the strong Cumbrian accent.

Half asleep, Pauline and I grope for money in the semi-darkness.

As my brain slowly clears, I wonder where she was at midnight when the whole campsite was alive like a fairground. I feel like asking her, but don't. The woman thanks us and moves off with her dog to the next tent.

Despite the overgrown grass and the toilets being old and rickety, the field is a real honey pot, being the only real campsite for several miles. Surrounded by glorious fells, it attracts campers in with very little effort.

So, what does it matter if the grass is long, the toilet block is old-fashioned and people party here until dawn? For the woman, the field must seem like a large fishing net, which draws in campers because of its unique position. All she has to do is turn up with her dog every morning to harvest her catch and see how many tents she's trawled. It's just another farming activity, like the daily round of checking for eggs laid by her hens.

Too awake now to go back to sleep, I watch the

woman as she makes her way from tent to tent, growing richer with every call. Is it just a coincidence that she collects her fees when the campers are still half-asleep?

A buzz suddenly goes up around the camping-field, there's some sort of kerfuffle going on. It's coming from a large Italian holiday coach parked at the entrance to the campsite. It must have arrived here late last night, along with all the other fairground attractions. Apparently, the coach driver has paid in full for the whole of his party of Italian students. But the woman's confused, as there seems to be more Italian campers here than has been stated. She's now remonstrating this fact with him.

It would appear that some of the other campers in the field have caught onto the ploy that when she calls at your tent, if you point at the coach and utter one or two words of Italian, like the real Italian campers are doing, then you don't have to pay for the long grass and the late night.

Several naturalized Italian campers have been pointing at the coach and gesticulating with gusto as they speak words like, 'Buongiorno, Prego, Scusi and Non-Capisco', this last phrase proving particularly popular.

As these quasi-Italians mutter anything they can remember from their holiday phrase book, the woman's baffled. There should only be twenty Italian campers on the coach, and yet she seems to have come across several more. She has herself now joined in the gesticulating, pointing towards the many tents as she tries to extract further currency from the now fiery Italian coach driver.

Meanwhile, the pretend Italian campers, like the real Italian campers, are hurriedly taking down their tents, filling their backpacks and leaving the field. They markedly walk towards the Italian's coach, but as they reach it, instead of boarding, for some strange reason they pass by it, and with a final 'Arrivederci Rosthwaite', disappear off into the morning mist.

On those Glorious Cleveland Hills

The rocky path on Haystacks

Chapter 19 – Far from Easy in Easedale

After our coffee and biscuit breakfast, I take down the tent. Despite its occasional drawbacks, we've stayed at this campsite many times over the years and quite like it here. The noise that night has also generally not been repeated.

Packing away the tent at this site on a typical wet Borrowdale morning has, however, always proved difficult. We would carry out a by now well-practiced routine of packing as much stuff as possible into my backpack from inside the tent. But as some items needed fitting into specific places in the sack, and the tent had to go in first anyway, this was always limited. Pauline would then run with her filled sack and leave it in one of the old outdoor toilets. She would then keep making trips back and forth to collect my backpack and the remaining items, and store them in another toilet cubicle. Finally, in the pouring rain, I would take the soaking wet tent down and drag it to the ablutions block to join her. After shaking it as best I could, I would retire into the cubicle and recommence filling my backpack.

Fortunately, a few years ago, management of the campsite changed hands, and facilities were improved. A barn was opened where campers could fill their backpacks and sit in out of the rain. It has proved so much better.

The day is warm and dry. An early morning mist that hung over the fell tops, seems to have disappeared. Leaving the camping ground, we detour off into Rosthwaite to purchase a few goodies from the village store. Over the years, it has provided backpackers with the odd creature comfort, such as a banana or a bar of chocolate when they've come off the fells. Sadly, the store would close a few years later, and even these small luxuries would no longer be available to future walkers. But today, it provides a source of refreshment for our journey. Leon and I buy some sweets whilst Pauline more conservatively settles for a packet of mints.

Once the shop had gone, backpackers staying in the village overnight and not carrying their own food would be at the mercy of the few, relatively expensive, local pubs for their meals.

We've decided to take Wainwright's advice and attempt another exciting high-level ridge-walk, but that comes later. First, we have to get over Greenup Edge. I'm hoping that there'll be no mist up there as our guidebook tells us that we'll have to negotiate a path off an extremely boggy fell top.

The walk begins easily enough. We follow a track running alongside a stone wall which borders a beck flowing down off the fells. There is just a steady rise as the stony path gradually climbs its way up towards the rocky facade of Eagle Crag, which is over on the other side of the beck.

A Walk to the Sea

Today's section of the walk is only nine miles long, so we're once again carrying our own heavy backpacks. Despite this, in the warm morning sunlight, we're so far sauntering along the path with relative ease. There is a high rocky ridge in front of us, which we must climb over to get to Far Easedale. But at the moment, there is little chance of us going astray.

On reaching a gate, the seriousness of walking in the High Places is suddenly brought back to us. A metal plaque on the gate looks old and interesting, and we stop to read it. It records that a university student succumbed at this place during the 1930s, when three friends were returning from a winter walk out on the fells. Because of the intense cold, the young man appears to have had no strength left to carry on. His two companions, also spent, had little choice but to leave him there while they went to get help in the nearby hamlet of Stonethwaite. When they returned with some local farmers, they found that the student had died of exhaustion. It was just a winter's day walk, and they were less than an hour away from civilization and safety.

Standing here with the sun on our backs and the weather bright, you wonder whether his companions could have dragged him. But probably all three of them were so weak that they might all have perished.

I would learn later that it's only when you're in danger yourself whilst out on the fells that you more fully understand the difficulties of the situation, you're in.

We're walking away from civilization and will have to negotiate our way over the fells to find the next pocket of it in Grasmere. The plaque provides a timely reminder that Lakeland needs to be taken seriously.

Continuing our walk, the dry-stone wall runs out. We're now on the open fell-side and following the beck, which has become a fast-flowing mountain stream. Walking by the side of it, we steadily climb as the water flows dramatically down over rocks, cascading into a small waterfall.

The distinctive rocky facade of Eagle Crag is being left behind, and the path is beginning to ascend much more steeply. With the extra effort involved, we begin our regular pattern of stopping every twenty yards or so. Standing with our hands on our hips, we look back at the fine views.

Climbing higher, the panorama is becoming even more spectacular, and we can trace the way we've travelled over the past few days. It's not long, however, before the track turns a corner, and the view becomes hidden by the bulk of Eagle Crag.

The rising path meanders amongst a series of drumlins. The first of these is almost the size of a small green pointed hill. Walking around them on a narrow track, we're disappointed to find that we're still not yet at the top of the fell.

Once again, because of our strenuous efforts, we have to stand and even more deeply gulp in the air. The path now almost levels out for a while as it crosses a wild, rising boggy plateau. Up ahead, we can see the route to be followed and are faced by what looks like a mighty climb up a high, rocky gully. This, we believe, is the final ascent, which will take us onto the top of the ridge, and eventually over to Far Easedale.

Standing at the foot of the gully looking up, we can see that it's filled its whole length with large boulders and that water is flowing gently down over them.

With trepidation, we begin the climb, trying to find the quickest route to ascend the maze of wet rock. Higher and higher up the gully, we go, negotiating a path through it using the fabled 'teeth and claw' method. Leon is proving to be the better pathfinder out of the three of us. He seems to be able to spot the easiest way up. Bit by bit we're edging closer to the horizon and the top of the ridge. But as we do so, the more fatigued we're becoming.

Once again, our task is being made more difficult as we've discovered that we have an audience. We're being watched.

Perched high above us on a large outcrop of rock overlooking the valley are a group of Coast-to-Coast walkers who have paid their dues. They've already negotiated the gully and are sitting, getting their breath back as they enjoy a well-earned rest at the top. Just like what we experienced on the small hill of Dent; the climbing seems even harder when you believe that every step is being observed. Gritting our teeth and using what's left of our sapping energy, we gird up our loins and make one final effort to climb the haphazard stone staircase towards the top of the ridge.

At last level with the horizon, but totally drained, we take it in turns to stagger onto the rocky outcrop. Throwing ourselves down, I rid myself of the proverbial 'Old man of the sea'.

Heaving off my backpack, it lays flat on its back on the rock like a beached whale. Thoroughly spent, it takes several minutes before we're able at last to gain the strength to enable us to look around at our surroundings.

To our front, we stare out at the side of Eagle Crag. Down below us we can trace the way we've come and watch other pathetic Coast-to-Coast walkers who are just rounding the large drumlin and still have to face the horrendous climb up the gully.

Looking behind us at the way we're soon to take, we're hit by the sudden realization that we're still not quite at the top of the fell. Although we're high, there's still a boggy plateau to get across before we'll arrive on the highest part of Greenup Edge and begin the descent to Far Easedale.

Our journey today is only nine miles long. We've

planned a short day because it makes sense to stop off in Grasmere and enjoy more time in the Lakes rather than rush through them and walk on further to Patterdale. To do so would involve us having to undertake strenuous climbs both this morning and afternoon.

Because this section of the walk is seemingly so short, we decided to once again have a go at carrying our heavy backpacks. Mine continues to play dead as it lays outstretched on the rocky outcrop like a prostrate body.

It's now our turn to look down on those Coast-to-Coast walkers who have yet to make the unenviable climb up the gully. We pity them, as like the other walkers resting on the slabs of rock, we appear to be sitting in judgement on their every move.

Totally spent on arrival, I wondered whether our bodies would ever recover. But just like a battery, after about ten minutes, the energy feels as though it is at last slowly returning to our legs, which at one point could not have gone a step further.

A light mist swirls around us as we continue to stare out across at Eagle Crag and down at a distinctive group of drumlins in the valley. This scene can't have changed in thousands of years. Surely some long dead ancient Briton must have once stood here holding their spear on this same rocky outcrop as they surveyed the valley on the lookout for potential enemies. Pauline reminds me that the drumlins go back much further in time and are probably a sign of the Ice Age.

Looking around us, we can see that we've caught up with the Romans, the Dutch Girls, and several other recognizable Coast-to-Coast walkers. The Dutch girl's blue and white striped shorts provide a great marker in the mist.

It's amazing how one moment our legs tell us that they can't go a step further, as they did when we reached the top of the gully, and now, after less than fifteen minutes, they're feeling recharged and ready to move on.

We're also finding that there is a definite amount of time you should stop for. To stay for too long can mean that our bodies grow cold and the more difficult it is to get moving again.

The Romans have already left. Their long-haired, warrior leader with his wooden staff, is keen to be at the head of all the walking parties.

Floating mist now covers the fell. It hangs in patches like steam as it drifts all around us. I turn and look at the trampled down track amongst the peat bog and reed-beds, which we're soon to follow. The path steadily rises over the squelchy peat. We're still not yet at the top of the fell; there's a little more climbing to do.

A chill is creeping into our bodies; it's time to go. Rising slowly, we hoist our backpacks onto our shoulders, and as though saddling horses, clip them back on.

Setting off again, we follow the initially well-tramped, boggy track towards the crest of the ridge. The mist is becoming so thick that the walkers up ahead of us can no longer be seen. The terrain beneath our feet consists of waterlogged peat and the trail on the ground is becoming difficult to follow. Fortunately, Pauline has memorized this part of the walk from our guidebook, and leads us twisting, turning, and jumping through the mist.

In his guidebook, Wainwright has warned us that we should not go too far off to the left along this ridge, or we could end up in the wrong valley. We're told to look out for an ancient metal fence post. This will both provide the landmark confirming we're still on route, and indicate where the climb down the valley begins. Unfortunately, until we see it, we won't truly understand what we're looking for. I've conjured up a picture in my mind, but like the 'watershed' on Dent, it could be totally wrong.

The mist clears for a few yards, and we spy movement up ahead of us. It must be the Romans. In the greyness, we can see walkers jumping over narrow rivers of waterlogged peat. Peering through the haze, we try to keep them in sight, there's safety in numbers. We desperately need to find terra firma, something solid to stand on amidst these estuaries of floating quagmire.

Pauline spots an old bent and twisted metal fence

post sticking out of the top of a large outcrop of rock. It's our beacon of hope, and we navigate our way towards it.

The mist clears and then closes in again. Our route isn't as straightforward as it first seemed. Between us, and the longed-for solidness of the rocky outcrop, lies a wasteland of bog. All the time we're having to keep circumnavigating it, negotiating a way through wet floating peat that stretches for yards. We jump over it, hoping that what we'll land on isn't part of this soaking boggy morass. We sink into it, getting our boots full of bog water.

As we try to make our way across it, we're forced further and further away from the stake. But it's our lifeline, and we endeavour to keep it in view at all times.

At last, we stand on the top of the hard-won rocky outcrop with the twisted iron fence post sticking out of it. These large rocks signal the head of the descent. Looking down from them in the mist, we can discern a narrow path that goes sharply down the first section of the steep valley. After just a minute of taking in our surroundings, it's once again too cold to linger, and we leave the rocks and begin the long descent.

As we twist and turn our way down the mist-filled side of the valley, every footfall requires watching. We can only progress slowly, tediously having to tread a path that is only loosely etched into a jumble of peat, scree, and rock.

A Walk to the Sea

But eventually, the fell for a short while plateau's out, and we traverse a wet grassy terrain. Arriving at a wide beck, which is constantly filling with water from the fell-sides, we look for the easiest place to cross it.

Wading over to the other side, the upper section of the valley is finished with. Looking down from a rocky shelf, a path drops steeply downhill in a final descent towards the mist-filled valley bottom. Instead of taking it, we aim for a path that climbs the nearby fell-side and should lead us up onto the top of the ridge.

On route for Kidsty Pike

Standing on the crag on Greenup Edge after the climb up from Rosthwaite

Chapter 20 – A Warning for the Hasty

Many years later, during an ill-fated solo attempt at the Coast-to-Coast walk, I would come a cropper when trying to climb over to Far Easedale.

I had begun the day well and had speedily made my way up to Greenup Edge. So speedily that I'd got in front of all the other parties of walkers, who, despite the pouring rain, were hanging back, admiring a waterfall on the climb up.

Standing all alone on the outcrop of rock on Greenup Edge overlooking the valley, the rain, which had been coming down in a deluge for hours, had stopped for a moment. But after a few minutes, it started to pour down again.

Not wanting my body to chill, instead of waiting for the other walkers to catch up, as there is always safety in numbers on such a wet day, like a fool, I plodded on.

Wading through reed beds over soaking wet peat, I tried to find the route. But what there was of a path over the compressed stalks soon ran out. As I floundered about, one of my legs sank nearly thigh deep into the morass. I should have immediately turned back and waited for the others. But spotting the beginnings of a track amongst the reeds about ten yards off to my left, I managed to pull my leg out of the bog and aimed for it. Arriving there, the track wasn't much better, and it took me even further off to the left. Following it, I ended up on a very distinct path running along the top of Greenup Edge.

Then, looking off to my right, I stared down into a mist filled, shallow valley. Not far down it was a high outcrop of rock. But instead of it having one old iron rail sticking out of it, as I'd expected, it seemed to have several. Was this the place I'd climbed down to so many times before, prior to the descent to Far Easedale. Had I somehow been able to make my way around to it by approaching from another direction? Perhaps in the past I hadn't noticed the other twisted iron rails, and the outcrop certainly looked familiar.

Instead of doing the sensible thing when unsure, and retracing my footsteps back to where the other walkers were coming up, I climbed down onto the outcrop. Then, dropping off it, began to descend the fell.

Almost at once. I realised I was wrong. There wasn't even a rough path down the fell-side. I should have immediately tried to climb back up onto the ridge. But looking towards the bottom of the fell, I could see a beck running along it. Surely this must be the beck that I had crossed over so many times on this section of the walk. So, I continued on down towards it, with the thought that following it would help me to get back on track.

The rain was pouring, and the grassy fell-side was so slippery that the only safe way down it was on my backside. Luckily, I had recently purchased a pair of waterproof over-trousers and used them to slide perilously down the fell. I was going at such speed that several times I tumbled dangerously over and was only able to stop myself by clinging onto passing boulders. Once, as I slid down the fell, my arm shot deep into a hole underneath a huge rock, and I expected at any moment to hear it snap.

Eventually, I arrived at the bottom of the fell and tramped alongside the beck in the pouring rain until I came to what looked like the only suitable place to get across it.

Wading over to the other side, my boots filled with water, but I stood at the top of a narrow valley. Did this lead to Far Easedale? After hesitating for a moment in the cold and wet, I began to make my way down it, following alongside an increasingly tumultuous beck.

The valley seemed narrower than I remembered it, and the rain continued to pour. To my dismay, I couldn't find a path to follow, which was strange, because if I was back on route, there should have been one. Was it simply that the torrential rain had changed the track into a flowing stream, and I just couldn't see it? If not, then I must be in the wrong valley.

But in this weather, there was no turning back. I was cold and wet and needed to reach civilization as quickly as possible. Wedged between the riotous beck on one side and a barbed wire topped fence on the other, I attempted to find a way down.

Walking between huge wet rocks on waterlogged peat, my progress was slow. Stepping into pools of water, I had no idea how deep they were and where I was putting my feet.

Sure enough, as my left foot disappeared into a water-filled hollow, it seemed to be going down forever. Then, with a sudden jerk, I felt a numbness down the back of my leg and had to grip onto a huge rock to steady myself. Clinging there in the pouring rain with my leg stuck deep down in the hollow, I couldn't move.

It had been difficult enough descending the pathless, water-logged valley on two legs, never mind one. And now injured, I knew that I was in trouble.

The rain continued to pour down, and I needed help. Having a mobile phone, I tried to ring Pauline, but due to the high fells, no service was available. I then attempted to send her a text message. But as the rain splashed down on the phone screen, and I pressed the different letters, the words came out as gobbledygook.

I was incapacitated and unable to summon help. Should I just stay there and hope that Pauline would eventually realise that I must have got lost and gone down the wrong valley? When she did, she could send the local Mountain Rescue team out to find me.

But what if they didn't come? I was already soaking wet and cold, so they might not get to me in time. Was this remote gorge to be my final resting place?

I suddenly realised just how vulnerable you are when one of your legs goes and you're out there all alone on the fells. Especially if you've gone off the beaten track and are making your way down what more and more seems like a rarely frequented valley.

Looking around me at my austere surroundings with the unrelenting noise of the thunderous beck filling my ears, I realised that remaining there wasn't an option.

Holding onto the huge rock, I slowly pulled my leg out of the water-filled hole it had plunged into. As it resurfaced, the whole of the calf muscle on the back of my leg felt numb, but I just about managed to stand. Then, with one leg feeling lifeless, clutching onto huge boulders and dragging it behind me, I continued my descent.

With the rainwater running around them like islands in a stream, and the fear that any minute one of my legs might disappear down another water-filled hole, I began to limp my way through a maze of rocks.

As I slowly followed the beck down, the landscape started to look similar to how it would have done had I been in the correct valley. But it was so much narrower, and I was hemmed in between the beck and the boundary fence. The descent was therefore comparable, and I realised that the beck must eventually descend to the valley floor.

With tremendous effort being required, I limped my way down, literally inches at a time. But possessing only one working leg, it was difficult to maintain my balance, and I often fell over amongst the rocks.

I knew, however, that the beck was my lifeline, and as I followed it down, it began to cascade into a series of waterfalls. Then, on turning a corner, I could see that it dropped down into what looked like relatively less wild pasture in the valley below.

Eventually the beck levelled out, and I was able to cross over it via a wooden bridge. But any hopes that there was a path off it at the other side were immediately dashed. There wasn't one, and the only way to continue on down the valley was to scale a fence. Somehow, by dangerously putting all of my weight on my good leg, I managed to climb over it and hobbled on.

Then miraculously, despite the pouring rain, in the distance, I saw two walkers across on the other side of the beck. To get as close as I could to them, I had to climb down through the bracken onto the beck side. As I neared it, the noise of the flooding water was deafening. Incapacitated on one leg, I must have looked a strange sight to the men as I kept falling over in the high, wet undergrowth. Managing to get back onto my feet, I kept crossing my arms above my head, waving to the two guys as I tried to shout above the sound of the water that I'd hurt my leg. After seeing my antics rolling about on the beck-side, inquisitive, one of them eventually came as close as he could get on his side of the beck. Attempting to be heard above the uproar of the tumultuous flowing water, he spelt out that if I followed the beck down, it would lead to civilization about four miles away. He then climbed back up on his side of the beck and proceeded on his journey.

Four miles! With all of the effort required, I would be lucky to manage one. Stumbling my way back up through the bracken, another sodden wooden fence blocked my way. Managing to climb over it, by again putting all of my weight on my good leg, I continued on down the valley.

Still attempting to find some sort of track, the first impressions of one began to appear on the ground. As the land flattened, the walking at last, despite my dragging leg, became slightly easier. Looking over across the beck, I could now see the roof of what looked like a white farm building in the distance, and it was getting closer. Then, to my great surprise, I saw a car drive past it. My heart sang. There must be a road down there.

My feet hobbled on, and I noticed that the beck was flowing under an old stone bridge. I couldn't believe it, if there was a bridge, then it must be on a road and linked to civilization.

Passing through a hedge, I suddenly found myself standing on it. The nearest village might still be three miles away, and I didn't have either the strength or the physical ability to be able to walk to it, but at least I was back on solid ground.

As I came onto the road, I noticed a municipal car park about twenty yards down it. Hobbling my way towards it, I approached a sign that read Steel End Car Park. I could at last tell Pauline exactly where I was. But as the rain poured down, I discovered that there was still no mobile phone service available. So, I again attempted to send her a text message, telling her where to come and pick me up. But the rain once more fell on my phone screen and made the words appear like gibberish. I tried writing it again and again until eventually I got the message to make as much sense as I could and sent it.

I now had nothing to do but stand around feeling cold and wet in the pouring rain and hope that Pauline would receive the message and come and rescue me. But what if she didn't get it, or didn't understand the message, or couldn't find the Steel End Car Park?. Perhaps I should try to get help at the white house? Leaving the car park, I slowly hobbled my way down the road towards it. On arriving there, I discovered that the building consisted of two semi-detached cottages. Which door should I knock on? I decided to try the cottage on the left. Rapping on an old, round, metal knocker, there was a sound of someone in the house, and a dog barked as they came to the door. A young guy in his mid-Twenties opened it. I must have looked a terrible sight as I stood there with rain running off my bog-stained hat, and my over-trousers covered in peat and moss.

In a distressed state, I explained to him about coming down the wrong valley and damaging my leg out on the fells. I then asked if it was possible for him to telephone a taxi to take me to Grasmere. The young guy immediately invited me inside and offered me a cup of tea, before saying, "I can't find the number of the local taxi service, but I can give you a lift into Grasmere!" With that, he picked up his car keys and drove me all the way to the Traveller's Rest on the Ambleside Road, where I had originally planned to meet Pauline, and where I hoped that she would be waiting.

I couldn't thank the guy enough, and he refused to take any money for his petrol or time and effort. Such kindness in this modern world, who would believe that it still existed. My back was to the wall, and a total stranger gave me the help that I so desperately needed. He should be proud of himself.

How I got down that valley I will never know. I later discovered that I had ruptured my Achilles Tendon and had to wear a large boot for twelve weeks. Pauline also didn't receive the text message I sent her for a further five hours.

Walking over the High Stile Ridge

Chapter 21 - The Lion and the Lamb

Our plan today is to follow another of Wainwright's recommendations. We intend to undertake a ridge walk over the tops of the fells making up the side of the valley of Far Easedale. Starting with Calf Crag, these should eventually culminate in us arriving at the famous landmark rocks known as the Lion and the Lamb.

Having successfully climbed over Greenup Edge, we hesitate for a moment. In this mist and now with the rain coming down, might it not be a better idea to descend directly to the valley floor and what looks like the promise of flatter walking.

Quickly dismissing the thought, we put our trust in Wainwright and follow the path as it climbs up the fell and onto the top of the ridge.

On future walks, we would discover that the path along the valley bottom has its own difficulties. It isn't flat and makes for far from easy walking, often being waterlogged and rock strewn throughout its whole length.

Arriving at the top of the ridge, tracks lead us first left and then right as one by one we cross over the tops of a series of mist-covered fells. The walking is easy as tracks take us higher and higher above the valley. Looking down from our lofty height, the mist has cleared a little, and a long way down below us, we can see the meandering tiny strip of a path on the main route. The rain has turned it into a narrow stream, and it continues to come down. We're the only walkers up here and have the fells to ourselves.

As we arrive at the start of a climb onto the next fell, the mist clears for a moment, and there in front of us stands a high tower of rock. Surrounded by floating mist, it appears quite mystical and could be the legendary Isle of Avalon. The tall, dark, rocky outcrop sits perched on the edge of the next fell and a long steep path leads up to it. In the mist and rain, it looks for all the world like a castle keep.

Walking along the rising path, we climb up towards it. Under a blackening sky and in the pouring rain, we could be three medieval travellers on a pilgrimage, desperately seeking shelter in the rocky fortress. But as we approach it, the castle keep magically turns back into just another towering outcrop of rock.

This has been the highest climb so far on the ridge walk. Beyond it, we begin to follow a narrow track along the edge of the fell. We're walking high above the valley. Suddenly, by the side of the path, we see a small plaque. Pauline bends down to read what it says.

It's a dedication to a walker who had a fatal heart attack on this very spot. As we're now quite exhausted, we don't feel any better for knowing this.

"Perhaps the man died doing something that he

A Walk to the Sea

loved, surrounded by the fells on a beautiful summer's day." suggests Pauline,

I do hope so.

Continuing along the narrow path on the edge of the fell-side, there is a sheer drop to the valley floor just inches away from our feet. It looks a long way down. The path goes on for a while, and after having read the plaque, we now even more cautiously pick our way along it. It would be quite a tumble to the valley bottom.

As the mist and rain clears, a popular group of rocks known as the Howitzer appear. They sit up ahead of us on the edge of the fell of Helm Crag.

Knowing from our guidebook that this signals not just the final fell on this ridge walk, but also the way down off the tops, we're spurred on by it, and quicken our pace towards them.

We stand below a distinctive pile of rocks which point to the sky like a long cannon. Because of their shape, the rocks are well known. At a distance, they could be one of the big guns used in the trenches during the First World War. From another angle, they appear like a woman playing the organ.

Pauline attempts to climb them, having read that their summit is one of the few places in the Lakes where Alfred Wainwright never stood.

Leon and I are impressed by her efforts as she almost reaches the top. Climbing back down, we follow a rough path that continues over the fell until it culminates at another group of rocks, known as the Lion and the Lamb.

Despite the drifting mist and falling rain, these popular rocks have a large number of day walkers sitting on them. From a distance, they do actually look like a lion with a lamb between its paws.

On arriving there, the archaeologist in Pauline comes out, and despite the rain, she spends ten minutes scraping the ground beneath the rocks, looking for any sign of buried ancient artefacts.

Having studied archaeology at Hull University, Pauline never misses an opportunity to remind me that tribes of ancient Britons once peopled ridges like these.

Climbing onto the back of the rocky outcrop making up the Lion, we can see the main road into Grasmere. Beyond it lies the distinctive shape of Great Tongue, alongside which the Coast-to-Coast route will take us tomorrow.

Despite it being a short day, with all of the climbing and carrying our heavy backpacks, we're beginning to feel jaded. Leaving the rocks, we make our way off the fell, following a long winding pathway that will lead us down to the valley floor.

Although feeling spent, we're glad that we took the ridge route and feel elated that we've conquered a few more of Lakeland's tops. It also seemed easier walking up here than it would have been taking the lower route. Staring down from our lofty height, the rocky track along the floor of the valley looked like a narrow beck as it filled with rainwater.

Now, on tired feet, I'm also glad that we decided not to do the long day and carry on to Patterdale. One or two walkers we've met up with along the trail have planned to go on. These include a lone walker who we've been quite chatty with. Today we part ways. Unless he takes a day out at Kirkby Stephen, as some walkers do, he'll always be a day ahead of us and will meet a whole new set of walking companions along the way. We might see him again in Robin Hood's Bay, if he spends the night there. Another couple we've met on the trail are also making this a long day. So, we may not see them again.

The twisting track down the fell-side finally ends, and we arrive at the bottom on a rocky path. Despite having only just covered eight miles, they've been hard-won, and we're both feeling tired. Our pace slackens.

I don't envy the passing day walkers, several with children, who are just beginning to make their way up to the Lion and the Lamb. I'm glad that we've done our bit for the day and can now relax and go on autopilot as we stroll down into Grasmere.

Not being exactly sure which is the way into the village, but ever hopeful of a shortcut, we leave the tedious rock-strewn track, which has been contouring the bottom of the fell, and go through an ancient metal gate.

We're now making our way along a pathway through old dark woodland that looks as though it was once the grounds of a grand Victorian house. By the side of the path there is evidence of several discarded landscaped features, including some long since dried-up ponds.

A Victorian family must have once played here and spent their summers beside these pools. As we pass down through an avenue of trees, there is a timelessness about this place. Ghosts appear to be etched into its shadowy landscape. Eventually, we arrive at another old gate. Going through it, we find ourselves on a road. Following it, we meander our way through the environs of Grasmere.

We're heading towards the centre of the village, where we hope to visit the Tourist Information Centre. At this moment, we're unsure where we'll be spending the night and don't yet know where the campsite is, or even if there is one. But we have faith as it's only two-thirty in the afternoon, so we have time to sort it out.

At the Tourist Information Centre, we're informed that there isn't a campsite in Grasmere. Then, after a pause, with a nod and a wink, a member of staff quietly suggests that there is a farm on the outskirts of the village, who do occasionally, and quite unofficially, take one or two tents.

Armed with this knowledge, we saunter through Grasmere looking for Wordsworth's cottage. Then, after visiting his grave, look around a few of the local shops.

As walkers, we need sustenance, but most of the shops seem to be selling handicrafts or oil paintings, items which aren't required when you're spending your night in a tent. We're looking for something to eat, but apart from expensively priced cafes, can't find anything.

Where do the residents of Grasmere buy their groceries? Do they have to travel to the nearest large town?

Every eatery here seems hell-bent on ripping off the tourist by treble charging for cups of tea and fancy named sandwiches and cakes. Even if I wasn't on a budget, my penurious childhood, rather than any sort of parsimony, means that I couldn't enjoy paying out around six pounds each for a sandwich or a pasty. Staring in the windows of the various cafes at the day-trippers, many of them have arrived on coaches and are hostage to the steep prices and what little else appears to be on offer in the village. Are they simply grasping the nettle or getting a taste of living the high life?

After visiting Wordsworth's cottage and touring the shops selling useless artefacts, what else can they do? The real beauty of Grasmere resides in the lakes and fells surrounding it. There seems to be little in the village for the backpacker or even the day-tripper, only exorbitantly high prices.

Disillusioned, we take the Ambleside Road out-of-town and as we walk down it, finally find a grocery store.

Here we're once again like children in a candy shop. This is the first chance we've had to buy any real goodies since day one of our walk when we visited the store in Cleator Moor.

Perusing the shelves, we go up and down the aisles several times in case we've missed anything. I purchase a few items to supplement our evening meal and at last find some reasonably priced sandwiches for our lunch. I buy an iced cake; Leon buys more sweets, and Pauline purchases a bottle of wine.

Leaving the store happily laden down with both backpacks and carrier bags, we follow the Tourist Information Centre's instructions and make our way out of the village.

Following the busy Ambleside Road as directed, we head towards the farm. On the way, we pass the Traveller's Rest Inn and earmark it for a drink later.

Approaching the farm, a welcoming sight greets us. Several tents have already been pitched. They stand in a field at the back of some old farm buildings alongside the main road. Accompanying them on makeshift washing lines, like a message in semaphore, hang lots of wet socks and other rain-soaked clothing. Far from keeping a low profile, the wet clothing is signalling the presence of campers to every passing motorist making their way to and from the village.

It's a great sight, and we can now relax, knowing that we'll have somewhere to sleep this evening.

Identifying the array of tents, I can see that the Romans have arrived here ahead of us, as have the Dutch Girls. Both parties must have taken the faster valley route, as we never saw them up on the ridge.

Paying the farmer his camping fees, he once again repeats what the Tourist Information Centre has told us. The pitch is quite unofficial, and he doesn't know why he does it, as the local council won't give him permission to turn some of his land into a proper campsite, which he would like.

A fraternity is developing amongst the backpackers, and as we enter the field, the Romans, the Dutch Girls, and several other walkers greet us quite heartedly.

Heaving off our sacks, we set about pitching the tent. We've now developed a system; Pauline takes the lead in putting the tent up at the end of a weary day's walking, and I take it down again in the morning. Once again, I consider that I've got the better deal.

Removing my boots and socks, I enjoy anew the ecstasy of having warm grass massaging my feet.

Since leaving the fells, and dropping down two thousand feet, the rain has stopped, and it's turned into a lovely sunny afternoon.

I think about those walkers who have carried on

and are suffering the long day to Patterdale. They'll now be toiling their way up Great Tongue under this same warm sun.

On future walks, we would ourselves occasionally continue onto Patterdale. This would be to limit the number of days walking to fit in with our holidays.

Leaving Grasmere, after first spending half an hour refreshing ourselves at the Traveller's Rest, the day would be long. We would never arrive at Patterdale much before teatime. Hobbling into the village feeling utterly spent, there would be little time to relax and enjoy the glorious views of Ullswater that are available from the campsite.

With the tent up, our backpacks emptied, and items sorted, the three of us explore the farm. We discover that the toilet facilities are housed in an ancient lean-to outbuilding. Inside there is an old toilet, a sink, and a misty old mirror. As primitive as it all is, it feels good to have somewhere to stay. Despite today's journey only being nine miles, with all of the climbing and negotiating of bogs, and carrying a full backpack, it's physically been quite a hard day.

A few years after this, there would no longer be anywhere to camp in Grasmere. Even this quaint old place wouldn't exist. Walkers would have to endure the long trek to Patterdale or bear the expense of bed-and-breakfast or youth hostel accommodation.

As teatime approaches, the sun has become a

A Walk to the Sea

golden ball in a deep blue sky. After an initially wet day, we bask in its rays.

The mother and son have turned up. The boy once again looks all in, but happy, after being treated to a feast in a café in Grasmere. The Romans have left their tents and are partaking of refreshments at the Traveller's Rest. We follow them down there later for a drink. Leon is really enjoying the experience of being able to go into pubs.

Afterwards, laying in the tent with our flaps tied back, we watch as the sun slowly sets. High up on the top of the fell opposite, we can see the rocky outline of the Howitzer gradually disappearing in the dusk. I recall once again Wainwright's occasional nighttime sojourns spent up there on the fell tops as he became as one with the mountains.

I noticed a flat patch of grass just after dropping down from the Lion and the Lamb. We could have wild camped up there. But we would have missed the relative luxury of the Grasmere food store and a long cool drink in the Traveller's Rest.

Standing high up on the top of the fell at night, a walker could look down on the world below them and see and not be seen. They could watch as the lights go on and off in the valleys, both near and far.

There might even be somebody up there tonight, sitting on the Lion and the Lamb, keeping a lonely vigil amidst the solitude of the mountains. Like the Greek God Argus on Mount Olympus, they could keep watch as the world slowly goes to sleep. There would just be them and their thoughts, perhaps looking back at their lives and reliving it all over again.

Climbing into our double-sleeping bag, I once more begin my nightly fight for my share.

Wainwright's seat on Scandal Bridge

Chapter 22 - Why Does It Always Rain on Me?

A wet and misty dawn greets us. Through the tent flap, the sky looks grey. We were hoping to climb Helvelyn today, via Dolly Wagon Pike, and then to come down by Striding Edge. I had therefore planned to get my backpack carried by the Packhorse Service rather than heave its weight up and down the fellside, especially over Striding Edge. Despite steadily eating our way through a mountain of packet pasta, my sack is still much too heavy. Taking Pauline's would make it easier for me on the climbs, even though hers is far from being light.

Sadly, I must concede that the weather is too bad and looks set in for the day, so we daren't risk the climb. Instead, we'll have to take the lower Grisedale Pass route, and as the journey will only be nine miles long, we won't get our pack carried.

We've decided to walk into Grasmere to see if we can buy some Compeed and a strip of Elastoplast. Walking in our wet, peat-stained socks yesterday has caused damage to our feet, and now all three of us have blisters and broken skin.

Despite it generally being accepted that you shouldn't, last night we had a blister bursting session. I believe that it's better to get the water out of them and allow them to dry up.

Pauline has become quite expert with the needle

and needs little urging when asked to prick my blisters.

The walk into the village will add a further two miles to today's journey, one mile there and a further mile back. But it will enable us to purchase a few goodies from the food store. However, it's also likely to mean that once again most of the walking parties will get ahead of us. So, there'll be no one protecting our rear if we get lost or become uncertain along the trail.

After our journey into town, we arrive back at the start of today's walk, the turnoff for Great Tongue. Looking down the Ambleside Road, we can see that all the tents have gone from the farmer's field, so everyone must be ahead of us.

Turning off down a wide track, we head towards Great Tongue, which we've discovered is a rounded green area of fell.

As we near the tongue, we can see that the mist is down. On reaching the start of the fells, it has become so thick, it's as though we're walking on the seabed.

Following Wainwright's recommendation, we take the path on the left of the tongue as it steadily climbs up along the side of the valley. Wainwright claims that walking on this side of the tongue is best because the view back is so inspiring, but we can hardly see each other let alone any views.

On later walks, we would find the path on the right-hand side of Great Tongue to be so much

A Walk to the Sea

quicker and easier.

Higher and higher, the narrow path climbs. We must now be at some height above the Tongue, but obscured by the grey haze, we can't see it.

Eventually, we reach a junction of paths at the waterfall of Sour Milk Gill. The furiously frothing milky foam makes for an extraordinary sight, but in the mist and rain, we daren't linger here for too long lest our bodies chill down. Despite it only being about eleven o'clock in the morning, the mist has grown so thick that it's almost dark. Stepping out through the greyness in our rocky surroundings has become like walking on the surface of the moon.

A huge boulder looms up out of the mist in front of us. It must be over ten feet high. As we walk towards it, through the grey swirling veil, we suddenly come face-to-face with an apparition. From behind the gigantic boulder, two hooded ghouls have appeared, and they seem to be moving in slow motion.

For a moment, we're taken aback at the sight of them. The figures look like two spacemen wearing astronaut suits with breathing apparatus attached to their backs. The mist clears slightly for a few seconds, and we can just make out that it's two walkers wearing some kind of new-fangled, over-the-head, waterproof capes. These fit over their backpacks, and make their bodies appear huge. What causes them to look even more strange is that the capes have a see-through, fishbowl like hood attached to them, so that the occupants can see where they're going. The grey veil closes around them again, and the figures disappear.

Twenty yards further on, we come to another huge boulder. This is also at least ten feet high. Reading up later, Wainwright suggests that these gigantic rocks must have rolled down the valley during the Ice Age. I wonder if on the way down whether they might have run over some primitive man or woman and if they were ever lifted, would they find some poor Ancient Briton laid flattened out underneath them? We've also learnt from our Wainwright dictionary that isolated out-of-place boulders like these are known as erratic's. From now on, whenever we see a large rock sitting on its own, we shout.

"Look, there's an erratic!"

The rising path beyond the boulder zigzags its way up through a wasteland of rocks and scree. In the mist and rain, we're making slow progress. The weather has become atrocious. In our make-do Cagoules, we're already wet and feeling the cold.

The time has come for us to don our bin liners. But it's too chilling to stand and root in our sacks to find them, let alone cut out any head and armholes.

As we continue to make our way up through the field of rocks and scree, through the mist, we can just discern that the path's leading up to a wide rocky lip, the point where the sides of the valley come together.

A Walk to the Sea

Slowly and steadily, we move towards it, there'll be no discernible progress until we get beyond it. On arrival there, we will at least feel as though we have nearly completed the first section of today's walk.

The narrow, rocky plateau is now just above us. Climbing up to it, the wind suddenly picks up and blows us backwards. As it does so, it howls, and the cold intensifies.

Arriving on the rocky lip, we stand amidst the swirling mist and driving rain under a dark sky. The way up the valley has been hard-won, but we're here at last. Turning around to face the grey world that we've just come from, the wind, like some wild creature, buffets us, attempting to blow us over. The sensation, despite the rain, is thrilling, but once again, we're feeling cold and daren't linger here for too long and must move on.

The terrain is levelling out. Our guidebook claims that there should be a pool of water somewhere around here, but in the mist, we can't yet see it and plod on further. According to Wainwright, Grisedale Tarn will mark the top of the pass.

"But what's this?"

Through the haze, a sheet of water has come into view, but it's not a tarn, it's a whole ethereal sea.

Wainwright must have got it wrong because something has appeared out of the mist that looks like a vast, turbulent ocean. Down below us, foam topped waves roll quickly in and crash on the shoreline before hurriedly rolling back out to sea again. As they disappear off into the mist-filled distance, we stand and gaze down on the stretch of water in awe. It's such a mystical sight that I'm half expecting to see a hand holding a sword to appear out of it at any moment.

Are our eyes playing tricks with us, surely this can't be a sea as we're on the top of a mountain? It must be that the mist is so thick we can't see the far side of the tarn. Spellbound, we linger for a while as the scene is so spectacularly stunning. But then the wind and rain pick up again, and we're urged on.

Grisedale Tarn is a place where we need to take a decision. Should we attempt the climb up Dolly Wagon Pike and onto Helvelyn, or do we continue following the path down Grisedale Pass?

We're already wet, and with the wind howling and the rain now pouring down, even my optimistic self tells me that it would be better to leave it until another time. Pauline looks at me wistfully, hoping that I make the right call. She knows that I want so much to climb Helvelyn and walk over the infamous Striding Edge. But sadly, in this weather, even I realize that common sense will have to prevail, and we'll have to postpone it for another day.

On later trips, we would sometimes take the Dolly Wagon Pike route onto Helvelyn and then climb back down to the valley via Striding Edge and occasionally Swirral Edge. Once on Helvelyn you could have played football on its smooth, grassy surface. It was easy walking, but with the final sting in the tail of having to get safely over Striding Edge.

One time when we did it, it must have been the hottest day of the year. The sun shone gloriously down on us from a deep blue sky as we carefully walked along the Edge. The hardest part was always the climb down onto it from the windbreak on Helvelyn.

On an occasion when Pauline and I did the Coast-to-Coast walk backwards, we walked over Striding Edge the normal way. The difficult bit was getting off it at the end. As I climbed down the side of the Edge, and attempted to drop off it, the shoulder strap on my backpack got caught on a rock. I swung perilously in the air for a few moments before somehow being able to shake myself free.

That was quite a miraculous day all-round, as I'd climbed Striding Edge carrying a full backpack and with a badly swollen ankle. I'd damaged it the previous afternoon when coming down from Boardale Hause to Patterdale.

We had that day safely walked sixteen miles, and were about to leave the fell, when a party of walkers came towards us along a narrow path. Being polite, I stepped to one side. But as I did so, an agonizing pain shot through my ankle, and a wave of nausea swept over me. A noise like thunder suddenly filled my ears as I was about to black out.

Feeling myself going, I had visions of the passing walkers telephoning the local Mountain Rescue Team and booking me an airlift to hospital.

So, I fought it, and in great pain, attempted to maintain consciousness whilst trying to keep an expression of 'No harm done' on my face, as each of the walkers went by. Grinning innately at them, I clutched handfuls of the grassy fell-side as I endeavored to stop myself from falling into oblivion. Somehow, I managed to hold this pose until the whole group had gone by, before finally being able to slump down.

I lay there feeling nauseous, and in great danger of evacuating my bowels. Despite only being about ten minutes away from the campsite, I couldn't move for over half an hour, and eventually had to limp off the fell holding onto Pauline.

I slept in our tent that night with my ankle throbbing, and the next morning it was so swollen that Pauline urged me to visit a local cottage hospital. But I knew that if I did, our walk would be over. So, I carried on, climbing over Striding Edge on one leg with a full backpack.

I still have a slight lean over to the right on that ankle.

Chapter 23 - Pouring in Patterdale

Beyond Grisedale Tarn, the rocky path drops down slightly, we're descending. Wainwright tells us that there's another two hours of this, but at least it's now going downhill, albeit on slippery wet rock. The wind has dropped, and the mist has almost cleared, being left behind at the tarn. But the rain continues to pour down.

We pass by a place known as Brothers Parting, believed to be the location where William Wordsworth said goodbye to his brother John before he went off to sea. They were never to meet again.

Just beyond it, we arrive at Rutherford Lodge, a university owned Mountaineering Hut. I estimate that we must now be only about four miles off Patterdale, but all three of us are soaking wet, drenched through to the skin. So, despite it being a short day, with all the buffeting from the inclement weather, we're already feeling fatigued.

A few years later, the dangers of Lakeland would be brought back to us. I read about a poor woman out walking with friends on a winter's day who, on reaching this place, couldn't go on any further. Exhausted, one of her companions went off to get help, but in the cold wintery conditions, the woman later died of hyperthermia.

We too must force ourselves forward, its midsummer, but we're walking in waterlogged boots and drenched clothing. My jogging pants are so wet that they drape around my legs like two soaking towels. We're fast becoming so chilled that I wonder if we'll ever get our bodies warm again.

Leaving the lodge, the track bifurcates. This is yet another word we've picked up from our Wainwright dictionary. There are paths now on both sides of the valley bottom. Fortunately, we choose correctly. Crossing over a wooden bridge, we follow the path along the right-hand side. It would be easy to go astray here as there are several trails.

As we steadily make our way down the pass, the environs of the valley are gradually beginning to change. They are transforming from one of an austere wilderness to that of a pastoral setting. But the rain continues to pour.

We're now on a farm track below the high fell of St Sunday Crag. Just before reaching the farm, we pass by a stone barn. I recognize it as the place where in 1954 Alfred Wainwright spent the night of the Queen's Coronation, the same day that Edmund Hillary and Tenzing Norgay climbed Mount Everest. Despite a notice on the gate declaring 'No Path', we go through it and pay homage to Wainwright at the barn entrance.

We're staring in at a place that can't have altered much since he spent the night here, all those years ago. A place where he once sat and smoked endless cigarettes because he was apparently too scared to sleep in case the farmer came along and caught him in there.

Once again, we daren't linger here for too long, as our cheap plastic jackets have really let us down today. The three of us are soaking wet, right through to our skin. My underwear hangs off me like a soggy nappy, and my socks and boots are awash. Leaving the barn entrance, we retrace our footsteps back through the gate.

Spent and on autopilot, we begin to make our way along a tarmacked road that should eventually take us into Patterdale, where we hope to find the sanctuary of the campsite. Feeling desperately cold, the road out of the valley seems much longer than it should. But even in the rain, there is a timelessness about this tramp along the valley floor.

The road is becoming tree-lined, and we pass by a group of isolated cottages. They stand empty and silent, in need of repair, but you can't help wondering about the lives that must have once been lived here. Despite their dilapidated state, the cottages would soon be redeveloped and turned into very expensive holiday homes.

Arriving at the main road running between Glenridding and Patterdale, we turn right and follow it as it heads towards the now prominent Patterdale Hotel. As we walk along the pavement, a sign points the way down a farm road to the campsite.

The fells have chilled us right through to the bone. We're on our last cylinder of energy and the borders of hyperthermia. If the campsite isn't at the end of this long trod, we'll be in trouble.

Crossing over a wooden bridge, high fells tower up in front of us. Continuing on down the road, we arrive at the reception counter for the campsite.

A sign on the wall displays a range of camping fees. It's not simply a case of how many tents have you got and how many people are sleeping in them. These are just the mandatory charges. There is a further list of fees for the camper. For example, if you've arrived by car, if you're carrying a canoe, if you possess a dog and if you've brought along an awning, then financially, you're going to be in big trouble.

Standing before her, three shivering, dripping wet wrecks wearing sodden anoraks and leaking backpacks. An assertive female student, home from university for the summer, asks if we've arrived by car. Satisfying herself from our drenched state that we haven't, she wastes further time reading through the long list of charges. Are we carrying a canoe, do we have an awning tucked away somewhere, do we possess a dog? After receiving negative responses to each of the items on her list, she reluctantly settles for charging us for one tent and three very wet people.

Years later, the camping fees would be a lot more

straightforward and the welcome so much sweeter. There would also be an excellent makeshift café where you could enjoy homemade tea and cakes.

Paying the girl, we're directed to follow a rough farm track down to the actual camping ground. Tired and drenched to the skin, it takes a further quarter mile of tramping before we arrive there. This extra trek will add distance to tomorrow's journey.

Entering the camping field through a farm gate, we're immediately met by a sensational vista. Despite the rain, the views across Lake Ullswater towards St Sunday Crag and Helvellyn are superb. Therefore, in retrospect, the fees charged here are quite reasonable.

Chilled to the bone, Leon and I have no other thought than to want to rush off for a hot shower. But Pauline bravely takes the lead in putting the tent up. Once erected, we've developed a well-organized routine as to what goes where. Looking in my backpack, I discover that our sleeping bag has got soaking wet. The relentless rain must have found a way down into the plastic shopping bag in which it was wrapped. Having only a few plastic sacks, we've had to use thin shopping bags for some of our items. Unlike the sacks, the tops of the bags have been open all day and so the rainwater has crept in. Taking off our anoraks, we put them into one of the plastic sacks to try to keep the wet things out of the tent. I then dash off with Leon to the shower block, leaving

Pauline to finish off before she follows us.

The shower water is boiling hot, but it still takes about twenty minutes under the glorious steaming spray to bring life back to my frozen body. I leave the ablutions block feeling warmer and so much more alive. Back in the tent, I find a dry tee-shirt amongst the wet things in my backpack.

Pauline joins me, and now dressed in dryer clothing, we feel somewhat revived. The rain has almost stopped, and leaving Leon to rest in the tent, we decide to go down into Patterdale to look for a few goodies in the village store.

We have to once again walk the whole length of the long farm trod. Just before arriving at the store, we pass by the garage attached to the Patterdale Hotel. Built for a single car, it has its doors flung wide open and there inside is an electric clothes-dryer. On the top of the machine, a sign reads.

"Fifty pence pieces only!"

Pauline and I immediately assume that this must be some enterprising way that the hotel earns additional income from passing wet walkers. Why else would the sign be there and on this rainy day, the garage doors flung so invitingly open?

Looking at each other, we both get the same idea. We could dry our soaking wet sleeping bag here. Rushing back down the farm trod to the campsite, we collect it. Having got so sodden coming down Grisedale Pass, it desperately needs drying out, and here is the perfect opportunity. It seems almost miraculous that we should have found this place, and with the garage doors standing wide open on such a wet day, they're clearly touting trade.

Luckily, when we arrive back there, no other walkers have turned up during our absence. Placing our sleeping bag into the dryer, I drop a coin into the payment slot, and the machine starts. Standing watching the bag as it spins around and around, we gain comfort from the heat that the dryer is throwing out.

The fifty pence runs out after about ten minutes. Feeling the sleeping bag, it's not perfectly dry, but it's warm and so much dryer than it was. Putting it back into the machine, we have a further fifty pence worth.

This is just so thoughtful of the hotel. What a brilliant idea to cater for the wet walker. It benefits them, and I imagine makes the staff a little bit of money as well.

As we wait for our second fifty pence to finish, the Dutch Girls pass by the garage and Pauline sticks her head out to tell them about our great find. They've also got soaking wet coming down Grisedale Pass and happily form a queue behind us to wait to dry some of their gear. Soon the Romans pass the garage and, greeting the four of us, ask what we're all doing in there. Pauline explains about the clothes dryer, and the Romans, impressed by our find, join the queue. They heave off their backpacks and begin to sort out their wet clothing. They also shout to other passing Coast-to-Coast walkers they've met on the trail, making them aware of this amazing service. A few more rain-soaked backpackers join the long queue to wait their turn to dry their wet gear in the machine.

The garage is packed, but nobody seems to mind the wait as everyone is busy chatting about today's relentless rain and their misty adventures out there on the fells.

Removing our sleeping bag from the machine, the Dutch girls happily take their turn and place their wet clothes into the dryer.

Just as we're about to leave the garage, I notice that a couple of people with frowning faces have sheepishly joined the rear of the long queue of backpackers. They're not wearing cagoules and don't appear to be walkers as they're carrying bag loads of wet bed linen. They must be staff from the hotel, and by the look on their faces, perhaps the use of the dryer isn't quite as straightforward as it first seemed. With our heads down, we skulk out of the garage past them.

On subsequent trips to Patterdale, we've noticed that whenever we pass by the hotel, the garage doors are now always kept firmly shut. Perhaps we did make a mistake that day, but that night we slept so much dryer in our sleeping bag than we would have done.

As the day turns to early evening, the rain finally stops, and the sun comes out. Tying back our tent flaps, we stare out at the glorious views of Ullswater and beyond it towards the fells of St Sunday Crag and Helvellyn. The campsite slopes its way down to the lake and the rays of the setting sun shine silvery on its surface. This is such a well-positioned site. All around us, the views are spectacular.

With the improvement in the weather, campers are beginning to appear at the front of their tents. Many of those pitched on the site are jumbo-sized family affairs with encampments formed around them. The sound of music comes out of a plethora of portable radio sets, and smoke rises lazily from the numerous barbeques that have been lit.

Screams suddenly go up from one of the nearby encampments. A party of campers have been sitting around their barbecue and a grass snake has dared to enter their territory.

Being close by, we can see that the snake, frightened by the incessant screaming, is attempting to side-wind its way back out into the undergrowth. Sadly, before it can escape, the brave men of the encampment pounce on it, attacking it with broom handles, tent poles, pans, and anything else to hand. Beaten into unconsciousness, the snake is then gingerly tossed onto the barbecue. Pleased with their exertions, the men and women, like primitive ancient

Britons, sit around and watch it smoulder. It was a close thing; the wife and kids have been saved from being bitten, or even possibly from being eaten alive.

It's strange how people, who have presumably come out here to enjoy the countryside, are so often afraid of it.

Pauline has been talking to the man in the next tent. She's discovered that he's the person who camped at the foot of the small hill of Dent during the first day of our walk. He's carrying a heavy backpack and, feeling that he had already done quite sufficient walking decided to pitch his tent. Tired out from his journey, he climbed in and was soon fast asleep. Waking up at midnight in the pitch black with trees swaying all around him, for a moment, he wondered just where he was.

Whilst he's also doing the Coast-to-Coast walk, he's not taking the usual two weeks like everyone else. Being early retired, he plans to allow himself a month to saunter his way across England. Whenever he arrives at a decent campsite, he spends several days there before moving on. The man is single, in his late fifties, and has no one to rush home to. Rather than sitting isolated at home, he's spending his summer surrounded by people and chattering voices. He keeps meeting friendly strangers even if they just nod at him on the site or in the washroom. He doesn't work, so if he were at home, he would be carrying out the same daily routine, possibly locked in the house for most of the day, not seeing or meeting anyone. Out here, there's a pulse of life on these campsites. People are friendly. The country code of saying hello to everyone you meet helps him to communicate with the world.

He's not the only person we've met doing this. Later we came across a very old man in Ulverston on the Cumbrian Way, who, for a couple of months every summer, pitches a tent on a campsite. Sitting outside it all day, rather than staying isolated at home on his own, he gets to talk with complete strangers.

The sun is finally setting. The fells start to disappear in the dusk and Ullswater flows even more silvery in front of us. It's nearly 11 o'clock and smoke from the last of the barbecue's floats in the air. Snatches of music can still be heard coming out of portable radio sets and people continue to chatter loudly behind the various encampment awnings.

We turn in, wondering if tonight will be like the night at the campsite at Borrowdale, where the campers' held parties and laughed and chattered until dawn. But at exactly eleven o'clock, just as though a switch has been flicked, the site falls silent.

This wouldn't always be the case. Many years later, when we were camped here, we had to endure hours of monotonous chatter from two guys in a nearby tent as they slowly sipped their way through can after can of beer. As they did so, one of them kept explaining to the other (and the rest of the campsite) in painstaking detail why his wife would never leave him. Apparently, she simply 'had it so good'. The other guy occasionally interjecting with the obligatory, "Yes" and "No" at appropriate intervals, as he partook of the free ale.

By two o'clock in the morning, and after having listened to several hours of this mundane, insane babble, Pauline decided that she'd had enough and shouted to let the guys know it. I was fully expecting a string of imprecations and a raging bull at our tent entrance. But thankfully, the men immediately shut up, and not another word was uttered.

Most of the people from the other fifty tents on the campsite that night must have heard the constant chatter, but no one else dared to intervene.

On Striding Edge

Chapter 24 – As I Walked Out One Misty Morning

The day breaks with rain hammering on the tent roof. Last night, we read through today's section of the walk in our guidebook, and Wainwright suggests that it could be tricky if the weather is bad. Through a crack in our tent flap, I can see black clouds covering the tops of the fells, and the rain is lashing down.

During the months of planning our walk, today has been a day that in some ways we've been dreading. We have no backup OS map to cover this part of the route, and only the basic maps and descriptions in Wainwright's guidebook to navigate by.

We live with an unspoken fear of getting lost out on the fells. Of going off route and wandering aimlessly about in the High Places with no idea of how to get back down again. Straying off the track would also mean adding to the mileage on what is already a long, hard day. I've studied the guidebook, and the first part of the walk steadily climbs until it eventually culminates at the top of Kidsty Pike. We've also learnt that the higher you climb on days like today, the colder it gets.

Wainwright has suggested an alternative bad weather route via the lakeside hamlet of Howtown, which he claims is much flatter and less remote. But from the first day, I've been a purist, and have trodden every inch of the trail. I want to do the walk the proper way and not theoretically cheat. Even on St Bees Head, I followed the path as close to the cliff edge as I could, as it twisted and turned its way high above the sea. There were places where I could have gone straight across, saving both time and energy, but I continued to contour. I've even climbed stiles when there was an open gate.

Another more pertinent fact about changing our plans is that I consider it's too late to study the Howtown route and be able to take it in. We've read through this section of the journey from Patterdale to Shap many times, and I believe it's better to stick with what we know rather than to attempt something new.

It's now half-past six in the morning, and the rest of the campsite has yet to wake. Pauline boils water and makes coffee, and we each eat a flapjack. Apart from a few competitively priced toffees on route, this will be our sole sustenance for the sixteen-mile trek which lies ahead, seven of which involve a continuous climb up to Kidsty Pike.

Not eating meat or fish, our diet on this walk has been even more restricted than it is back at home. How I envy those backpacking carnivores who carry those precooked sausages that come in sealed foil packaging and don't require refrigerating. I imagine that they could be used to spice up a pan of beans or spaghetti or to knock up a quick stew. I finish my flapjack.

If we can only stay on route for the first seven miles and make it to the Pike, from there we ought to be able to see the track down to Haweswater. The rest of the journey should then be relatively easy to follow. A four-mile walk alongside a reservoir followed by gently meandering our way through a pastoral landscape until we arrive at Shap Abbey. The abbey is just a mile out from today's destination of the village of Shap.

However, because of our lack of confidence and the inclement weather, we don't really want to attempt the first part of today's walk alone. What we need are some pathfinders, a party of Coast-to-Coast walkers we can follow, who will unwittingly lead us through the wilderness of the fells until we arrive at the promised land of Kidsty Pike. Or at least stay ahead of us until we've gained our confidence.

Last night, before we went to sleep, Pauline and I lay plotting. Our plan is to wait for the first Coast-to-Coast walkers to rise from their tents for their morning wash. When they do, we'll fill our backpacks and be ready to take down the tent. Then, as soon as any of the other walking parties set off, we'll stealthily follow them. There's safety in numbers, especially in weather like this.

Despite a brief respite last night, the rain has continued from where it left off yesterday. Nobody is moving, so there's little chance of us getting off to an early start.

Pauline sits keeping a vigil at the tent flap. Looking out at the other tents, she watches to see if any of the Coast-to-Coast walkers have stirred yet, so that when they do, we're ready to follow them.

This remains our main plan of action, our modus operandi. The journey over the fells looks difficult until we reach the former lake, now reservoir, of Haweswater, and we really don't want to get lost out there in the wild.

Pauline leaves her post and rushes out through the rain for her morning wash, and I take over her duties. On her return, she tells me that she's met one of the three University girls in the washroom.

These are a group of young walkers who are mixing camping with Youth Hosteling and who we keep meeting up with along the trail. Because of the mist and rain, they claim that they daren't risk taking the high-level path and have decided to follow the lower level Howtown route.

Hearing this has made Pauline even more anxious about today's journey.

"Suppose nobody else is going up there!"

"We could be all on our own and there'll be no one to help us if we get lost."

I try to reassure her, but I'm feeling apprehensive about it myself. The blackened, mist-covered fell tops with the rain coming down do look daunting. But haven't we made it safely across Lakeland so

A Walk to the Sea

far? If only we can get through today, then we'll have finished with the High Places and tomorrow we'll be walking in a very different type of environment.

Unfortunately, today's fells are more remote and less frequented than those in central Lakeland. So, there are likely to be fewer people around. Especially in this weather.

Do the University girls know something we don't? I haven't really studied the Howtown route and still think it's too late to start that now. But in case we go off trail and cover any extra mileage, we do need to get away early, and I'd like this to be by eight-thirty at the latest.

I'm sure I'm not the first, but I've devised a way of measuring how long it's likely to take us to complete a day's walk. By settling on a walking speed of two miles per hour, it gives some indication of the slowest time we're likely to arrive at our destination. Today's journey is sixteen miles long, so according to my method, even including breaks, it should take a maximum of eight hours to reach Shap. Therefore, if we set off at nine o'clock, we should be there by five this evening at the very latest. We simply adjust our time of arrival as we go along.

Things are looking desperate. It's now nine o'clock, and the rain is continuing to pour down. The fell tops surrounding the campsite remain obscured by black rolling clouds. Worse still, nobody is leaving their tent and making a move, and I can tell by Pauline's face that she's worried.

"What if the rest of the walkers decide to take a day out, we'll be up there all alone?" she repeats, perhaps trying to coax me into putting our journey off until tomorrow.

If only one of the other parties would go for it and set off, it would give us the strength and encouragement to follow them. Knowing that someone else is up ahead of us and that others may be following, so that we won't be the last ones making our way across the fells, would boost our confidence.

It's now almost nine-thirty and still no one seems to have stirred, let alone set off. Either they're waiting for a break in the weather, or they've decided, as Pauline suggests, that it's so bad they're going to take the day out.

There's no alternative, we're running out of time and will just have to go for it, raining or not. Packing things haphazardly into my backpack, I run through the rain with it to the shelter of the old ablutions block. I identified this place yesterday as somewhere to keep our gear out of the wet while we pack.

Returning to the tent, Pauline and Leon pass further items out to me and I rush them in relays to the former washroom. By doing several trips, the tent slowly empties. Finally, like bailing out of an aircraft, wearing her own well-stuffed backpack, Pauline makes a dash for it off to the new toilet facilities and Leon quickly follows her. Here they'll get themselves ready for the day ahead while I take down the tent and refill my sack.

The tent is soaking wet, and I know from bitter experience that if I'm not careful, it will pervade the contents of my backpack. Unfortunately, we badly underestimated the number of plastic sacks required to keep things separate and dry. As we've gone along on our journey, we've also lost some and don't have enough left to cover everything. So, we're having to use plastic shopping bags.

To limit the damage caused by the rain coming off the wet tent, I put our sleeping bag inside one of our two remaining thicker plastic sacks. I've already learnt on this walk that this is essential.

After shaking the tent, I fold it up on the concrete floor of the old shower room and try to make it as small a shape as possible. I then fit it into our last plastic sack. This should stop any residual rain from permeating the rest of my backpack, and wetting our sleeping bag and my few dry, clean clothes.

As well as carrying far too much, the wet tent is expanding, and my backpack is becoming difficult to fill. I try to find a place for everything, including all of the useless items I've brought along with me. It takes time, but eventually everything is squeezed into it.

Glancing at my watch, it's now ten o'clock, we're packed, and will have to grasp the nettle and go for it. Today's journey is long, and we're already well-behind our planned schedule and fast running out of time.

Using my estimated walking pace of two miles per hour, it suggests that we're unlikely to arrive in Shap much before six o'clock this evening. This means that the tent, and everything else that's wet, will remain in our sacks until then, and won't have a chance to dry.

I hitch my backpack high up onto my shoulders. Despite us continuing to eat our way through the packets of pasta, my sack still weighs heavy, and I once again stumble forward like an overloaded mule.

Meeting Pauline and Leon at the new toilet block, she tells me the good news that the Dutch girls have just left. She doesn't, however, know which route they're taking.

We set off quickly behind them, following at a discreet distance. But instead of them turning off the farm road towards the path marking the start of today's walk, they continue on along it and look as though they've decided to stock up on refreshments at the village store. Walking there and back will add a further mile, and an extra half hour, to their journey time. So, they'll be of little use to us, even if we knew for certain that they were going our way. We can't wait for them and now have no alternative but to go for it.

Leaving the farm road, we begin our first ascent

of the day. A climb up a high fell. After initially scrambling straight upwards, we continue along a steadily rising path situated halfway up the fell-side.

On reaching a commemorative bench dedicated to Queen Victoria. The path suddenly veers dramatically uphill as though it's decided to make a dash for the summit of the fell. Following along it, we arrive on the edge of the fell top.

I'm soaking wet with both rain and sweat and my backpack is once again weighing ominously heavy. Without speaking, the three of us shudder to a halt, and stand and deeply suck in the air. Our hands rest naturally on our hips as we look back towards Ullswater.

With our breath returned, we saunter onto what appears to be the crest of the fell. Arriving at a featureless crossroads of paths, we assume from our guidebook that we're at Boardale Hause. Here, after our exhausting climb, we stop once more.

The rain continues to come down, but even more worrying, a dense mist has closed in. It surrounds us, rolling around the rocky moonscape of the fell top like a Sherlockian fog. Once again on our journey, we can only see a matter of a few yards in front of us.

We're now facing a choice of paths we could follow, and it would be easy to go wrong. Reading through our guidebook last night, Wainwright stressed that we should be very careful here, and warns walkers not to follow the path off to the valley of Martindale by mistake.

Pauline suggests that we should take an extreme path off to the right, which whilst we can't see where it goes, must contour the edge of the fell. I think she's wrong and suggest that we take a nearby path that enters a narrow pass situated between two mist filled fell-sides.

As we stand in the haze, considering which path to take, we can hear faint voices. Straining our ears to listen, we try to identify where they're coming from. We can just discern the figures of another walking party. They're stood a distance away from us in the gloom. The voices don't sound familiar, so we can't have met them before, which suggests that they must be Toast-to-Toasting.

The party emerges for a moment from out of the murk. There are three of them, they're consulting their guidebooks and talking earnestly, as though they too are apprehensive, and wondering which path they should take.

This mist is a Pea Souper, of which Victorian London would have been proud, so no wonder they're nervous. The party seem hesitant, as though waiting for us to move off and show them the way. But we're also uncertain and hoping that they'll be able to direct us.

In the mist, our surroundings appear even more like that of a stark wilderness. We're once again walking away from civilization and will need to hold our nerve if we're to get over the fells and find it again.

The chilling weather forces us to take a decision. Standing at a distance, the other party are clearly not going to make their move. Taking the plunge, we make ours and set off down the mist-filled void between the two fell-sides.

I'm hoping that this will encourage the other walkers to follow us. If they do, then hopefully they'll be confirming that we're on the right path. If they don't, then it's likely to suggest we're not.

Every ten yards or so we look back, but it's difficult to see anything through the grey veil, and we're relying on hearing their voices. After a few minutes, Pauline spots movement behind us in the mist. After some initial hesitation, the other party do appear to be following us, albeit at a distance. We still can't see them, but can occasionally hear their faint voices. But it's us that should be following them. This was meant to be our ploy.

Further down the pass, we tentatively go. The mist is growing denser. It swirls like fiends around us, and the wind howls in our ears. Our heads are bent low as it drives the rain sharply against our faces. We're apprehensive, but at least we now have the comfort of knowing that there are other people around if anything goes wrong. Straining our ears, we can still occasionally hear their voices and odd words of conversation. But as we continue on down the pass, the voices are becoming more distant.

It's a good job we didn't wait any longer at the campsite. The weather is getting even worse, and we might not have set off at all. Despite it only being about eleven o'clock in the morning, the mist has made the sky almost black like the night. We're walking through a murk and the rain has now turned into sleet.

Without speaking, fear has again entered our minds and both Pauline and I are silently considering whether we should turn back and give it up for the day. This weather can't be normal for the time of year. It seems so extreme that surely nobody should be out here walking in it.

But what if we do turn back? There would be little solace as we would have to set up camp again and endure a whole day laid cramped together in a wet tent, on a wet campsite. It would also put us back a day and there might still be bad weather this time tomorrow.

I try to think of the positives of going on, such as tasting the gorgeous, golden fried chips rumoured to be had at the fish shop in Shap. I salivate at the thought of them and the possibility of mushy peas, pickled onions, and a buttered bread cake. Positive luxuries after our usual evening meal of packet pasta. There will also be the opportunity to spend the night camped at the rear of a quiet village pub with our tent pitched just a few yards away from the bar. If we can only get to Kidsty Pike and down to the Haweswater reservoir, then after that the route finding should be easy.

Urged on, but apprehensive, Pauline and Leon reluctantly follow me. As we walk, we continue to strain our ears, listening out for the voices behind us which have become worryingly quiet.

Stopping for a moment in the mist and rain, we hope to catch a crumb of comfort, to hear another human voice again amidst this maelstrom. We need the reassurance of knowing we're not alone if we get lost or require help. And seek confirmation that we're not being reckless in continuing on.

I suddenly recall one of Santos's army training exercises in which he claimed he was taught the North American Indian technique of listening out for distant enemy voices. All we apparently have to do, according to Santos, is to open our mouths and turn our heads slowly from side-to-side as we listen. Coming to a halt, like three grotesque clown masks in an amusement arcade, we stand with our mouths agape as we gently gyrate our heads from left to right, left to right. Sadly, there is only silence.

The voices have gone, suggesting that the party following us has turned back. Does this mean that they've realised we're on the wrong path, or has the mist, the wind and the rain forced them into retreat? If so, then should we also turn back?

All alone now and deeper into our journey, Pauline looks even more apprehensive. Should I tell her that we'll give it up for the day? Does that party know something we don't? Is this weather beyond that normally accepted as bad for the time of year, so that walkers shouldn't really be out in it? It certainly feels so.

We hear later, on the grapevine, that the people following us had indeed headed back to Patterdale and would resume their journey in the morning, by which time they hoped that the weather would have improved.

But now committed, and once again in danger of hyperthermia in our cheap plastic jackets, we urge our feet forward. With our heads bent low in the howling wind and driving rain, we reach the end of the mist-filled passage.

Standing getting our bearings, the mist clears in patches, and I can see that Pauline was correct in earlier suggesting that the path we should have taken was further off to our right. Luckily, our trail has at least gone in the same direction, and so we're not far off route.

Joining Pauline's path, it soon takes us along the side of a fell which, according to our guidebook, towers high above a road. The path is close to the top of the fell and the mist beneath us is so thick that it gives no indication that there is a road somewhere down there in the valley below. Despite the wind and the rain, the path is flat, and the going is easy.

We're stepping out through the mist with a solid blanket of grey at our feet that can't be seen through.

Walking in an eerie, dampened silence, it feels like we're edging our way along the top of a netherworld. Below us is a mist-filled nothingness, and we must keep on along this narrow path or tumble down into it. As we step out through the greyness, it seems as though we're the only souls left alive in the world. We're three acrobats, walking on a tightrope, with only the crest of the fell showing above us. One stumble on the path, and we could descend into that grey abyss.

The path turns a corner, and we're back on the top of the fell. This is a decisive moment. If we're still on route, then we should soon come to our first major landmark of the day, the small mountain lake of Angle Tarn.

Straining our eyes, we attempt to peer through the mist, hoping to see an expanse of water. But as we step through the muffled greyness, there's nothing to be seen but rocks and boulders.

Then suddenly, from out of the haze, a magical stretch of water appears, which has some small distinctive islands in it. The scene looks exactly like the photograph in our coffee table, Wainwright.

We've found Angle Tarn.

Until seeing Innominate Tarn on Haystacks and the mist filled Grisedale Tarn, neither of us had ever seen a mountain lake. They look such magical and yet lonely places. Grisedale Tarn, with the mist cloaking it and the waves rolling into the shore, looked so ethereal. But now Angle Tarn in the mist looks even more like a scene from the Dark Ages.

In this weather, it would be easy to believe that this is the actual pool of water into which Sir Bedivere eventually threw King Arthur's sword Excalibur.

It's such an enchanting place, and as the mist clears for a moment in patches all the way around the tarn, we can see that we're no longer alone. A few other hardy souls have gone for it and are walking up ahead of us on the far side of the water. We never saw them leave the campsite, so they must be a party of Toast-to-Toasters or Youth Hostellers. Unbelievably, there is also a tent pitched alongside the tarn. Somebody wild camped here last night.

"Hurray!"

It feels good to know that we're no longer alone and don't appear to have been as foolhardy as we perhaps thought we might have been. We've also arrived at our first real landmark of the day, so we're still on route. Our hearts sing.

Chapter 25 – Wondrous Place

Despite the savage beauty of the tarn, because of the chilling weather, we daren't spend too long here beside its icy waters. But as we make our way around it, we keep stopping and gazing down on it in awe.

Angle Tarn must have looked exactly as it does now, over a thousand years ago. Has anyone ever stood on those tiny islands, I wonder? Did ancient man and woman once kneel down here to collect water?

Despite its primitive loveliness, this is an austere place. There is no shelter from the cold and its wide open to the elements.

The rocky path continues to make its way around the tarn, and we follow it. As the mist for a moment clears, we spy a party of walkers moving off about thirty yards up ahead of us. This is our chance to freeload, to trail in their wake. They can become the pathfinders we waited for back at the campsite. With frozen fingers, I put my guidebook away.

This whole section of the walk between Patterdale and the Haweswater reservoir we've long since identified as being the most difficult part of today's adventure. Now, with the mist and rain coming down, it's even more of a challenge. It's a long day, and we're unlikely to arrive in Shap much before teatime, so we really don't want to go off route. To do so would add both extra time and distance to our journey. Having no Ordnance Survey map for this part of the walk, if we lose the trail, we might not find it again and could wander off aimlessly over the fells. And if we do eventually get down off them, we would then have to try to road walk to Shap. This could prove impossible, and we may well have to give up, so we're grateful for our pathfinder's help.

As the party in front move off, like Red Indian braves, we stalk them. Staying just out of sight, we hang back when they stop or show any signs of hesitation. The rolling mist helps us in this, as we're led over sodden terrain and through rocky outcrops. The mist remains, but doesn't seem as dense as it was, and the rain has also eased. We gratefully follow our scouts as they plot a course across a wide, wet, bog ridden plateau and begin the climb up the fell-side of the Knott.

As they ascend, we use stealth as we track them, always keeping at a discreet distance. But they're slowing down, and we're catching up with them. The group disappears around a bend near to the top of the fell, and we follow. But as we turn the corner, we're practically on them, they've decided to stop for lunch.

Please don't stop now, I feel like pleading, we're so close to Kidsty Pike. But I don't, and simply grin and acknowledge them as we pass.

Did they realise we were following them; I wonder?

Getting my guidebook out, the route finding is

now back with us. But judging by the steepness of the climb, we must be somewhere close to the summit of the Knott and can't be that far off Kidsty Pike.

The steadily rising path we're on is wide and looks straightforward enough. As we follow it, the mist is clearing, and now just hangs in patches like steam coming off the water in a bath.

Arriving at the top of the fell, the path levels out, and we can see the trig point on the summit of the Knott.

On a later walk, we would go off route to touch it and claim the fell, bagging ourselves another Wainwright.

The wide, stony path now only has a slight rise to it and makes for easy walking. Arriving at a junction, a track branches off to the left and the wide trail continues straight on. Our path looks much more well-trodden, and we're uncertain whether this is the point where our guidebook tells us to turn off.

But looking on the ground, help is at hand. Someone has kindly made an arrow out of some small stones, and it points straight on. Underneath it, neatly arranged in pebbles, are the letters C2C. How helpful this suggests that Coast-to-Coast walkers must often go wrong here. So, it's not yet time to turn off towards Kidsty Pike.

Continuing along our existing path, it begins to rise, and rocky outcrops start to surround us. The mist is also growing thicker again, and something tells me that this isn't right.

As we stop to consult our guidebook. From out of the mist appears a middle-aged man sporting a tweed jacket. Worried that we might go wrong at this crucial moment, Pauline takes the opportunity to clarify the situation.

"Are we on the right path for Kidsty Pike," she asks politely.

"Haven't you got a map?" the man answers curtly

"Not for this section," replies Pauline.

We then receive a lecture on why people without maps shouldn't be out walking on the fells.

Yes, I know, but we're on a budget and while we don't have an OS map to cover these six miles, unless we get lost, we can usually rely on the route map and instructions in our guidebook. It's only when we've gone too far off the trail that we really do need a map.

Dismissing us as fools, the man begrudgingly informs us that we should have turned off down the path where the stone arrow pointed the route as going straight on.

We've been duped and should have stuck to our instincts. Instead of heading towards Kidsty Pike, we've been continuing along the old Roman road of High Street. Somebody must have switched the head of the arrow, some joker thinking it's funny to get walkers, possibly on the border of hyperthermia, lost in the High Places.

A Walk to the Sea

Retracing our footsteps back to the turnoff, we head down it. We must now be walking above the Straits of Riggindale, and the path should eventually lead to Kidsty Pike. But the remaining mist is still floating above the top of the fell, and we can't see anything. It hangs like a dense cloud above Riggindale, blocking out any views down into the valley below.

But after about fifteen minutes of steady walking, the path swings off to the right. The ground here's covered in small white rocks and leading off from them in the mist-filled distance looms the distinctively pointed shape of Kidsty Pike.

On a later walk, we would once get too complacent on this section. After turning off the High Street path for Kidsty Pike, chatting away instead of veering off towards it, we walked straight on. Following tracks on the ground, they soon became faint and eventually disappeared altogether.

The mist that day was the worse we had ever seen it, and probably accounted for our mistake. Normally, as you walk along the path to Kidsty Pike, you can look down from the Straits of Riggindale at the lake of Haweswater. But this day, the mist was once again so thick that we couldn't even see the Pike. Having walked off route for twenty minutes, we could tell by our desolate surroundings that we were totally lost. My suggestion to Pauline was for us to continue on a general compass direction heading east, the way the Coast-to-Coast walk is going. But she was convinced that she could find her way back to Kidsty Pike. And on a flat barren fell top, in thick mist, with no landmarks to go by, she traced her way to the Pike and safety.

As we arrive at Kidsty Pike, most of the mist has cleared from the fell tops. We're now able to stare down at the end of the former lake of Haweswater, and gaze across the valley towards the fells of High Street.

As we do so, Pauline suddenly catches sight of an eagle as it soars high up above us and points it out to me.

Despite patches of floating mist, the intermittent views of the fells and the end of Haweswater appear dramatic from our lofty height. Mist hangs in the air like clouds of steam that slowly float over the fell of High Street. Down in the valley below, we can see the head of the lake or reservoir as it now is. Our eyes eagerly scan it for glimpses of the drowned village of Mardale Green. There is little to be seen other than old stone field boundary walls that disappear off into the water, and a very distinctive-looking island of fir trees.

Some years later, when Pauline and I walked the Coast-to-Coast Walk east to west, huge flies would attack us on this spot. Thoroughly exhausted after our climb up to Kidsty Pike from Haweswater, we collapsed down on the rocks here to take a well-earned rest. But within seconds, we were surrounded by hundreds of giant flies, who, like Kamikaze pilots, kept buzzing in on us in constant attacks. Despite almost being out on our feet after the climb, we had no choice but to get up and leave. The only explanation I could make for their behaviour was that they were being attracted by the streams of sweat, which, due to our recent exertions, were pouring freely down our faces and backs. The flies were probably simply after a drink.

The cold is beginning to seep into our bodies again, and it urges us to leave the Pike. We can now clearly see the route we have to follow; a wide path which winds its way down the fell-side.

Once again, we'll soon lose all the height we've spent the morning sweating to gain.

I'm beginning to dislike this side of walking in the Lakes. Spending hours slowly grinding your way up a fell to gain height and then at the top, all your efforts often almost immediately being wasted, as you head straight back down again.

Once you've achieved the summit of a fell, you should at least be able to gain some significant mileage along it before you have to descend. When you don't, you feel as though you've given it away far too cheaply and have wasted all your earlier efforts.

We've been steadily climbing all the way from Patterdale. But we're now heading back down again.

After the slog of continually ascending all morning, we feel weary, and our pace slackens. But as we tentatively begin the climb down from the Pike, the path is wide and provides for easy walking.

Looking back, it's plain to see why Kidsty Pike and other pikes bear that name, as the rocky fell-side comes to such a dramatic point.

After several rotations down the grassy fell, we stand on a rocky lip high above the valley of Mardale. We've reached a long final section of the fell, where a series of outcrops lead dramatically down towards the valley bottom. The remains of the village of Mardale Green lie somewhere in the valley below us, but a precipitous route down to it requires all of our attention.

Commencing the descent, we begin to zigzag our way through each of the rocky outcrops known as Kidsty Howes. At times, we have to revert to the fabled 'teeth and claw' method to stop ourselves from sliding down scree ridden, inclined paths. We're forced to go-slow to avoid accidents, and time has to be spent carefully negotiating the route through each of the outcrops. As we descend, the rough paths through the Howes are dropping ever more steeply down and are becoming both narrower and trickier.

Beyond the Howes, a pleasant grassy fell-side slopes its way dramatically downhill for the final drop to the valley floor. About halfway down it,

Pauline decides to hold a conversation with two walkers who are coming up.

Even though we've left the rocky outcrops behind us, the path remains sheer, and we'll need to dig our heels in all the way before we'll arrive at something which vaguely resembles flat earth.

Keen to rid ourselves of the sloping fell, Leon and I push on, and finally stand at the bottom of the valley. Looking back, Pauline is still busily chatting away, but eventually, having exhausted her conversation, joins us. It has taken almost an hour of descent to reach here from the Pike.

Surrounded by the huge, lonely fells of High Street, we stand and survey the silent valley. It's such a wondrous place. There is a rough path along its grassy floor, which will take us to the reservoir. After resting for a moment, we follow it, and it soon leads us to the lapping waters of the former lake of Haweswater.

Arriving at a series of broken-down, dry-stone walls close to the water's edge, we explore the end of the lake. We're looking for any signs of the submerged remains of Mardale Green, the village that was drowned during the 1930s. The Old Dun Bull Inn and the church were once situated somewhere around here. But now there are no traces of them to be seen.

Sadly, we're seventy years too late. But we still look for clues to ascertain where the church and the inn might have once stood. Both have long since been demolished, but we're hoping to see some evidence of their foundations.

There has recently been a drought, and one of the village's old stone bridges has re-emerged from the water. On an old photograph that we've seen, the Inn stood close to the bridge.

Failing to find anything, we make our way across to an interesting island of fir trees at the end of the lake. As we climb onto it, we immediately sink deep into its surface of thick mud and think it wise to leave.

After the exertions of the high fells, what a natural stopping point on the walk this village would have been, especially on a hot summer's day. To be able to step inside the Old Dun Bull for refreshments to see us on our way.

And what a wonderful place it would have been to spend the night. Breaking the journey here, we could have camped alongside the lake and enjoyed an evening at the inn.

The most difficult part of today's walk is over, and this seems like such a natural stopping place. It could have altered a walker's plans for the Coast-to-Coast, with some perhaps deciding to stay here before moving onto Shap or Orton the following day. The views of High Street and Haweswater from the tent would have been glorious.

As we stand and look across the valley at the

surrounding fells, there is a stillness in the air, a timelessness. It could still be seventy years ago, and the men of the village are busy working in the fields; the landlord of the inn is serving passing wayfarers, and the local vicar is going about his rounds.

Wainwright came down here to view Mardale Green during the 1930s, when it was being demolished. And as he himself said, it was a sad sight.

There is a stillness about this place, which seems to say, 'There was once a pulse of life here. People were born and died here, laughed and cried here as they lived their lives tucked away from the world. Their voices must have once floated out on the wind over the lake and the high fells. Now there is only a profound silence, and the fleeting shadows of time-honored ghosts.'

Coming down to Grasmere

Ray Moody

Haweswater and Mardale Green

Chapter 26 – Watching the Detectives

Magically, as we've dropped down into the valley, the rain has stopped, and the mist remains above us in the high places. The journey so far from Patterdale to Kidsty Pike has been dire, with our heads bowed in the thick mist and driving rain. But now we've rounded the Pike and made our way down through the Howes, we're feeling safe. The hard work in terms of route finding appears to be done. The rest of today's walk, albeit still strenuous, should be relatively easier to follow, especially the next four miles alongside the reservoir.

Leaving the site of Mardale Green, we continue along a rough path that trails the left-hand side of the former lake. The path is overgrown and rises steeply as it climbs towards the top of an embankment. Walking between head high rushes, we can no longer see our feet. But we quickly gain height and soon find ourselves out in the open again, looking down on the reservoir.

Resting for a moment by a large rock, we adopt our usual pose of standing with our hands on our hips as we stare back at what once was Mardale Green. With our breath returned, we move on towards the site of a reputed ancient British hill fort that appears to have been on a cliff top high above us. Below it, the place is dense with thorn bushes and as we arrive there, movement in the undergrowth suggests that some animal has recently taken cover. By the sound of it, it must be quite big.

There have so far been no sheep in the area, so we wonder what it could have been and whether there are any wild cats out here. I've often read about people abandoning their exotic pets in remote places such as this. This side of the lake seems so isolated, and with plenty of water being available, it would make it an ideal place to adapt to living in the wild.

The lakeside path continues to rise and fall, or 'undulate' as our Wainwright dictionary would say. Coming to a section, high above the waters of the lake, we pass alongside a distinctive series of concrete fence posts which house rusting wire. They look old and must have been put here when they first built the reservoir, sometime before the Second World War. On the other side of the lake, we can now see the prestigious hotel built to replace Mardale's ancient inn, the Old Dun Bull. Situated on the wrong side of the water, it's of little use to Coast-to-Coast walkers, but we still look across at it with envy.

A few years after this, we would enjoy a drink at the Haweswater Hotel, and it would be well-worth the visit. The place has, like a time capsule, been immaculately preserved, permanently stuck in 1937. Photographs on the walls show the valley and former lake as it was before the flooding, with isolated cottages dotted here and there. It was easy to imagine as we looked out of the hotel windows and walked out on the veranda that you could still see and hear the men busy working on the construction of the dam. The hotel has become a wonderful token, recording forever the death knell of the drowning of the village of Mardale Green.

Continuing our trudge along the four miles by the side of the reservoir, it's easy walking, but it's becoming a slog. Sometimes, we walk just above the lapping water at the edge of the lake and at other times, move away from it as it becomes hidden by trees. Looking back, the Mardale end of Haweswater can still be seen, but with a bend in the valley, it disappears.

The continuous tramping is making our feet feel sore, and we're longing for it to stop. Now looking towards the other end of the reservoir, we can make out the retaining wall which signals its finish.

Passing by a small waterfall, it's claimed that there was once a Victorian school standing somewhere around here. But there is no evidence of it to be seen. Soon after it, we join a wide flat vehicle access track, which suggests that we must at last be getting close to the end of the lake.

Like the winning post in a race, the reservoir wall is a long time in coming. Until we reach it at the settlement of Burnsbank, we won't be on the final section of today's walk and the finish won't be in sight.

The path returns to the water's edge for a last time. We're now walking directly towards the huge stone retaining wall and the reservoir's end. Our hot feet quicken their pace, and we almost gallop past it.

Sadly, on reaching a sign detailing the building of the Haweswater dam, there is the sudden realisation that we're leaving the lakes and fells behind. Our first taste of Lakeland is over and another milestone on the Coast-to-Coast Walk has been reached. Whilst it's sad that there'll be no more mountains to admire in the landscape for a while. There will be the bonus of not having to continually walk over paths of rock and scree and having to perpetually make hard climbs and descents.

Even though I've already learnt on our journey that there's no such thing as flat earth, the ground from now on should be softer underfoot and there'll be much less climbing for a while. At least until we reach the Pennines, and later the North York Moors. At this moment, it's a good thing, as the three of us feel somewhat tired and jaded as we limp our way through the hamlet of Burnsbank.

Here, in an encampment of deteriorating wooden huts, the men who built the reservoir once lived. A few years after this. The old huts would be transformed into luxury bungalows and be sold at luxury prices. But today, the few remaining wooden buildings, appear run down, warped and dishevelled.

Some budding entrepreneur out here at Burnsbank

could make a regular income by selling tea and coffee from their garden to passing Coast-to-Coast walkers. But so, far, none of the residents have taken up the idea.

Leaving the small pocket of civilization behind, we follow a path through a wood. Catching up with a group of German Coast-to-Coast walkers, we trail each other in single file through the trees. A badger suddenly crosses the path up ahead of us.

"Skunk, skunk!" shouts an excited German walker as he points at the passing animal.

Leaving the wood at a road bridge, we find the first of many honesty boxes that we'll come across on the walk. From now on, there will be a veritable cornucopia of them along the trail.

We're beginning to flag and are badly in need of energy. So, the honesty box has come at a very opportune time. To help us through the final leg of today's journey, we lift the lid off the box, and each select a bottle of soft drink, putting our payment for it in a jar. Suitably refreshed, we feel like we now have a little more petrol in our tank to enable us to complete the last bit of the walk to Shap.

Climbing down from the bridge. We follow a trail across country. The route has become pastoral, and we now meander through fields and over pastureland. The walking is immediately so noticeably different to that in the Lakes. But despite it being softer underfoot, our aching feet are letting us know that they're about ready to stop.

After making our way across a boggy reed bed, we climb a steep lane and, on entering a field, follow a series of telegraph posts.

Passing by a derelict farm cottage, in an old outbuilding, we can see a large, ancient copper washing boiler. Some poor farmer's wife must have once stood here and toiled away at the weekly wash.

There at last in the distance stands the venerable tower of Shap Abbey, today's final longed for landmark. Our guidebook says that it's just a mile out of Shap, and it draws us on like a magnet. Despite our aching feet, we quicken our pace towards it.

Arriving at the abbey. Pauline's archaeological bent overcomes her tiredness, and we spend half an hour exploring the ruins. Then, with tired legs, and our backpacks hanging low on our hips, we drag our weary bodies up a steeply rising country lane to join the main road into Shap.

Slowing down almost to a halt, we grow wearier and wearier the closer we get to the village. Today's fells have taken their toll and as cars and fast-moving farm vehicle's speed down the narrow lane towards us, they make it a very dangerous place for weary walkers. Without concern for our aching feet and tired limbs, they race by, paying us little heed. They don't know or even care that we've barely got enough strength left to get out of their way.

A sign points to an off-road side-track for use by

pedestrians. Sadly, we've learnt from bitter experience that such places are often long and full of nettles. We've fallen for this once before, near Ennerdale Bridge, where we had to fight our way through thick undergrowth. Once committed, there is usually little chance of being able to turn back, and at the end of a tiring day, it's tedious and not amusing. As our goal lies directly ahead, we stick to the road and finally pass the metal sign that declares we're entering the village of Shap.

The main street is busy with rural traffic and commuters returning home after a hard day at work.

We've completely forgotten about work. Here we are in another world, where all that matters is not getting lost as we spend our days wandering from A to B, so that eventually we'll be able to say that we've walked across England. How distant and unimportant work at this moment seems.

Passing by two Toast-to-Toast walkers, their soiled clothes show that they've had a rough day's journey. But they look smug as they head off towards their bed-and-breakfast accommodation. And with soft beds, hot showers, and prepared evening meals to look forward to, why not?

Halfway down the high street, a sign outside a public house proclaims that camping is available at the Bull. Entering, we pay our fees to the landlord and pass through to the rear of the premises, where we've been directed to pitch our tent in the small back garden. Before pitching, we carefully examine the narrow stretch of grass in a vain attempt to find an area free from dog faeces.

Some Coast-to-Coast walkers have already pitched and there's a merry buzz about the place. A hard day is over, and we're all camped ten yards away from a bar and twenty yards away from a fish and chip shop. Sheer Hedonism!

With our sacks off and the tent up, Pauline and I are both feeling better. But sadly, Leon has developed a bad headache.

The news soon spreads that the fish and chip shop is open. Things are looking rosy. Before heading off to it, we intend to visit Shap's Aladdin's Cave of a mini supermarket.

Leaving Leon sleeping in the tent, we make our way out through the pub. As we do so, the iconic scene from the classic black and white British movie 'Ice Cold in Alex' springs immediately to mind. Sitting cosily together in a row on bar stools are the four Detectives from Scotland Yard, and they each have a cool glass of lager in front of them. They're not camping, so must be bed-and-breakfasting at the pub. All four of them look fresh and clean as they sit and grasp their glasses. They must have arrived here a lot earlier, as they look as though they've already changed and showered. We'll have to make do with a quick 'spit and a lick' using the single wash basin in the pub toilets. It seems strange that we didn't see these guys out there today along the trail. They must have got away pretty early to arrive here so far ahead of us. But we did set off quite late.

Leaving the pub, directly opposite, lit up in all its electric glory, is Shap's wonderful fish and chip shop. The added advantage of reaching Shap is this place. The chance for us to have a hot meal, which we don't have to cook, and the further bonus of a night off from the dreaded packet pasta. Pauline checks that the fryer cooks in vegetable oil, so that tonight we can enjoy hot potato chips, pickled onions, mushy peas, and the luxury of a buttered bread cake.

We'll also be able to supplement our meal with a cheese and onion pasty bought from the mini supermarket. This is the biggest store we've come across since starting the walk.

Going around it, I feel like a child in a sweetshop, as there is so much choice.

Later, back at the tent with our spoils, Leon only eats a little, and sleeps for the rest of the night. But Pauline and I selfishly gorge ourselves on the wonderful hot food, enjoying a veritable feast for the Gods. This includes a battered pineapple fritter, which I discovered the fish and chip shop also sells. I finish my meal off with a bottle of banana milkshake and a cake from the supermarket. Sadly, for the next few hours, I feel quite bloated and regret my gluttony.

It's a lovely sunny evening and I think about those walkers who turned back or didn't set off because of the morning's mist and rain. They're now a whole day behind us, and who knows what the weather will be like tomorrow. The Dutch Girls are camped here, so too are the Romans and several other walking parties. The remaining tent space on the small piece of grass at the rear of the pub is becoming quite limited.

Sitting in the bar later, we greet the University girls, who tell us that they took the alternative route to Shap via Howtown and wished that they hadn't. It proved to be a lot more arduous than they'd expected.

Pauline reminds me that a backpacker on leave from the Navy, who's walking with his young son and a small dog, hasn't turned up yet. So, they might still be out there. We suspect this because the Packhorse Service has delivered the man's heavy backpack, and it stands forlorn in the pub entrance. Should we inform somebody? As the beer flows, nobody else appears to have even noticed, and no one mentions it. We resolve to give it until ten o'clock, just in case the man has decided to bed-and-breakfast and is spending the night somewhere else in the village. Perhaps he'll come to collect his sack later.

Just before ten o'clock, looking somewhat weary and dishevelled, the father and son turn up. The man is carrying his small dog and almost collapses as he sinks down on a bench beside us. Despite it being late, he still looks very relieved to be here.

Getting his breath back, he tells us that they got lost on the high fells and totally missed Kidsty Pike (as we would also do several years later). Having gone off route and not knowing where they were, he kept on an easterly direction and eventually got down off the fells and onto a road. Finding the nearest village, they discovered that they were miles away from Shap, but not wanting to give up, they road walked all the way here. What slowed them down even further, was that the man had to carry his dog. The animal's feet had become so sore and bloodied that he couldn't walk any further. Sadly, the fish and chip shop has closed, but fortunately, the man is just in time to order two pub meals and a sausage for his dog.

As the night draws on, there's a merry throng in the bar. There are several pubs in Shap and if he had been relying on locals, the landlord's custom would have been minimal. The Coast-to-Coast walk has given his trade a great boost.

The consensus amongst most of the walkers in the pub is that we have the worse of the walk behind us in terms of terrain and sheer physical exertion. Everyone is sad that they're leaving Lakeland but looking forward to a change of environment.

We agree with them. From those first tentative steps up St Bees Head, our bodies now seem much fitter. Even though we're still carrying far too heavy backpacks, and now fully realise that there is no such thing as flat earth, the terrain tomorrow over a limestone landscape, although covering a greater distance, promises a kinder form of walking.

The bonus for us in arriving at tomorrow's destination of Kirkby Stephen is that we'll have a chance to jettison some of the unnecessary weight we've both been carrying. I intend to take a day out and carry home with me all of the useless artefacts from our backpacks that we've brought along with us.

The Railway Viaduct near Kirkby Stephen

Chapter 27 – The Wild Man of The Moors

Morning at the Bull, the doors to the premises don't open until eight o'clock, and so we have to wait with sticky faces and throbbing bladders for the cleaner to unlock them. When they do at last open, we take it in turns with the rest of the campers to have our morning wash in the pub toilets.

When the pub later closed and became a private residence, we would stay at the nearby, walker friendly, Ings Lodge. There, we would enjoy a whole range of accommodation, including camping, bunkhouse, and bed-and-breakfast. The place had a great common room and was unique in that the building featured an ancient stone pillar, which looked suspiciously as though it once formed part of Shap Abbey.

Last night, we replenished our supplies from the local supermarket and bought a few goodies for today's journey. After brewing a cup of coffee and eating a biscuit, we take the tent down and pack our sacks.

It's a long twenty-two-mile trek today, so we want to get away as soon as possible. The earlier we arrive, the longer we'll have to spend exploring the fleshpots of Kirkby Stephen, which we've heard should be able to supply us with anything we need.

Heaving on our backpacks, we leave the Bull and

walk up Shap high street. Some of the campers left before the pub doors opened, with the idea of having a wash in the public toilet block, which we'll pass on the way.

Shap was once on the trunk road to Scotland. With the building of the M6 during the 1960s, the town was bypassed. But it's still easy to imagine Shap high street as being part of the main route up North. Heavy motor traffic used to be constantly making its way through the village. And tarpaulin covered, freight lorries often got stuck here during the winter snows. The noise of traffic now comes from the nearby M6 motorway. It's arguable that the pubs, shops and boarding houses of Shap would be a lot emptier if it wasn't for Coast-to-Coast walkers spending the night here.

As we continue along the high street, well-groomed walkers emerge from their bed-and-breakfast establishments. Trailing behind them, we look somewhat dishevelled in our crumpled clothing. Opposite the King's Arms, we turn off down a side street and start to leave Shap.

Making our way towards a bridge over a railway line, we pass by some local men who are piling wood into a shed. One of them doesn't seem too friendly and scowls at us as he makes a disparaging remark. Perhaps he thinks we're the idle rich, people with nothing better to do all day than to meander their way across England, when we're just two romantics out on an adventure with their son.

Passing over the railway line, we cross a field and the sound of motor vehicles on the nearby M6 immediately hits us, growing louder with every step. Pauline spots a pedestrian footbridge over the motorway, and we aim for it. The noise of the traffic is becoming deafening.

Nearing the bridge, we meet up with a trio of North American Coast-to-Coast walkers who've been putting on a brisk pace. They've been going so fast that it's been difficult for us to catch up with them. Despite appearing to be very efficient walkers, we don't see them again.

So far on our journey, we've come across several walkers like this, charging their way through the countryside and then resting up for half an hour or so. One minute they're well-ahead of us, the next we're passing by them as they lay in the long grass.

Since the first day of the walk, when everyone speeded by us, we've developed our own steady plod. Sometimes we'll take a couple of minutes' rest, and a little longer at extra strenuous places. But now, despite our still far too heavy backpacks, we're beginning to occasionally pass other walkers. This could be a combination of building-up the necessary muscles and having fewer packets of dried pasta shells to carry.

The noise of the traffic crescendos as we arrive at the motorway bridge. It's shaking with the vibrations caused by the endless charge of speeding cars and lorries. On the top of it, I look back at the way we've come. It's probably the last time we'll see the skyline of the Lakeland fells again until we reach the Pennines.

Today we're leaving behind the constant rocky, scree-laden paths of the Lakes and entering limestone country. Here we should be able to enjoy softer walking underfoot. Beyond the M6, we'll be passing through a vast expanse of pastoral semi-isolation. There will only be small villages and rural homesteads on our journey from here to our next stopping place of Kirkby Stephen.

As Pauline and Leon walk on ahead, I linger on the bridge for a moment and stand and watch the pace of the real world, a place we've escaped from for a while. Down below us, people are rushing to their destinations whilst we amble our way towards ours. The sun shines down on my face, and a light breeze blows through my hair. The drivers inside those cars are locked away from this natural environment. As they speed through it, this other world just passes them by.

From the bridge, we follow a narrow path that leads to a quarry. In the distance, it shines white in the bright morning sunlight. Despite being able to see it from a track above the M6, we continue along the path for too long and have to retrace our steps before climbing higher up onto a grassy embankment towards it.

As we pass over the quarry road, it gleams white with the limestone dust that covers everything. The quarry lies warm and quiet in the early morning heat.

Beyond it, we come to a small group of cottages which make up the hamlet of Oddindale. Wainwright famously once stood here on the corner of the road leading into the settlement and lit his pipe. I stand and imitate him, whilst Pauline looks earnestly across the landscape for a glimpse of a reputed stone circle, which is claimed to be hereabouts. We make a limited attempt to find it, and do spot some large boulders, but can't be certain that this is it and return to the main path.

Now, following a broad grassy track, our journey over limestone country begins. Today there are wide-open spaces to traverse, we've left behind the mountain paths and passes, and the walking already seems so much easier. There's no longer the constant jarring of our toes on loose rocks. It will be a long day, but at the end of it, there'll once again be the lure of edible luxuries and the added comforts of a commercial campsite.

There'll also be the quaint old-fashioned market town of Kirkby Stephen to look around. It's rumoured to contain a wide choice of pubs, shops and eateries, such treats we haven't known for days.

But most importantly, there will be the opportunity for us to take a day out. This will enable me to catch a train home and take with me all the unnecessary items from our backpacks.

Despite our bodies slowly building up the strength to be able to cope with the weight, taking our surplus goods home will make the second half of our walk so much easier.

As we follow along a wide grassy track, we leave behind the hamlet of Oddindale, and can now see for miles across a vast, open green landscape.

Wainwright tells us that when we reach the corner of a bield, we should head off towards a stake on the far horizon. We keep looking for something that resembles a bield, but like the watershed on Dent, we have no real idea what one looks like. The walking is so pleasant and straightforward that even though the bield, whatever it is, seems a long time in coming, we assume that we can't have arrived at it yet and continue on along the track.

Suddenly the track ends, and we find ourselves standing on a quiet country lane. We must have somehow gone wrong. This road's not on the Coast-to-Coast route. Luckily, we now have a map covering this section of the walk. It shows that if we follow the road, it will take us down into the village of Orton.

Wainwright claims that the time it takes, or the way you go on your walk across England, matters not. But I really do want to stick to the designated route, so we reluctantly turn around and retrace our steps back along the track.

Where is the bield?

We can't remember passing anything, but now look even more intensely at our surroundings.

Eventually, we come to the corner of a ranch style fence that encloses a small plantation of trees. Could this be it? We scan the wide green horizon, looking for a wooden stake that our guidebook says we should aim for. I have poor eyesight and, not wearing my glasses, can't really see anything. But Pauline thinks she's spotted it. Having wasted half an hour of extra walking on what is already a long day, we head off towards the stake.

We're stepping out across a vast, open, grassy limestone plateau. There is only a slight rise to the ground and the white limestone rock appears on the green surface as it cuts its way through the earth. The walking remains easy, and on reaching the top of the plateau, we continue straight on, following a rough track. Crossing over a stream, we walk alongside a wall that takes us down to a dried-up riverbed. Climbing up the other side, we pass through several more fields before eventually coming out onto a quiet country lane. After the undulation of the past few days, it feels good to be on fairly flat ground again.

Whilst it will be a long day, the walking is already so much easier than it was back in the Lakes.

The road is long, and it feels warm in the bright sunshine. Our hats are on, protecting our heads from the sun. But to let the metaphorical steam out, like pan lids, we keep lifting them on and off whenever it goes behind a cloud.

After a distance, we arrive at a junction and, leaving the road, go down into a farmer's field. Here, signs help to steer us away from getting too close to the farmhouse. Being careful not to stray from the authorised track, we follow faint paths on the ground and eventually come out onto a narrow country lane.

Wandering idly down it, our guidebook shows that if we turn off the lane too soon, we'll end up in Orton, a village bypassed by the walk. We would then have to face the problem of how to get back on route. Consulting our Wainwright, Pauline makes sense of the twisting lines of the hand-drawn map, and after turning with the lane, we almost immediately go through a farm gate. Walking down a long trod, we head towards another farmhouse.

Later, at the campsite, we hear that several of the walkers went off route here and entered the village of Orton before following the long road down to Sunbiggin Tarn, which we would do on occasion.

In the future, the route near the Tarn would also change, and some walkers would purposely take the longer road journey there from Orton.

On reaching a farmhouse, we go through a gate and find ourselves on yet another quiet country lane. Plodding along it, once again, the walking on this lovely sunny morning is so pleasant.

Eventually, a sign indicates that the Coast-to-

Coast walk goes through an open gateway into a field. We have to enter on tiptoe as we wade through yards of deep liquid manure.

Beyond the muck, the walk follows a high grassy ridge. Through field after field and hamlet after hamlet we go, seemingly in a straight line. On the way, we meet up with yet another party of North American Coast-to-Coast walkers. These guys always look so clean and spotlessly dressed. How do they manage it?

As the days have passed, I've become almost tramp-like as I roam the countryside. Sadly, it comes to me quite naturally, and I don't really care. I've discovered that long-distance walking has enabled me to once more taste the freedom that I last felt during the halcyon summers of the late 1960s. Years when, as a teenager, anything seemed possible. Not that I was ever a hippie, but combining a wide-brimmed hat with my long hair and a colourful headband, has allowed me to metaphorically re-enact my pilgrimage to Britain's Woodstock, the 1970 Isle of Wight Rock Festival. The place where I witnessed Jimi Hendrix's last stand. I've turned into that carefree spirit again, not concerned with work, the bills and the worries of everyday life, but simply with wandering safely on foot across England.

Each morning I put on a clean tee-shirt, selecting it from the fourteen I've rather foolishly brought along with me for the trip. And most days, within an hour of strapping on my backpack and starting walking, I have a river of perspiration running down my spine. On the rare occasions when we rest up for five or ten minutes with my pack off, when I put it on again, I have to endure the very unpleasant feeling of having the cold sweat on my tee-shirt pressed firmly against my back. It's not a nice sensation, and I'm beginning to not look forward to it.

At the end of a day's journey, I take off my sodden tee-shirt and leave it to dry, flapping in the wind on one of the tent lines or on a fence wire. If during a day it's rained, and we've got wet, I've learnt from other backpackers to sleep with my tee-shirt and socks in the bottom of my sleeping bag to dry them out. This usually works well, but sometimes they can still be damp.

I'm beginning to think that it's a complete waste of time putting on a clean tee-shirt every day, only for it to almost immediately become wet with sweat. And it's certainly foolish for me to be carrying fourteen of them. So, I'm wondering whether it would be better to just keep wearing the same tee-shirt during the day and smell 'Au natural', only putting a clean one on, on an evening. That way, perhaps packing about six would be a much better idea.

We have, however, discovered that it's essential to have the luxury of a nice dry tee-shirt to change into at the end of a wet day. Unfortunately, after just a few days of walking, our expanding wet clothes bag has grown bigger, and now elicits a pungent odour.

From our grassy ridge, the waters of Sunbiggin Tarn loom up in the valley below. Birds swarm above it like vultures, squawking as they circle around before swooping down to drink and fish from its icy waters.

Wainwright's original route went on a wild path on the other side of the tarn over a lonely barren moor. But today, on reaching a moorland road, the Walk continues along it. Moving away from the tarn, it heads towards a crossroads from where the trail turns off down an isolated country lane.

Even though we can see the crossroads in the distance, as we tramp along the road, it seems to be taking an age for us to reach it. Looking across the landscape, Pauline spots a vehicle driving down the narrow lane we're aiming for. She suggests that we should head off over the moor directly towards it, thereby cutting a large corner off. Stepping out over the heather, our shortcut works, and we soon emerge out onto it.

In the future, the route would change yet again. It would revert to following a much more straightforward path across the moors, passing by the right-hand side of Sunbiggin Tarn.

Wandering down the lonely narrow lane, we pass by several sleepy farmsteads. There is a distinct feeling that we're beginning the second part of today's journey. Despite the easier conditions underfoot, today has already been quite a trek and our energy levels have drained a little. Walking under a hot sun on a tarmacked road, it's noticeable that as easy as it is, our legs have slowed their pace. Sauntering along under a wide blue sky, huge white clouds float high above us. The long, winding road we're on disappears off into the far distance.

We're hoping to see a cattle grid that, according to Wainwright, will mark the place where we leave the tarmac and climb back onto the moor. Arriving at one, we grow excited, but discover that there's no turn off after it. Tramping onwards, the road begins to rise, and eventually we arrive at the correct grid.

The walk today has so far been pastoral. But as we turn off the narrow lane, we're immediately into a different type of terrain. Walking on remote moorland, parallel to a solid stone-built boundary wall, we're now heading in a beeline for Kirkby Stephen.

The smooth rounded green hills of the Howgill Fells appear in the distance. Before reading my Wainwright, I didn't know of their existence. The distinctive shape of Mallerstang Edge, the photograph which first awakened me to the Great Outdoors, now also comes into view.

Signs of an old coaching road begin to appear on the ground. A wide, deep sunken cutting in the earth that runs alongside the very solid-looking wall.

A Walk to the Sea

The road constantly rises and falls, so any passengers in the coach must have had quite a ride. Following it, we pass by a sign that announces, 'Bent's Farm'.

We would occasionally camp here. Whilst taking tents, the farm also offered bunkhouse accommodation. On one trip, deciding that we'd like to spend longer in Kirkby Stephen, instead of camping, Pauline and I elected to pay for a night in the bunkhouse. Stopping there would leave us only a short six-mile journey the following morning, giving us the rest of the day free in Kirkby Stephen.

The bunkhouse looked as though it had been built from an old stone barn and contained everything you might need during your stay.

Inside, we found it to be quite dark, having all of its main windows positioned at the front of the building. No other walkers were staying there that night, and so we had the sixteen-bed accommodation to ourselves.

Later, on looking around the place, we noticed that all of the windows, including a toilet window at the back of the building, were wide open. The bunkhouse stands on its own, well-away from the farmhouse. So, not wanting to get any visitors in during the night, we diligently went around, shutting them all.

As we settled down for the evening, we discussed the possible reasons why the windows had all been opened. Was it simply that the farmer's wife had been letting some fresh air into the place? Or was it, as Pauline's imaginative mind suggested, that being miles away from anywhere, some passing tramp might be using the bunkhouse when no one else is in residence. By leaving the windows open on their exit, they could easily climb back in after dark.

When it came time for us to go upstairs to bed, Pauline was perturbed to learn that there was no key or bolt to lock the front door. Rather than leave it unlocked, she encouraged me to find some way of preventing it from opening. I looked around the bunkhouse and found an adjustable walking pole, which I was able to wedge under the door handle so that it couldn't be pressed down.

On going upstairs to sleep, Pauline grew even further alarmed when she discovered a large steel rat cage under one of the bunk beds. The possibility that there might be rats roaming around the place after dark greatly disturbed her.

Closing the door of the room containing the cage, we chose the other bunkroom to sleep in. To make any rodents aware of our presence, we decided to leave the light on all night. Then, as a further precaution, I got my portable radio set and tuned it into a programme, hoping that the sound of voices would help to further deter any rats from appearing.

Selecting our bunks from the eight available, we both automatically chose top ones. Sealing our sleeping bags tightly around us, we tried to ensure that even our faces were almost covered. After talking for a while, Pauline dropped off to sleep.

But she had stoked my imagination, and true to character, I had by now become a quaking coward. Unable to fall into slumber, I lay there wide-awake, keeping a lonely vigil.

Wedged in my sleeping bag on a top bunk, I stared up at the dusty roof space and noticed its rodent friendly wooden beams, ideal for small creatures to run along. With my vivid imagination for company, I now had the fear of both a rat infestation and the possibility of a visit from a moorland vagabond to contend with.

The combination of the light, the worry, and the noise of the radio meant that I couldn't sleep. I lay there wide-awake, sweating profusely in my constricting sleeping bag. My eyes constantly scanned the floor and the roof space, looking for any signs of movement. At the same time, I listened out intently for the slightest sound of anyone trying to get in at the front door or through one of the windows. In the meantime, Pauline slept soundly on.

After a few hours, I kept drifting off to sleep, but only for about ten minutes at a time. Waking up with a start, I would resume my sentry duties.

Fortunately, the night wore on, and after having listened to a whole succession of radio programmes, at around five o'clock in the morning, Pauline finally awoke from her slumbers, and we resumed our conversation.

Almost immediately she did so, I distinctly heard the sound of the front door being pushed against, in an attempt to open it. Someone was trying to get in. Had the tramp left it until dawn to call?

Not wanting to distress Pauline, I ignored it and didn't mention the obvious noise I'd just heard coming from downstairs. Then suddenly, there was a much louder bang on the door. Somebody definitely wanted to be in, and unfortunately, this time Pauline heard it.

"What was that?"

Was it the farmer? Did he need to collect something from the bunkhouse, or want to use the toilet rather than walk all the way back to the farm cottage? Or was it Pauline's mysterious tramp, calling in for his morning wash before disappearing off onto the moors for the day?

The same sound at midnight, or during the early hours of the morning, would have petrified me. I would have frozen in my bed. But at 5 am, the witching hour was practically over, and despite it still being fairly dark and us being tired, I decided that it was better to go downstairs to face our demons rather than to remain vulnerable in the bunkroom.

Standing by the front door, armed with brooms, we waited anxiously for the sound of another attempt to get in. Sure enough, within minutes, there was another tremendous effort at opening the door.

'Bang, bang!' The door fairly rang as it was forcefully pushed against.

"What do you want?" I shouted in my deepest, macho voice. But there was no reply. Instead, the door was once again loudly banged.

Now waking up a little, girding up my loins, I removed the walking pole. It had been doing an excellent job of holding up the handle, stopping the door from opening. Then, with both of us stood resolutely gripping our broom handles, we steadied ourselves for the onslaught. There wasn't long to wait. The door almost immediately received a further hefty blow and flew wide open. Petrified, we both stood there, half expecting to see the Wild Man of the Moors staring in at us. But instead, sitting on the doorstep with its backside pressed firmly up against the door frame, was a large sheep. Relieved, we tried to shoo it away, but it kept on returning and banged the door several more times. We later surmised that the changing occupants of the bunkhouse must feed it scraps of food, and it had simply been calling in for its breakfast.

Grisedale Tarn

Ray Moody

On St Sunday Crag with Ullswater in the background

Chapter 28 - A Place for Licking Wounds

Our guidebook tells us that we need to turn off through a gate just after Bent's farm. The trouble is that there are two gates, and neither of them is marked. If we're not careful here, we could go off route and add extra mileage to our already long, twenty-two-mile day. This would also leave less time to spend exploring the fleshpots of Kirkby Stephen. Holding our nerve, although there isn't a sign on it, we go through the second of the gates.

On later trips, busy talking, we would occasionally ignore these unmarked gates and continue along the old coaching road, wandering aimlessly alongside the high wall. The problem is that once you've missed the correct gate, there is no way through the wall, as the gates run out for a while. You're then forced miles and miles further away from the trail as you walk further and further on, trying to find the next gate. Then, going through it, you flounder about as you attempt to get back on route.

On one Coast-to-Coast walk, realizing that we must have missed the correct gate, rather than go back to it, or carry on to the next one, Pauline and I kept a lookout for a lower part of the wall. The idea was for us to try to scramble over it.

We had noticed some thin wires stretched all the

way along the wall. And had earlier seen a sign claiming that it was an electric fence. Our experience of electric fences in the past was that they gave out a slight trickle of volts, just sufficient electricity to dissuade away cattle. Unfortunately, this fence was different.

When we eventually came across a slightly lower section of the wall, I led the way in attempting to climb over it, with Pauline following close behind me. Despite being careful, I must have accidentally touched one of the wires stretched along the wall. Suddenly, a powerful electric shock ran through me. Which in turn ran through Pauline, who at that moment was helping me over the wall and had the misfortune to be pushing me. The shock coursed through both of us, and just like in some animated cartoon film; we danced as the voltage surged through our bodies and threw us over backwards. As we landed in a heap on the earth, it felt as though the farmer had the wires plugged directly into his 240-volt mains.

Today, we've read our Wainwright well, and once through the gate, like Red Indian braves, look for signs on the ground as we attempt to pick up the trail.

We discover a track by the side of a wall running perpendicular to the one we've been following. Continuing alongside the new wall, we soon come to a stile. Climbing over it, a vast blue sky with fluffy white clouds opens up high above us. We're stood on

A Walk to the Sea

a rounded hilltop and below us a row of electricity pylons are spread out like a trail of staggered iron men as they disappear off into the distance across a valley.

Following the path downhill, below us, we can see the track-bed of the old Kirkby Stephen to Tebay railway line. Beside it stand two long-abandoned cottages. Climbing down to them, we arrive in front of these derelict, slate grey buildings.

Standing silent in the afternoon sunlight, they look such lonely places. But for the families of the railway workers who once lived here, with this wonderful green landscape surrounding them, and a regular pulse of passing trains, it must have been an idyllic place to spend their lives.

Crossing over the track-bed of the old railway line, we begin a steep descent down to an ancient packhorse bridge. In the fields alongside it, can be seen the outline of an Iron Age village. Close by there are also two large, raised disturbances in the earth, which are known locally as the 'Giants Graves'. These are claimed to have been places used for cultivating live rabbits.

Arriving down at the bridge, we sit on one of its side walls and watch the river flowing in the stream below. From memory, I sit in the same place that Alfred Wainwright once sat when he filmed his television series on the Coast-to-Coast walk.

Understanding this, Pauline pretends to interview

me.

"Can you put a date on the bridge, Mr. Moody?"

"Well, I think it's probably medieval, possibly built before the Conqueror, perhaps later."

Continuing to stare down into the flowing waters, we eat our last few remaining bits of lunch.

Our lunches rarely resemble anyone else's, which have often been made by the skilled hands of some bed-and-breakfast proprietor or Youth Hostel Warden. They usually simply involve splitting a flapjack or a chocolate biscuit between us. Other than this, and occasional gulps of water, the only other sustenance we have during our walk is that of a competitively priced toffee.

Today is an exception. At the Coop supermarket in Shap, we discovered that they sell a reasonably priced, yet tasty, cheese sandwich, and we bought some for the journey. Whenever we come across a similar store on the rest of our walk, we'll look forward to buying some more.

At this spot on a later walk, Pauline found herself in difficulties. The sun had beaten down on us all the way along the trail, so much so that she had become severely affected by the heat. So hot was it that day, that when we arrived at the Packhorse Bridge, the only shelter we could find to hide away from the sun was to crouch down amongst the shadows cast in places by the side stones of the bridge. Taking refuge on the stone slabbed floor, we sought what coolness we could get. Luckily, two passing Swiss Coast-to-Coast walkers saw Pauline's plight and lent her a folding umbrella, which she used as a parasol to keep the heat off her head for the rest of the day's journey.

Slowly, very slowly, we drag our weary limbs away from the bridge and follow a rising path, which leads us over a series of hills. We're on our last cylinder of energy, but it's definitely feeling like we're on the final stretch of today's walk. Having covered nineteen miles, we've just three to go. Nevertheless, it's quite a steep climb up from the bridge. The path steadily rises over one hill and then continues over another until it at last reaches the top of Limekiln Hill. Our weary bodies ache, but we know that we're near the end of today's journey.

Over further wide undulating green mounds, we go before coming down to pass beneath a working railway line. As we approach it, a train shoots by on its way to Carlisle. Beyond the underpass, we join a quiet country lane, and strolling along it, soon climb a stile and cross over a field to go through a farmyard on the outskirts of Kirkby Stephen.

I never thought that I would, but I'm beginning to enjoy going through farmyards, where the combined smells of hay, creosote, cattle droppings and pig manure greet you. As I breathe it all in, it seems such a healthy smell.

Our bodies are weary, and from the farm we drag ourselves along the backs of the houses that flank

Kirkby Stephen high street. Finding an alleyway that passes between them, we suddenly emerge out onto a very busy main road.

The noise of traffic is deafening after the silence of the hills. It's teatime, and Kirkby Stephen High Street is a hubbub of activity. Cars, farm lorries, and tractors rush this way and that.

Turning away from the town centre, we make our way down the road towards the campsite. We've discovered that it's situated on the edge of town. Pennine View is a luxury of a campsite. Its well-mown lawns practically invite you to pitch your tent. Emptying our backpacks out onto a strategically positioned picnic table, hot steaming showers, and the possibility of clothes washing, and drying facilities awaits us.

Kirkby Stephen is a place where walkers meet up with civilization again. After roughing it for a week, for a moment, you almost come back to the real world. But Kirkby Stephen isn't like most of the towns and cities we come from. It's a quaint old-fashioned place, a market town, almost frozen in time. Even though we're coming face-to-face with the real world again, it's a different sort of world, quite unlike the one we're used to, so it's an acceptable world.

On our way into Kirkby Stephen, we met one of the solo coast-to-coast walkers. Just like us, he's roughed it in his tent throughout the rain-sodden days. But he said that tonight, instead of camping, he's looking forward to enjoying the relative luxury of bed-and-breakfast accommodation.

How unfortunate, with Shap having such a good campsite. There are so many other places along the Coast-to-Coast trail where booking bed-and-breakfast would seem to make much more sense. With the quality of the camping, it seems a shame that he doesn't spend his money somewhere else, some place more worthwhile, such as Keld or later at the Lion Inn on Blakey Ridge. The camping there will be a lot more primitive.

Several other Coast-to-Coast backpackers, including the Dutch girls, have also opted for a little more luxury tonight and are staying at the Youth Hostel. But the Romans have joined us here on the grass, as have the Sticks.

Wainwright suggests that Kirkby Stephen is a place for licking wounds, which totally sums it up. We're now practically halfway through the walk and tomorrow, on the top of Nine Standards Rigg, we'll reach the mid-point of our journey. Our rough undulating passage through the Lakes and the mileage that has slowly built up, including today's twenty-two miles, means that we feel ready for whatever lies ahead.

Talking to other walkers at the campsite, they too are feeling the same. Many have dragged blistered heels and toes covered in Elastoplast throughout the first week of the walk. One guy's feet hurt so much after just a couple of days walking, that in a last desperate attempt not to have to finish, he took the bus into Keswick from Rosthwaite, where he bought himself a pair of trainers and dumped his boots. His feet are now slowly healing, and it appears to have worked, saving him from both having to give up and from developing even more blisters.

We too have spent days wearing wet socks, and realize that because our boots aren't waterproof, we should be carrying many more pairs. Being on a budget, we grabbed every sock in our sock drawer that looked as though it could put up with some walking. We've also copied a technique from the Romans, who tie their wet socks to the back of their sacks to try to dry them as they walk. Whether this is effective, I'm not convinced.

Making it to Kirkby Stephen means that we can at last do something about the excessive weight that Pauline and I have been carrying. I intend to catch the first train home in the morning and take all of the useless items from our backpacks with me. I hope to return by early evening. Several of the other walking parties are also taking a day out here, including the Dutch Girls and the Romans. Pauline and Leon propose to spend their day relaxing in this quaint, old market town.

On making enquiries, I've discovered that the train station situated opposite the campsite is Kirkby

A Walk to the Sea

Stephen East, whose line closed during the 1960s. I'll have to walk over a mile out-of-town in the morning to find the working railway station of Kirkby Stephen West. But it will be worth it to get rid of all the unnecessary weight in our backpacks. It will mean that we'll both be carrying much lighter sacks for the rest of the walk. I've even persuaded Pauline to part with a pair of her high-heeled shoes.

After pitching the tent, we leave the campsite to visit the high street and the plethora of shops it has to offer. A rural market town, the first thing to greet us is a solemn-looking Temperance building, which reminds us to moderate our drinking. Beyond it, we find the marketplace and experience the pleasure of being able to shop in two supermarkets. Continuing on through the market square, we look for the Coast-to-Coast fish and chip shop, a place where Alfred Wainwright once had his chips. Finding it, I'm hoping to enjoy more golden fried potatoes. Because we're Vegetarian and don't eat meat or fish, we will only eat chips if they've been cooked in vegetable oil, like at the fish and chip shop in Shap. Sadly, we discover that this place cooks in animal fats, so we can't eat them. But rather than leave empty-handed, I buy a buttered bread cake, and get to speak to the shop's proprietor, who spoke to Alfred Wainwright during the filming of his television series. We also leave the shop via the same distinctive stone steps by which the great man himself once entered and left.

Ray Moody

On the bridge over the M6 motorway

Chapter 29 - Nine Standards Jig

Morning arrives, and we discover that the campsite at Kirkby Stephen also serves as a place where walkers about to commence the Coast-to-Coast walk are picked up by the Packhorse Service and transported to St Bees. The Packhorse apparently operates a minibus from here, which takes fresh-faced walkers to the start of the trail.

As they hang about waiting to take their seats on the Packhorse coach, the new walkers can easily be spotted as they look so clean and tidy. Once boarded, they stare out at the passing dishevelled, and often limping, group of 'bloodied' walkers making their way to and from the washroom. As they do so, I guess they can't help wondering about what lies ahead for them. But these guys are a week into their adventure and beginning to shine with the confidence that they've got this far. The new walkers look on, knowing that they still have it all to do.

The Coast-to-Coast grapevine has spread the news throughout Kirkby Stephen that the four Detectives have split up. All four of them were apparently sighted yesterday, attaching themselves to other walking parties. Last night, they were also all seen drinking in different bars, and they don't appear to be speaking to each other.

The further news is that the three University girls, who we have kept meeting up with along the trail, and who've been staying down at the Youth Hostel, have decided to give up. These are the same girls who took the Howtown route to Shap. Apparently, one of them has developed a problem with her knee.

Packed and ready to go, we leave the campsite and saunter along down Kirkby Stephen High Street.

Yesterday, I took home all of the useless items from our backpacks and now they weigh so much lighter that we almost have a spring in our step.

Outside the Youth Hostel, we meet the University girls. They're standing with a small group of Coast-to-Coast walkers who are trying to talk them out of finishing. They've come this far and once they're over the Pennines, with the change in terrain; the walking should be so much easier.

One of the students tells us that she actually completed the Pennine Way the previous year, an arguably even more arduous trek. And we know by their speed that they're all good walkers.

From the discussion, it appears that two of the girls don't really want to give up, but back at university, the three of them agreed that if one of them dropped out, then they would all finish.

I suggest to the girl with the bad knee that she could get a lift into Keld, the next stop on route, using the Packhorse Service. She could then opt back into the walk if her knee improves or could continue getting lifts along the rest of the trail until it does. The two fit girls brighten up at my suggestion, but the injured girl doesn't even consider it. Giving no thought to allowing her friends to continue the walk, she dismisses my idea out of hand. Selfishly holding the girls to their pact, they're gone.

Leaving the Youth Hostel, we visit the supermarket to buy a few goodies for the day ahead. Sauntering along the high street, we're looking for Frank's Bridge, the place where the Coast-to-Coast walk leaves Kirkby Stephen. As we do so, we pass by a deserted open-backed vintage double-decker bus, the type I used to collect fares on in my youth. The temptation is far too great. I clamber aboard the footplate and press the bell twice, giving the signal for the bus to move off. It all comes back to me so very easily.

The problem with having enjoyed the luxuries available in Kirkby Stephen is that today we're heading for the relative austerity of the isolated village of Keld, where comforts will be at a minimum. There is apparently no pub, no shops, nothing except a few houses, a Youth Hostel and several waterfalls.

In future years, the hostel would be sold and transformed into a posh hotel with a bar. Walkers would be able to get a drink there. It would replace Keld's long-lost infamous watering-place, the Cat Hole Inn. Down in the village, there would also be a fairly well-stocked camp shop. Today it seems that there will be nothing except a short day.

At Frank's Bridge, we leave the high street and

the comforts of Kirkby Stephen behind us. We initially stroll along a tarmacked path, and the walking is easy. But as we reach the hamlet of Hartley, it starts to become more difficult. Joining a road, we begin to climb steeply up beyond a quarry. After it has twisted and turned several times, we continue straight on, following a narrow road that appears to be heading in a beeline for the top of the fell. As we do so, the local post van shoots by at speed on its way to making a delivery at an isolated farm.

Apart from other walkers, this is the last we'll see of civilization for a while until we've crossed over the Pennines and come off them at the other side.

Since leaving Kirkby Stephen, the weather has begun to change, and a storm is brewing. The sunny morning has gone, and now looming up in front of us on the horizon sits a dark, foreboding cloud. It's only ten o'clock, but the sky is fast turning black, and a thick enveloping mist covers the top of the Pennines.

The narrow road we've been following goes through an open gateway and enters the wild fell proper. This final wall, dividing wilderness and civilization, we now know from our Wainwright dictionary, is called the intake wall. Beyond it, the road immediately becomes a muddy, rocky track, but it continues to follow a stone wall on our right. To our left is a mass of undulating dark boggy peat.

The fitness gained during the first half of the walk

is paying dividends. Now, combining it with our much lighter backpacks, we're beginning to catch up with other Coast-to-Coast walkers who set off before us.

Keld, our target for today, lies twelve miles away over the top of the Pennines. We've heard on the grapevine that a couple of walkers are continuing a mile further on to the village of Muker, and that one maniac is hoping to reach Reeth.

Between Keld and all the walkers lies a climb over the wet boggy peat of the Pennines. To make matters worse, it will now have to be done in thick mist and under a darkening sky.

We've read through this section of the walk in Wainwright's guidebook many times. It's yet another part of the trail we've long since identified as being scary. It would be easy to get lost up here on the wild fells. And judging by the look of the peat, it's very likely that our bog rope will be required. Wainwright suggests that the peat bogs around here can get waist deep in places.

I'm scared of bogs, and have been since my childhood when I first saw the Hound of the Baskervilles, the Sherlock Holmes movie, where, in the grand finale, the villain sinks slowly out of sight into the mire. This fear was reinforced during my student days, when on the Lyke Wake Walk I experienced a peat bog for myself, sinking up to my waist in one on the North York Moors.

The Pennine crossing provides a brief taste of the infamous National Trail, the Pennine Way. A relatively tougher, boggier and much more of a wilderness walk than the Coast-to-Coast.

Reading through my guidebook, I have, however, discovered that even though the Pennines are a wild and lonely, often trackless place, where you could easily get lost, there is apparently an escape route off them.

Looking at the map, a narrow ribbon of tarmac road threads its way around the isolated moors and fells between Keld and Kirkby Stephen. Should we go astray on the top of the Pennines, then the map in our guidebook suggests that if we keep heading off anywhere south, we should eventually come down to meet the road. For this reason, one of the first purchases I made was to buy a compass, and I've had it tied around my neck since day one of the walk.

I'm currently wearing a travel-stained, wide-brimmed white hat, which now has a large seagull feather stuck in its jaunty headband. I'm also sporting several days' growth of beard. So, with a compass hanging around my neck, I've moved on from my original image of a horse dealer and look like a wild, intrepid explorer. A persona I cultivate, especially on a morning when we're leaving a campsite. I stride out, pretending that I'm not noticing the weight of my backpack, like today when we left Kirkby Stephen. Wet socks tied to the bag straps swinging in

A Walk to the Sea

the breeze add to the effect. Once I've turned a corner and I'm out of sight, my shoulders do sag a little and my pace slackens. But when passing rows of lethargic caravan owners, I imagine that the various wives must glance at their pot-bellied husbands and for a moment, in my head, I think I might appear to be such a fine figure of manhood.

The path moves away from the wall and as we follow it onto the glutinous moorland; the mist grows immediately thicker. In the gloom, we can just make out walkers up ahead of us clambering over the peat as they climb towards the horizon. Nowhere in sight are the Nine Standards, the amazing nine or more high pillars of rock that stand on the edge of the summit of Hartley Fell, and according to our guidebook, we should by now be seeing.

Despite its apparent scariness, Pauline and I have really been looking forward to today. A chance to examine these mysterious, and seemingly strategically placed group of monoliths. I keep peering through the mist, expecting to see nine sinister columns of rock standing on the ridge above us, just like the photograph in our coffee table Wainwright. Unfortunately, as we near the top of the fell, the mist is becoming so thick that little can be seen except the deep sloppy wet peat beneath our feet. The rain is also coming down, and yet again on our journey we're surrounded by a veil of grey. Our walk has once more become like walking in slow motion on the seabed.

As we climb up towards the shrouded ridge and the place where we imagine the Nine Standards are likely to be, we try to follow occasional fleeting glimpses of figures in the mist.

Peering through the murk, I can just make out that we're nearing the top of Hartley Fell. And I can discern what appears to be a Trig Point with a whole bunch of Coast-to-Coast walkers gathered around it.

On arriving there, I count about twenty walkers of various shapes and sizes surrounding the concrete obelisk. These include the Romans, the Dutch Girls and several other recognizable faces. We all appear to have missed the Nine Standards, and yet, according to our maps and guidebooks, they must be situated somewhere close by. We can only be about a hundred yards away from them at the most. But the mist is so thick that we can't see a thing. Feeling disappointed, I wonder whether we should try walking blindly towards them along the ridge.

Years later, when you now approach the top of the fell, there is a well-defined, albeit boggy path, which leads straight up to the Nine Standards. Occasional boulders on either side of the path form an avenue amongst the peat, before finally a stone seat and a high cairn act as a gateway. Once through which the peaty track followed pops you directly out at the Nine Standards.

Today, I resist the urge to be swallowed up in the

mist, believing that there's safety in numbers. The rain has brought with it a chill. We need to get off the top of this fell as quickly as possible.

Standing shivering together around the trig point, the mist envelopes everything. When for a moment it clears for a few yards, the peat hags and bogs surrounding us look particularly evil.

In the pouring rain and gathering gloom, walkers can be seen desperately consulting their maps and guidebooks. A path off from here across the peat is barely discernible, let alone one going in the right direction. No one appears to want to take the lead, and the situation is looking dire.

Suddenly, a couple of walkers, who look as though they know where they're going, leave the trig point and make a dash for it off into the murk. Believing that somebody must know something that the rest of us don't, on seeing this, everyone quickly follows them. Slipping and sliding amongst the peat hags, they soon disappear off into the mist.

Bringing up the rear, we attempt to follow them. We don't want to lose track of the other walkers. The rain suddenly turns to sleet and comes down viciously. As it does, the now distant front markers put on speed and practically hop, skip, and jump across the boggy wasteland of peat and soon disappear in the mist. Panic sets in. The long line of walkers chasing after them also begin to frantically run, including ourselves. Nobody wants to get left behind.

Already on this walk, we've endured mist and driving rain and slid our way along Grisedale Pass and through the peat bogs of Far Easedale, but nothing compares to this.

Worried thoughts again enter my head. Do the more experienced walkers consider this to be particularly extreme weather, or why else would they be running? Knowing Pauline, the same thoughts must also at this moment be going through her head.

As the fleeing walkers spread out and disappear amongst the peat groughs (deep ditches of peat that appear like First World War trenches), Leon, who is a few yards behind me, suddenly lets out a cry. He's lost one of his trainers in the bog. It's been sucked off his foot, and now lies stuck deep down in the peat.

I'm desperate for us not to get cut off from the other walkers, but reluctantly stop. While Leon hops around on one leg, I go down on all fours in a frantic effort to retrieve his trainer. With my arm reaching far down into the Pennines, I manage to grab it before it sinks out of sight. As I resurface with my trophy, I suddenly realize that the rest of the walkers have gone.

We're all alone, marooned, just the three of us standing isolated amidst a mist-covered wasteland of bog. Silence has fallen all around us. We're on our own and can barely see more than a few yards in front of us. Balancing with one hand on my shoulder, Leon puts his trainer back on. Chilling sleet encourages us to move on, and we set off in the direction the rest of the walkers have gone. But we're having to make our way across a desert of bog and are finding it impossible to walk in a straight line.

Faced by deep, glutinous channels of peat, we stumble awkwardly down into them, sliding down the sides of these wide trenches dug deep into the soaking wet peat of the Pennines. At the bottom, we stand for a moment in the clinging morass trying to spot the best place to clamber up the other side to enable us to get back out again. These are easy places to lose direction and go off route.

Back on the surface of the Pennines we're forced to stray off the barely discernible paths to make our way around huge rivers of water-logged peat. Gradually, however, we begin to climb over the top of the oozing fell and drop slowly down into the Pennine valley.

In some ways, it's been a good thing that we couldn't see more than a few yards in front of us. With the mist narrowing our view, it has allowed us to concentrate only on that which lies directly ahead.

After what has seemed like an eternity of floundering about amongst the peat, we sight a shooting hut. Built out of corrugated iron, it looms up out of the mist like a ghostly apparition.

On reaching it, I try the door handle and miraculously it opens. As it does, to our great surprise, we find the rest of the Coast-to-Coast walkers cowering in there. As the door closes behind us, a violent storm blows up, sleet hammers tunefully down on the hut's iron roof, and the wind howls like a banshee as it practically lifts it off.

Seated on benches around a large wooden table, we sit and shiver in silence with the rest of the wet walkers. As we do so, I muse that it's probably a safe bet that at this moment in time, there are one or two people here wishing that Wainwright had kept his idea of a long-distance walk to himself.

Nobody seems to want to speak. So, I look around me, scanning the roof and walls of the hut. Then I almost gasp in utter amazement and total disbelief at what my eyes behold.

Alfred Wainwright appears to have posthumously signed his name in large bold letters along one of the roof beams. Intrigued, I check to see how he has written it in my guidebook. Yes, that confirms it, that's definitely Wainwright's signature. He must have come all the way down here to autograph it during a night off from his lonely vigil on Haystacks.

Chapter 30 - The Witches of Keld

The storm is dying down, and despite the protection of the iron walls of the hut, our bodies are beginning to chill. Deciding to resume our journey, we leave the shelter and follow a well-defined path.

But instead of it continuing on across the moor as we'd expected, it brings us out onto the tiny snaking strip of moorland road that flows between Kirkby Stephen and Keld.

In some ways, we're relieved. We've had enough of slipping and sliding amongst peat bog for the day. It does, however, mean that unless we follow a suggested narrow road down to it, we won't be able to enjoy a cup of tea at lonely Ravenseat Farm at the foot of the Pennines. Nevertheless, it feels good to be safely back on terra firma again, especially when surrounded by such magnificent desolate Pennine scenery.

We're on an isolated, yet lovely, moorland road, with low green fells on one side and boggy terrain on the other. It makes for such pleasant walking that we begin to relax, knowing that the most difficult part of the day is behind us, and we're not going to get lost on the wild Pennines. We also can't be far off Keld and plod blissfully on along the tarmac.

As we walk, the landscape is gradually turning from one of austere moorland to becoming almost pastoral. There are views of occasional remote farmsteads and distinctive looking stone barns down in the shallow valley below us.

But as we approach Keld's first waterfall, we're suddenly stopped in our tracks by the sound of spine-chilling screaming. It doesn't appear to be human and must be coming from some distressed animal hidden from view behind the stone wall of a nearby field.

Looking over the wall, there is nothing to be seen. But as another scream goes up, I notice that it came from the direction of a small, beehive-shaped pile of rocks in the corner of the field.

Taking off my backpack, I carefully climb over a line of barbed wire on the top of the wall and make my way towards the pile of rocks to examine them.

As I approach, the almost unbearable screaming continues, and I gingerly remove the large top rock from the pile. As I do so, I cautiously lean back and wonder just what I will find.

I'm half expecting to see a small animal being preyed upon by another, and I'm ready to jump back should I need to. But inside the hollow of the rocks, I discover a weasel whose bloodied leg has been caught in the jagged teeth of a gin trap.

Now receiving the full force of its screaming, I look around for a twig and use it to lift the trap and the attached weasel from out of the pile of rocks. As I do so, the screaming crescendos. The weasel has become hysterical, and I wonder just what I should do. Could I, as a vegetarian, use a rock to club the poor distressed animal to death and put it out of its misery? That would certainly stop the unbearable screaming. Or would it be possible to lever its leg out of the trap?

The weasel is growing increasingly hysterical by the second. In a frantic effort to escape, it keeps damaging its sharp teeth by trying to bite through the metal of the trap. I suddenly have a brainwave and ask Pauline to pass me a tent peg from the side-pocket of my backpack. I then use it to try to lever apart the jaws of the trap. Far from seeing me as its saviour, the weasel turns its attention away from the trap and towards me.

It keeps trying to bite my hand and displays a very dangerous looking set of crocodile teeth. Avoiding the snapping mouth, I manage to lever the jaws of the trap slightly apart and free the creature's leg. Not stopping to thank me, the weasel shoots out, and dragging his bleeding limb behind him makes good his escape. Despite not a word of thanks being uttered, I feel that we've done our good deed for the day. Climbing back over the wall, we continue on along the quiet strip of tarmac towards Keld.

On later walks, in terrible weather, rather than climb over the top of the Pennines, we would occasionally take this isolated moorland road all the way from Kirkby Stephen to Keld. The views everywhere were primeval, dark but glorious. It was a great feeling to be safely walking on a narrow-tarmacked carpet of civilization in the middle of almost a wilderness. Austere looking fells and shallow valleys lying on one side of us and rolling boggy moorland on the other. There was a silence on the wind and never a soul in sight. Apart from the road, and occasional glimpses of remote farmsteads down in the valley, this place must look exactly as it would have done over a thousand years ago, when the road was probably just a track.

Last night, I spoke to the leader of the Romans, and he reliably informed me that there is only one campsite in Keld. So, as we walk in along the road and come across a field of people and tents down by the flowing river Swale, I assume that we must be there.

Leaving the road, we enter the camping ground, and Pauline and I take off our backpacks. As we do so, I notice that several of the campers in the field have stopped what they were doing and are staring at us. Some are even pointing. I guess that after our Pennine crossing, we do, look a bit disreputable. So, ignoring them, I continue to undo my backpack. I'm about to get the tent out of it when a woman approaches.

"You can't camp here!" she says.

As this is claimed to be the only campsite in Keld, I demand to know why.

"Because you wouldn't like it," she replies, and

I'd swear that she appears to be winking at me.

"Why wouldn't we like it?" I ask.

The woman seems reluctant to answer.
"Well, we've, we've hired the whole field from the farmer," she says rather hesitantly.

How selfish, the only campsite in the village, and she claims that they've hired it all. They've not given a thought or care for any weary Coast-to-Coast walkers like us who need somewhere to pitch their tent this evening.

I also think that the woman is bluffing, and for some strange reason, doesn't want us to stay here. But I'm adamant that we're going to and suggest to her that we'll go and speak to the farmer.

The woman suddenly changes tack, becoming much more appeasing. Continuing her winking, she now suggests,

"There's a much nicer campsite down in the village!"

She's just saying that to get rid of us, I think. But now I'm beginning to look around me and can see that close by, there is a blazing log fire with a large black caldron of a cooking pot hung over it. The sort you see being used by cannibals in those boys' adventure stories, which often featured desert islands and shipwrecked sailors. I can also hear the bleating sound of a goat tethered in a nearby makeshift covered pen. At the same time, I'm noticing that the people on the campsite don't quite look like walkers, or even like ordinary campers. Their attire, to say the least, is a bit strange.

The penny suddenly drops, and I do an immediate turnabout in attitude. Now furtively winking at Pauline, I suggest that the woman is probably right. It might, after all, be worth going on down into the village if there is a better campsite.

Hurriedly repacking my backpack, we leave. Pleased that we're going, the woman shouts after us.

"We'll try to arrange good weather for you!"

We fairly fly out of the field and scurry on down the road towards Keld. I'm fully expecting there to not be another campsite, but I'm proved wrong. Just after a crossroads, where a signpost points the way to the only pub in the area at Tan Hill, we find the real campsite on the edge of the village. In fact, we discover that there are two, learning that there is a further one down in the centre of Keld.

We had stopped too early. Those people must have hired the whole field from the farmer for whatever purpose it is they have planned. We were at the wrong campsite, and with all the flowing water around Keld, it suddenly dawned on me that we were in the company of a group of witches.

Pauline and I remind each other later that we had better keep our tent flaps securely fastened tonight. Having possibly annoyed them, we might well be due a visit!

Chapter 31 - Down by the River

The first campsite is very basic. It has a chemical toilet which is housed inside a small barn, where an old tractor is stored. Campers stand cooking at a communal stove just feet away from the loo. So anyone using it must carry out their toileting duties as quietly and discreetly as possible. Meanwhile, campers are nonchalantly standing around brewing tea and eating their meals as they hold conversations whilst trying to ignore what's taking place a short distance away from them.

The campsite had only just opened. A few years later it would go upmarket and greatly improve its facilities. So much so that whenever we pass the field today, it's always full of tents and yurts.

After learning that there is another campsite in the centre of the village, we decide to try our luck and plod on down the road towards it. Staying there will have the added advantage of there being slightly less walking in the morning.

Passing Keld Youth Hostel, we call in to see if we can pick up any extra goodies to go along with our evening meal. On opening the large outer door, we're greeted by a whole host of Coast-to-Coast walkers who are sitting in there waiting for the hostel to open. They're apparently not allowed in until four o'clock.

The cost of staying at Youth Hostels is arguably becoming almost as expensive as using the cheapest bed-and-breakfast accommodation. And yet here are both adults and young people, being treated like children, as they seemingly sit on the naughty-step, waiting for the place to open. Couldn't they be trusted to wait in the Common Room?

Leaving the hostel, we follow a quiet back lane, which leads us down into the heart of the village. Passing by a public toilet block, we approach an old chapel, which has an ancient sundial on its wall. I'm reminded that Wainwright once said that time in Keld is measured in centuries. The sundial confirms this.

Just beyond it, in the front room of a cottage, we find the booking-in place for Rukin's Park Lodge Campsite. We're further pleased to discover that it also serves as a small makeshift shop.

The farmer's wife offers us a choice of pitches. We can either camp in a field next to the public toilet block, which we've discovered has a machine that dispenses soap and warm water for a morning wash. Or, pitch our tent on a green grassy mound, which has Portaloo facilities situated close by. Alternatively, as an afterthought, she adds that if we wish to, we could also enjoy a more idyllic setting down by the river Swale.

True romantics, after the surprise of being able to buy a few goodies from the farm shop, we head off towards the river to pitch our tent beside its flowing waters.

The riverbank is situated a distance away from the

A Walk to the Sea

Portaloo block. And we have to clamber down a grassy embankment to get to it. It means that there is a 200-yard walk back to the toilets and the water tap. But we love the idea of the tranquillity of watching the river flow and the possibility of lighting a campfire later.

Fantastic. With the tent pitched, the afternoon wears on. No other campers have joined us, and we have the river to ourselves. Beaming in the warmth of the sun, we sit and idle our time away while Leon paddles in the soothing waters of the Swale.

As we relax, our sockless feet are in recovery mode, recuperating from the soaking they got from the bogs on our Pennine crossing. Wet, peat-stained socks hang from the outside of the tent, drying in the sun.

As the afternoon turns to evening, we can't help but wonder why none of the other Coast-to-Coast walkers haven't chosen to come down here to join us at this idyllic spot. They're missing out on a real treat, a mini paradise.

Having got off our feet early, we've relaxed all day and are slowly regaining our strength as we recharge our batteries. The whole experience has been so therapeutic.

I dig out a packet of pasta from my backpack and cook our evening meal. Then, while Leon explores the riverbank, Pauline reads, and I press my ear to my portable radio set, as we all continue to unwind.

It's as dusk falls that the first stealthy creatures appear. Initially, it's just a few scouts giving us the occasional nip so that we're unsure whether we've actually been bitten and think that it might be an itch. Then, as though losing their inhibitions, the main party of midges arrives. They come on in droves, in full-scale attacks. As we sit there, bite after bite is taken out of our faces and heads. Having not brought any midge repellent with us, there's no escape from them, we've no defence. How I wish I still had access to that farmer's rub-on magic portion.

My memory returns to my puffed-up face after the night spent at the campsite in Ennerdale Bridge alongside the river Ehen. Why don't we learn from our mistakes?

We hurriedly taking everything into the tent. Inside, we're still far from safe. Once again, there are no zips to fasten the flaps, and no midge net to keep the 'Wee Beasties' out. Our tent only has ties to hold the flaps together, and so we need to secure the end.

After tying the flaps, we try to block any gaps by putting our backpacks up against it and pile clothes on top in an attempt to seal the slightest opening. Sadly, it's too late, we're still being bitten. Some of the midges must already be in the tent. The sheer strength of numbers of them living by the river means that they'll get anywhere.

Trapped inside our canvas abode and desperate, Pauline comes up with the idea that we should have a midge slapping session. By blindly clapping our hands together in the general vicinity of the tent roof, where the midges appear to be hiding, we should be able to see some of them off. Even though they can't be seen, we know that they're up there, lurking away, giving us the occasional bite and waiting until we're asleep to present their coup-de-grâce.

Like fervent worshippers in a Baptist choir, the three of us clap our hands vigorously together in the narrow space above our heads in the hope that this will at least stun some. The triangular-shaped roof of the tent makes it difficult, but memories of my swollen face back at Ennerdale Bridge spur me on.

After a while, I try a different approach and come up with a new ploy. While Pauline and Leon bend down, I whirl a hand towel around my head to see off any stragglers. After about five minutes of constant whirling, I stop, and we attempt to make ourselves comfortable for the night. There will be no more going out this evening. The midges surround us and are laying siege to the outside of the tent.

Still getting the occasional nip, I come up with another of my camping brainwaves. Even though we can't see them, by holding our cigarette lighter close to the tent roof, but not so close as to burn it down, with luck, any remaining midges might be attracted by the light and fly into it. As cruel as it seems, especially for vegetarians, it's now either them or us. When your head and face have been bitten for the umpteenth time, there is no parlay.

Peering through a crack in the front flap, the midges continue to keep a vigil outside. Flying in black clouds, they're looking for another victim. As darkness falls around our barricaded abode, we climb into our sleeping bags and lay listening to the soothing sounds of the Swale as it gently flows over the rocks and stones of the riverbed. Slowly, we begin to drift off to sleep.

Waking up suddenly, I check my watch, it's almost midnight, and half asleep, I can hear voices. Faint at first, but gradually becoming louder as they get closer. Pauline has also woken up and wonders what's going on out there. The voices crescendo as the sound of the feet of a small party of people tramp by our tent. Whoever it is, they're certainly full of joviality, which suggests that they've just left the pub, probably the one at Tan Hill, about a mile away.

Carefully undoing the tent flap to avoid any attempted rush by the midges, I cautiously peer out. I can see a group of guys wearing full evening dress and carrying musical instrument cases.

It's midnight, pitch-black, and we're tired and trying to get to sleep, and yet here are these people wide-awake and making their way along the riverbank full of joie-de-vivre. The voices grow fainter as they move further away down the river.

Thinking no more about it, we return to our slumbers. But a few minutes later we're suddenly awakened from our sleep by the sound of a small impromptu orchestra playing what I must assume to be Handel's 'Water Music', down by the river Swale.

Cellos are being plucked, violins are being bowed, and flutes are being blown. The music begins with gusto, and the orchestra soon gets into their stride as the individual musicians become as one with the river.

It's a unique experience, but after a while, we realize that this heavenly sounding music might go on all night and keep us from our slumbers. We have a hard day tomorrow, walking through the lead mines of Swaledale, so as quaint as it all is, we wonder just how long it will go on for.

But we've no need to worry, for the midges soon come to our rescue. We're beginning to hear notes being missed as the various musicians are being bitten and the flute players swallow mouthfuls of them. Startled voices and distressed yells begin to accompany the music until finally it stops altogether. The sound of yelling, however, increases and is now accompanied by the clicking shut of musical instrument cases. This is shortly followed by the thud of the feet of stampeding musicians as they run past our tent, desperate to get to the safety of their cars. Silence reigns, and we return to our sleep.

Morning arrives and the wet dew on the grass, and on our tent, guarantees that the midges will be out there, lying in wait for us. Through a crack in the tent flap, I can see swarms of them already circling about as they wait patiently to breakfast off us.

Pre-empting this, to outwit them, we've devised a plan. Pauline and I have haphazardly gathered together all of our belongings into our two backpacks. This just leaves the tent to be taken down.

Our plan is for Pauline and Leon to bail out of the tent and rush with her filled backpack up the grass slope and onto the portaloos. There they'll wait for me inside one of the toilet cubicles. I'll then emerge from the tent wearing my own fully stuffed backpack, and after quickly taking out the pegs and poles, drag the tent as fast as my legs will carry me up the slope and follow her.

"Go, go, go!"

Pauline and Leon bail out of the tent and I'm right behind them. Like Bats Out of Hell, they disappear up the grassy embankment and dash off at full speed towards the ablutions block. I'm left to take out the tent pegs and poles as speedily as possible. But having missed breakfasting off Pauline and Leon, as soon as I bend down to remove the first peg, the midges immediately swarm around me and totally cover the backs of my hands. My head and face are being bitten as they start to gorge off me. But each bite encourages me to take the tent pegs out even faster. Finally, with them all out, I desperately remove the tent poles and shake the dew-laden tent.

A big mistake, hordes of midges fly up into the air

and I'm now being bitten from all angles. Feeling as though I'm being eaten alive, with poles and tent pegs in one hand and my backpack on, I drag the tent up the embankment and away from the river towards the toilet block.

Clouds of midges follow my retreat. My hair is alive with them. It's even worse than midge attacks I've experienced in Scotland. My legs race beneath me like pumping pistons until finally, the toilet block, like the winning post, stands before me. In one mighty leap, I swing open the door of the nearest cubicle and plunge inside with the tent.

Unfortunately, some of the midges follow me in, they have a vendetta against me, I've taken away their breakfast. Despite slamming the door shut, dozens of them are in the toilet cubicle with me, still coming off the dew-ridden tent.

But now they're in my territory and it's time for more choir practice. I begin my insane clapping of my hands above my head, hoping to kill off any that come into range. They're still swarming around outside, but after about five minutes, I've seen off most of those indoors. Sitting on the toilet seat, I can finally relax. Pauline is in the cubicle next door, and we make contact with each other by shouting through the wall.

Ray Moody

The cairn on Helvellyn

Chapter 32 - The Lead Mines of Swaledale

By the time we re-emerge from the toilets, most of the midges have gone. We've repacked our sacks from the safety of our cubicles. Hoisting them up onto our shoulders, we set off for the lead mines of Swaledale. But the closeness of flowing water means that the midges haven't gone far. A few of them follow us all the way along the path by the river as it leads to a wooden bridge that crosses over the river Swale.

It's on this bridge that Coast-to-Coast walkers might meet up with their kindred spirits on the Pennine Way as they head north towards Tan Hill.

One day we, too, will cross over this bridge while on the Pennine Way. Only then will we be able to understand the look of sheer anguish that can often be seen on the faces of dishevelled Pennine Way walkers.

The midges make one final surge as we cross the bridge. But we lose them as we climb up towards the direction sign that separates Pennine Way from Coast-to-Coast walkers. Those on the Pennine Way turn left whilst those on the Coast-to-Coast turn right. As we climb higher, we thankfully leave the midges behind.

Just before leaving Keld, we met the leader of the Romans. He informed us that his party are taking the river route to Reeth, so too are the Dutch girls.

"There's naught but muck and clambering over old, discarded industry up there," he said, gesticulating with his thumb towards the top of the fells above Keld.

He also told us that the four Detectives have been spotted together again. Apparently, they've had to grasp the nettle as last night they were seen booking into the same bed-and-breakfast accommodation.

It seems that we're the only ones taking the high-level route, and the suggestion that there might be no one else up there has done little for my confidence, let alone Pauline's. I was already feeling slightly apprehensive about today's journey. But now there's the added thought that there could be just the three of us walking through those isolated old mine workings. We'll be on our own as we scramble our way through the leftovers of a deserted industry, the remnants of an austere past.

My vivid imagination easily allows me to consider the possibility of us coming face-to-face with the ghostly apparition of some half-crazed miner, who mumbling to himself, might declare,

"They're after my gold!"

Except that in our case, it will be lead.

The path above the Swale continues to rise. At the skeletal remains of an ancient farm tractor, it bifurcates or splits into two. Yet another word learnt from our Wainwright dictionary. We follow the

A Walk to the Sea

upper-level path, as it ascends high above the river, heading for our next landmark of Crackpot Hall, an abandoned old farmhouse.

The morning sun shines down on us and the walking so far is relatively easy. In the valley below, the silvery river Swale bends dramatically away towards the village of Muker or Mucker as we've decided to pronounce it. The view, from up here, is claimed to have been a favourite of Dales' vet and author James Herriot, and you can see why. The river route does look tempting.

As we climb higher, we're beginning to walk amidst the first evidence of spoil from the lead mines. Eventually, we arrive at the broken-down walls of Crackpot Hall.

This building must have been one of the first places of civilization outside the mines. The miners would have come down this way and, if they'd earned any money, might have been able to buy a few provisions here, such as milk, eggs or salted meat.

Standing in front of the derelict farmhouse, above each of its open doorways can be seen the heavy stone lintels that still hold up the brickwork. I can't help marveling at how, in those primitive times, they got them up there.

I also wonder about the lives that were once lived here and the people who would have stared out at these glorious views of the river Swale each morning. Would they have been able to appreciate their surroundings, or would the sheer austerity of the times have meant that their lives would have been one simply of survival?

Going around the rear of the farmhouse, we get back on route. The path appears to grow impatient and begins to quickly ascend the fell-side. We're getting close to the top of the fell, and as the path turns a corner, we enjoy sudden dramatic views down to the valley below.

We're now walking high above a narrow rocky ravine. Straight ahead of us, a small waterfall is slowly cascading water over a stone sill down to the bottom of a gully a distance below. As we turn our backs on the pleasant view of the Swale and spurn the picturesque villages that the other walkers will be passing through, there is a distinct feeling that we're leaving civilization behind. For a moment, we once again hesitate and wonder about going back down and joining the lower-level route. But quickly dismissing the thought, we hold our nerve and press on.

The path along the side of the shallow ravine is becoming narrower. We have to follow each other in single file as it bends in a U shape around its rocky walls. Before we can get onto the next fell, we must cross over the wet stone sill over which the water flows.

Safely across, the path climbs up onto the fell and the start of the lead mines proper. My heart sinks. It seems that the leader of the Romans was right. Desolation now stares us fully in the face. Having crossed over the gully, we almost immediately stand amidst the ruins of abandoned mine workings and dilapidated old stone buildings, all of which are trapped inside a dark narrow gorge. Scrambling up it, the river Swale and the security of the views of the world below us have gone and can no longer be seen.

With no one else around, we feel isolated. This is indeed a grim place. Water runs down the rocky walls and it really does seem like we've left civilization behind.

We're on our own amidst the debris shed here by an earlier generation, most of whom must have toiled away in this dark place for so very little reward.

We could have played it safe and followed the river Swale. Wainwright called it the royal road to Reeth. But on later walks, we would discover that it's not as majestic a journey as it first appears. Eventually, it becomes quite tedious, and when it does, there is no way of being able to rejoin the main route.

Nevertheless, it's quite an eerie feeling being up here all alone as we follow a rough scree ridden path alongside a stream of water which flows down from the side of the fell.

We're treading on debris that was washed out of the rock a hundred years ago by the miners and then left abandoned. Apart from occasional walkers, archaeology students and those on the Coast-to-Coast walk, there would appear to be little reason for anyone else to have trodden these paths since the lead miners deserted them.

The way out of the gorge lies directly above us, an inclined fell-side which we can see the light of the horizon above.

Slowly and gradually, following a sketchy track alongside a beck, we begin to climb out of the desolation. The track consists of scree scattered amongst boggy peat. It climbs in a zigzag pattern until we're at last on a short sloping section which leads to the top of the fell.

Climbing out of the dark confines of the gorge, we're immediately dazzled by the light as the full extent of Swaledale suddenly opens up to us. From our lofty height on the fell-top, there are glorious views all around. We're staring out over the Yorkshire Dales and beyond. Our early efforts have paid dividends, the restrictions of the gorge are being left behind, and we're now greeted by wide-open spaces.

Looking back towards the Pennines, I wonder about those walkers coming over the soaking wet peat today. Will the bogs be any better? Or will today's walkers, like us yesterday, be at this moment sinking deep into the mire?

The walking is so much easier now, a reward for keeping our nerve and not taking the river route.

A Walk to the Sea

We're traversing a flat stony fell top, a moonscape where limestone rock has been torn from the earth. The ground shines dazzling white in the morning sun. We pass by a piece of old rusting machinery, a leftover from the lead mining days. The trail is straightforward, and we relax. It feels good to be able to get our breath back.

The wide path temptingly begins to descend. But thankfully, having read our guidebook, we're not fooled by it and turn off onto a pathway along the edge of a moor. Almost hidden amongst the heather, the path soon brings us out by the side of a deep, narrow valley.

The view down it is sensational. The long valley has the ruins of several discarded mining buildings at its abrupt end. Walking towards them, we follow a narrow path that runs high along the valley edge. As we near the end of the valley, the path finishes and down below us stands the remains of a very distinctive-looking building, which has classical arched windows.

There are various other dilapidated structures down there and a stone slab bridge over a beck that drains water from the fell-side. Standing almost directly above the deserted ruins, we look for a route down to them. Spotting a precipitous sloping track, we follow it and descend to the valley bottom.

Arriving there, we stand on the stone slab above the noisy flowing beck. Looking around us surveying our surroundings, this place looks like it was once the centre of lead mining activity. The distinctive building with the arched windows stands close by. It's now silent, but there must have once been so much going on down here. There is a real sense of the past in the air, as though the mining has only recently ceased, and the men have just downed tools.

After contemplating the derelict environment from the bottom of the valley, we visit the building with the distinctive windows. Then, after looking around the other ruined remains, we decide that it's time to go.

From the end of the valley, we need to exit it by climbing up the other side. Pauline spots a steep track that ascends the fell. It initially goes almost vertically upwards, and we soon gain height. On reaching a narrow track running along the valley side, we follow it as it takes us back down towards the village of Gunnerside. Once again, it's easy walking, but as the path begins to descend to the village, we leave it.

We now begin a steep climb up towards the crest of the valley, through a scree-laden gully, which we hope will get us back onto the top of the fell.

It's hard going. Our feet slip on loose scree as we look for the shortest way up to the horizon. Despite our best efforts, the fell top is a long time in coming.

Finally arriving there, we once again take up our pose of standing with our hands on our hips while we get our breath to return. Having got the climb out of the way, we stare out across the valley to the other side and can see the path on which we came in. No other walkers appear to have followed us.

Now that we're back on the top of the fell, the walking has once again become straightforward. Plodding along it, the track gradually descends. After crossing over a bridge, we turn a corner, and there, to our amazement, stands the ruins of what looks like a whole deserted mining village.

We're walking amongst the skeletal remains of buildings belonging to the history of lead mining. We explore them, entering a few. But our feet are feeling sore from the pounding they've taken on the fell top, and we have to move on.

Arriving at a road, Pauline spots the bridge that features at the start of the classic television series 'All Creatures Great and Small'. Crossing over the road, we follow a gently ascending path as it twists its way up a rising moor. At the top, we descend into a narrow ravine that blocks our path.

Precipitously climbing down one side, we almost immediately climb straight back up the other. Finding a stile, we clamber over it and follow a green grassy path that runs along the edge of the high moor.

As the sun shines down, it has once again become easy walking. The world has opened up all around us. We can see for miles. Down below us in the green valley, a road contours the ridge we're walking on. After a mile, we take a path that goes down to meet it. Almost as soon as we arrive there. Just beyond a cottage, a sign points to another path, which climbs back up the fell-side.

We're now feeling tired, but can sense that we're on the final leg of today's journey. Back on the top of the fell, we resume our walk, following a well-defined path, which continues to track the road down below. As we meander along it, the walking is pleasant.

Arriving at a gate in a hedge, an arrow suggests that it's time to leave the ridge and turn off it for the village of Reeth. Going through the gate, we follow a steeply descending path down the fell-side.

Squashed between the fences of two fields, we carefully negotiate our way along the overgrown corridor through endless stinging nettles. The passageway should take us down to meet the road leading into Reeth. But it's both long and tortuous and literally provides a final sting in the tail of today's walk.

Despite my best efforts, as I make my way down it in my shorts, nettles come at me from all sides. Sting after sting I receive as I slip and stumble on the high undergrowth covering the path. Wearing shorts has not been a good idea today.

I can't help thinking that this path is some kind of joke being played by a local farmer who's required to provide a right of way through his land. It looks like he's purposely not cutting back the undergrowth.

A Walk to the Sea

If it isn't, then we must be walking down some long since abandoned common ground. Either way, this route off the fells can't be much used. It's so overgrown with nettles that it suggests there's another, easier path, which locals take to get up and down the fell.

The passageway finally pops us out onto a road in the suburbs of Reeth. We're directly opposite the village school. I stand for a moment and rub the many irritated places on my legs. But realizing that we've almost finished our walking for the day, we relax and saunter down the road, ambling our way into the village. Passing by a baker's, our spirits rise, and we stop and purchase three piping hot cheese and onion pasties.

Approaching the rounded village green, we can see a series of benches. Wainwright famously once sat on one of these when he made a televised visit to Reeth. I vaguely recollect that it was the end bench. Making our way towards it, we sit and eat our pasties as we watch parties of weary Coast-to-Coast walkers come slowly limping into the village.

The Walkers' grapevine has informed us that several of the Toast-to-Toasters aren't staying in Reeth. They will have a long day ahead of them as they continue on to the fleshpots of Richmond. We've heard that the four Detectives are also planning to do this.

With our pasties eaten, we hobble our way to the

campsite. It's only two-thirty in the afternoon, so we'll be able to get off our feet early and wash and dry a few clothes.

The campsite owner gives us a cheery welcome. Because we're the first Coast-to-Coast walkers in today, as a special reward, he lifts our backpacks onto his small electric vehicle and drives us down to the bottom of his camping field where he wants us to pitch our tent. On the way, we pass through an avenue of caravans.

After putting up the tent, we discover that the river Swale flows past the rear of the site. Visiting it, we sit on a line of large stepping-stones and cool our feet in its soothing waters.

Returning to our tent, the Romans have turned up with the Dutch Girls, and like a band of gypsies, we all camp together at the end of the field. We're providing entertainment for the caravan owners, who stare out of their windows and smile at the sight of us. Wet socks hang on guide ropes and a week's growth of beard can be seen on most of the guys' faces. The Romans' leader holds court, leaning on his staff with his followers around him. Everyone is going into the village for a drink, and we arrange to meet them there later.

A few years after this, a new and even kinder campsite proprietor would take over management of the site. We named him Saint Peter, as he would frequently identify any wet and obviously suffering

A Walk to the Sea

Coast-to-Coast walkers in need of care and attention.

Instead of camping, he would, at no extra cost, offer them the opportunity to spend the night in the relative luxury of one of his caravans.

Doing this would enable a walker to enjoy a more comfortable night's sleep. It would also save them from the time and effort involved in pitching and packing up their tent.

In the caravan, surrounded by some of the comforts of home, such as a table, chairs, television, cooker and a bed, it would give them a real chance to recharge their batteries.

Crossing Limestone country with Lakeland in the background

Ray Moody

The solitary tree before the Whitby Road

Chapter 33 - We Tea'ed on the Lawn like Landed Gentry

Today we're passing through the largest centre of civilization on the whole walk, Richmond.

The morning is dry and bright, and we stock up on a few goodies for the journey, buying sweets from a corner shop as we leave Reeth.

Our bodies have had more than a week to build up the required muscles. And the fact that Pauline and I are now both carrying less has meant that since crossing over the Pennines, the walking has become so much easier. The terrain has also changed, becoming gentler, and we stroll down country lanes, with cows and sheep grazing on either side of us with ease.

Passing by a field, a sheep has somehow managed to climb up onto the top of a dry-stone wall. The rest of the flock stand close by, bleating for it to come back down.

"Bah, bah!" they seem to say, "You shouldn't be up there!"

The sun shines down on our pleasant pastoral surroundings as we continue to roam down traffic free, quiet country lanes.

We soon arrive at our first landmark on today's section of the walk, the distinctive buildings of an old Priory. Cowled monks once found solitude here, but today it's an outward-bound centre.

The Priory signals the point where we must leave the road. Here the first real exertions of the day begin. Climbing over a stile, we head off towards a wooded copse where we find a flight of ancient stepping-stones hidden amongst the trees.

These stones were once laid and trod by the monks from the Priory. Clambering up the seemingly endless, continuous line of rounded boulders, at the top we stand breathless with our hands on our hips and deeply draw in the air. After a few minutes, with our breath returned, we continue on over farmland.

Passing through a small hamlet, an ancient sundial on the wall of a cottage tells us that, just like in Keld, we've once again stepped back in time.

Beyond an old schoolhouse, we cut across fields and arrive at a flowing beck near a farm building. Taking it in turns, we cross over it via a precarious wooden plank which serves as a bridge.

The environment has become one of continuous pastureland, with farms dotted here and there. Through more fields we go before eventually coming out onto a narrow country lane. The lane leads us through yet another quiet village.

Lying motionless in the gutter are several dying rabbits. Each of them has their eyes scabbed over, blinded by myxomatosis. The poisoning of rabbits must have been extremely effective around here.

A church in the centre of the village advertises that it has an honesty box available in its vestibule, where you can purchase cool soft drinks.

Leaving the village at a crossroads, we meander down yet another quiet country lane. Climbing over a stile in the hedgerow, we follow a well-trodden path across several fields. The path is leading us directly towards a high grassy ridge which is known locally as Willance's Leap. This is the place where a local dignitary broke his neck when he fell off his horse.

Passing over a beck, we climb up the steep embankment and onto the grassy top, where we stand gasping for breath beside a white-painted cairn. With our breath returned, we continue along the ridge as it passes through various farmsteads and past another outward-bound Centre.

Beyond it we follow a path that descends to a gate leading into a wood. Climbing over a stile, we enter the ancient woodland. Travelling down a tree-lined path over wet undulating earth, we soon come out at a gate on the other side. Just after the wood, we get our first glimpse of the red rooftops of Richmond and its distinctive castle keep.

Despite it so far being a relatively easy twelve miles from Reeth, we're feeling like we need a rest. Entering the environs of the town, our spirits rise, because today we've promised ourselves a few luxuries.

I'm looking forward to the possibility of there being a chip shop, a bakery, and the chance to visit a bank. Pauline wants to buy a couple of books to read and a bottle of wine. Leon hopes for more sweets. After shopping, we intend to sit in the market square and have our lunch. Apart from Kirkby Stephen, this is the only other place on the Coast-to-Coast route, where we can indulge ourselves in such hedonistic pleasures.

Just after entering Richmond, at the end of a street of terraced houses, we spot an old, round, yellow metal sign which is hung up on the wall.

Standing reading it, the sign celebrates the event of a total eclipse of the sun, which was experienced here back in 1927.

The town of Richmond was identified as being close to the central line of totality. As a way of celebrating it, prior to the event happening, the local council planned a week of entertainment.

People arrived here from all over Britain to witness the eclipse, including the author, Virginia Woolf. She came down from London by train, specially to see it. Like many others, she must have stood and watched as the moon totally blocked out the sun for exactly 24 seconds.

Making our way into the town centre, Pauline discovers a charity shop. While she searches for a book to read, and Leon looks at the toys and games, I support the weight of my backpack by sitting on a chair near the changing cubicle.

As I rest, I keep catching customers glancing at

me. I'm doing little for business.

I've not shaved for several days, and wearing a creased tee-shirt and stained shorts, I look scruffy and dishevelled. I fear that after the morning's exertions I might also just possibly smell of sweat. To crown it all, a large, discoloured white hat tops off my appearance and its jaunty headband now contains an even bigger feather. I guess that I could quite easily be mistaken for a tramp who's wandered in off the street to beg some fresh clothes.

Leaving the premises, we saunter around Richmond's market square. For walkers who've been absent from society for ten days, the hustle and bustle of it all seems strange. But like taking the lid off a box of chocolates, we don't know which shop to visit first.

We begin with the bank, drawing out sufficient money to cover our expenses for the rest of the walk. We won't come across another cash machine again unless we go miles off route.

Finding a fish and chip shop, we discover that it cooks in animal fats, so we can't eat the chips. But not far away is a baker, and as we stare in the window, I practically salivate at the range of cakes and pies available. It's a veritable cornucopia of confectionary and I don't know what to choose, there is such a selection. Eventually, we settle for buying some pasties for our lunch and some more to carry with us to supplement our evening meal.

Sitting in the sunshine on the stone steps of an obelisk in the market square, I'm enjoying an absolute feast for the Gods. I've bought a bottle of ice-cold banana milkshake, and like Billy Bunter, sit and greedily gulp it down. This is quickly followed by mouths full of cheese and onion pasty, and then topped off with an iced bun. I wonder if I should go back for more.

We've lived on almost nothing but tent food for the past ten days. Packets of dried pasta, supplemented by crisps or packet mashed potato and anything else that we've been able to buy from the few local stores. I've been inventive with our meals, swapping the crisps for packet mash, and making meatless, vegetable stew concoctions, whenever I've been able to get my hands-on tinned peas and potatoes, or something similar.

Not eating meat or fish has meant that our range of meals has mainly been restricted to tomato and cheese pasta, although I have occasionally used packet soup for our lunch. I might therefore be forgiven for behaving like a child in a sweet shop, as in Richmond I can buy anything I've been deprived of for a week or more. Also, after today, the few shops we'll come across are likely to have limited items for us, so I'm making hay while the sun shines.

The campsite we're staying at this evening is on an isolated farm deep in the countryside. It's only six miles away, so I calculate that I can manage to carry something to go with our pasties. I choose a quality tin of rice pudding and store it in the side pocket of my backpack.

As we entered Richmond, for the first time since Kirkby Stephen, we can hear people and traffic. It seemed like a good idea to experience civilization again. But after only an hour, we've had more than enough of the crowds and dodging cars and coaches.

Some of our fellow walkers on the trail have set aside a night of relative luxury here. They're bed-and-breakfasting in the town with a possible visit to the theatre, the castle or one of its many pubs. They'll get a day behind unless they make up the distance tomorrow, which will mean a 24-mile hike to the Blue Bell Inn at Ingleby Cross and an extra mile if they go onto Osmotherley.

Richmond provides a brief reminder of the world we've disappeared from, a world that's carrying on without us. The walk has given us the chance to get away from that world, to forget about everything except the daily task of walking across England without getting lost. Looking around us, we're glad to have left the real world behind for a while.

As we've rested on the steps of the monument, our legs have slowly regained their strength. They remind us that they've only done twelve miles and have sufficient energy left to go on a little further. We've extracted the most we can get out of the fleshpots of Richmond, and even feel slightly alien to it. So, it's time to leave.

Standing up, I heave my sack onto my back. The ubiquitous cold sweat on my tee-shirt has for once dried while we've been sitting here. But experience has taught us that it will take some time to get our legs going again and back into the rhythm of the walk.

There are four ways out of the market square, but having packed our guidebook, I have to identify what I believe to be the correct corner to leave Richmond by.

Descending a cobbled street, at the bottom of it, I discover that I'm wrong. This isn't the way out-of-town, and we have to climb back up to the square. I couldn't be bothered to get my guidebook out of my sack to check it.

Finding the right corner to leave the square by, we're soon back on the trail. Walking alongside the fast-flowing river Swale, Richmond castle stands directly opposite us on the other bank. Moving away from the river, we pass by a row of terraced houses. At the end of them, we follow the road out of town.

In a field next to the road, stand the fine architectural remains of Richmond's former railway station. I wonder how a town of this size, position, and historical significance could have had its rail link removed as part of the savage Beeching cuts of the 1960s. Such grand station buildings, and yet you can't use them to catch a train to or from Richmond. Virginia Woolf would have been sorely disappointed if the eclipse had been today. There wouldn't have been a train for her to arrive on.

In the past, Richmond used to connect with Darlington, where it joined the main line. Now, despite the town being so close to one of the UK's major army bases containing thousands of soldiers, you can no longer board a train to Richmond.

Leaving the road, we return to walking alongside the river Swale as it twists away from the town. After passing a sewerage works, the path becomes wooded and overgrown, and we slip and slide in the wet muddy puddles that cover the ground. The trees by the river are dark and dank, and we follow a slippery path as it eventually climbs and makes its way to the top of an embankment.

This is a place where for only a few times on the walk I've felt a bit isolated.

Several years later, the path would be greatly improved by the Army. They apparently carry out night exercises here amongst the trees beside the river. Today, when you make your way along the path, it's a more enjoyable experience, and it seems so much less remote.

At the top of the embankment, we emerge from the semi-darkness of the trees and back into the light. As we walk towards the site of a derelict farm, it feels good to be in the open again.

Standing checking our guidebook near the remains of some ruined farm buildings, a Coast-to-Coast walker, who we've never seen before, catches up with us.

"The route goes right!" he says, and then turns and walks that way.

Throughout the walk, we've suffered from the delusion that because we're new to long-distance walking, and the use of map and compass, every other walker must know more than we do when it comes to route finding.

The hand-drawn map in my Wainwright suggests that we go left, but we concede and follow the man, believing he knows something we don't. Within a few minutes, our surroundings tell us that he's wrong. The environs don't fit Wainwright's description. We turn back to find the correct path.

For yet another occasion on the walk, doubting ourselves and following someone else has proved erroneous, and we're now heading back in the right direction. This has happened a few times on our journey, being led astray by walkers whom we assume know better than us. However, as we've slowly gained our confidence in route finding, we're not so quick to follow them. On a long day, even walking twenty minutes in the wrong direction means that you have a further twenty minutes to walk back, and the whole thing can throw you out of sync for a while.

A Walk to the Sea

Fortunately, we haven't gone too far off route. According to Wainwright, we should now be only a few hundred yards away from the small settlement of Coburn, but we can't see it. Steering ourselves via a telegraph pole, it points the way to a path leading into a cornfield. Cutting across the field, we follow a well-trodden track and at the end of it find an opening into a magical Rupert Bear type wood. The passage through the trees is short, and it quickly brings us out into the hamlet of Corburn.

Passing by the Corburn Arms, we continue on towards Catterick Bridge. We're now walking on a green embankment high above the river Swale and can hear the constant hum of road traffic in the distance. Passing under a motorway bridge, the noise of motor vehicles above us on the A1 crescendos. The edge of a racecourse now appears, and we turn away from it as we head directly for Catterick Bridge.

Meeting the road at the bridge, it's busy with traffic. We stand for a moment, waiting for a gap in the long line of cars before being able to cross over to the other side. Climbing down off the bridge, we follow a path alongside the river Swale. The sound of traffic grows quieter the further we move away from the road. As it does so, for the second time today, I feel a little bit isolated.

Hearing voices, we suddenly come across a group of strange characters who are camping in the undergrowth close by the river. Quickly passing by them, we walk alongside the Swale as it bends away in a curve. Following it, we eventually come out onto a long country lane. Tramping down it, at its end we arrive in the village of Bolton-on-Swale.

Here we find the church where it's claimed England's oldest man lies buried. Standing in the churchyard, we spot an obelisk dedicated to him.

During his televised series on the Coast-to-Coast Walk, Wainwright visited this church and signed the Visitors' Book. We wonder if it's still here with his autograph and comment in it. Entering the vestibule, we discover that the door into the church is open and, going inside, look for the book.

Finding it laying there in full view, we eagerly search through it to try to spot Wainwright's entry. Turning over the pages, we eventually find it. We're further lucky in that there are still a few blank pages left in the book where we can add our own names and thoughts.

Visiting the church, a year later, a new visitor's book was in place, and the one containing Wainwright's signature had gone. It had probably been stowed away for posterity. And if it has, then it's good to know that our own names and comments have been stored away along with his.

Leaving the church, we're on our last legs and wearily climb a stile before following a path across fields, which soon leads us to Laylands Farm.

A Walk to the Sea

Arriving at the farm cottage, we slump down on a wooden picnic table situated on a well-mown lawn. Unshackling ourselves from our backpacks, we position them beside us on our seats.

With her breath back, Pauline knocks on the door of the cottage and an elderly lady appears. Pauline pays her the camping fees and then re-joins us at the table. With our packs off, we sit and laze in the late afternoon sun, allowing our bodies to return to their normal unshackled state. Removing my boots and socks, I enjoy the ecstasy of massaging my feet on the trim lawn.

The door of the cottage opens, and the woman comes out holding a tray. Approaching our table, she places a large pot of tea, cups, and a plate of biscuits on it.

"These will refresh you!" she says.

We're taken aback.

"How kind, how much will it be?" asks Pauline.

"Oh, they're on the house, a welcome for our visitors."

We thank her profusely.

I normally drink coffee, but it's strange just how refreshing a cup of tea is when you've been walking. We drain the pot, making as many cups as we can squeeze out of it. In the warm afternoon sun, the tea tastes like we're drinking from a cool mountain stream. I finish off by gulping down the remaining milk from the jug.

When you're long-distance walking, and living in a tent for two weeks, it limits how many hot drinks you can have during a day. Especially when compared with the number of cups you would normally have back at home.

Some experienced walkers of the 'old school' often talked about 'making a brew' during a day's walking. It seems idyllic, but we've found it to be far too impractical. For a start, you need to unshackle yourself from your backpack and unsettle it all by looking for the gas stove and the tea making ingredients. Then, you waste further time waiting for it to boil, and as we've discovered, stopping for too long can chill your body down. Setting off again, it can also take a while to get your legs back into their normal walking rhythm. So, we never stop to make a brew, but take every other opportunity we can get to enjoy one.

This isn't the first free cup of tea we've had on the walk. We also received one at Reeth from a woman in a caravan who had seen us setting off that morning from Keld. So impressed was she by us having walked all the way from there to Reeth that on our arrival, she made us each a mug of tea.

Pauline and I did once come unstuck, partaking of tea in out-of-the way places. On another walk, we came across signs for refreshments deep in a wood. The café was about half a mile off route. But keen to encourage anyone who takes the time to offer walkers a few perks out in the middle of nowhere, we tramped our way through the trees, following handwritten, tempting signs that said such things as,

"Nearly there!"

"Delicious pasties and sandwiches!"

"Homemade cakes and buns!"

'You certainly won't regret it!'

By the time we reached the café, our mouths were practically dribbling. Correction, by the time we arrived at a load of old wooden packing cases, out of which some kind of shanty town was being built.

Nevertheless, joining in the spirit of the thing, we sat ourselves down at some roughhewn tables made from an assortment of discarded pieces of wood.

No menu was on view, but having once run our own café, and being from Yorkshire, I played it safe by ordering two mugs of tea, which in most cafés are usually the cheapest item on the menu.

We gave our order to a man wearing a siren suit who was brandishing a chainsaw. He disappeared off into one of the larger packing cases, which was serving as a kitchen. Five minutes later, he returned with our tea. It was presented to us in an old, dented, tin teapot, the sort you'd find thrown out at any jumble sale. Accompanying it were a couple of mismatching mugs. How quaint, I thought, they're even recycling old crockery.

Once again, whether it's my Hull or Yorkshire poverty-stricken upbringing, I like to get the business end of the deal out-of-the-way. So, I asked our Eco-warrior, who had now picked up his chainsaw, just how much the tea was going to cost us.

I had already calculated a price in my head. Here we were, sitting in the open air on a wooden plank surrounded by a load of old packing cases, and our tea was coming out of a dented teapot. My conclusion, therefore, was that these rough-and-ready mugs of tea should cost us around a pound each.

"Six Pounds please!"

"How much!" I blurted out, spitting my tea all over, as the raised volume of my voice caused birds to fly out from the surrounding trees and wild animals to start stampeding in the wood.

"Six Pounds!"

The man wasn't joking. I had never paid six pounds for two cups of tea on the high street, yet alone two served from a battered old tea pot and mismatching mugs.

But I considered our situation. Here we were being fleeced, but we're on our own in the middle of an isolated wood with a strange man stood brandishing a chainsaw. I paid up, vowing never again to buy anything without checking the price first. The guy, however, hadn't finished. As though wanting to pour salt into my wounds, he insisted on taking a photograph of the two of us enjoying tea at his establishment for his Facebook page. Only with very strong coaxing from Pauline was I able to go along with this charade, but I must admit that I found it extremely difficult to smile.

The lawn at Laylands Farm is filling up with our fellow Coast-to-Coast walkers. The Romans are here, and their long-haired leader tells us that his group often camp at the farm. The Dutch Girls have also arrived, so has the mum and the boy and the family with the dog. We're all here with our tents pitched, exchanging tales from the journey so far, as we relax in the late afternoon sunshine.

Spirits are high, knowing that the North York Moors are getting closer. Everyone is feeling confident now about being in a good position to be able to finish the walk. Whilst there is still the barrier of the Cleveland Hills to get across, the really hard stuff does seem to be behind us.

However, one lone backpacker, who has only recently joined our tribe and who is on his second attempt at the walk, warns us all about becoming too complacent. He explained that he nearly finished the Coast-to-Coast walk last year but had tripped over the pavement at Ingleby Cross (tomorrow's destination) and broken his ankle and was forced to drop out. I think that I would have limped the rest of the way to Robin Hood's Bay.

Pauline at the Face Stone

Chapter 34 - Blue Remembered Hills

Departing the farm on another bright, sunny morning, how the weather has changed for the better since leaving Lakeland. Judging by the absence of several tents, some of the walkers must have got away very early as the lawn was full last night.

In later years, fewer Coast-to-Coast walkers would stay at this site, preferring to set up camp earlier at St Giles's Farm, just after Colburn. This might have coincided with tea no longer being served on arrival. The kind old lady had moved away, and the campsite near Colburn had adopted her practice. Eventually, camping at the farm stopped altogether.

There are quite a few miles of tarmac roads to trek down today. But I'm looking forward to it as it will make a refreshing change. You can't occasionally beat the solidness of a road under your boots, and it can help to zip up the miles on a long day.

As we walk down endless quiet country lanes, only the sound of birdsong accompanies our footsteps. But with the constant tramping on the tarmac, long before we get to our next landmark, the village of Danby Wiske, all three of us are hot and sweating.

There have been one or two off-road diversions along the way. We've left the tarmacked road and followed them, fighting our way down a few confined short side paths. Sadly, once again, we've soon regretted it. True to form, they've been overgrown and full of nettles. So, we now prefer to plod on down these long country lanes, passing by sleepy farms as the sun beams down on us.

A metal sign proclaims that we have at last arrived at the village of Danby Wiske. Just beyond it we pass by a parked car. Pauline notices that seated behind the driving wheel is one of the four Detectives. As we go by him, the man keeps his head down and clearly doesn't want to be seen. Where did he get the car from, we wonder, and who is he waiting for?

We've had regular updates on the Detectives throughout the walk. We had heard on the grapevine that by the time they reached Kirkby Stephen, despite them being on a team building exercise, they didn't appear to be talking to each other. They had often been spotted walking on their own, or with other parties of Coast-to-Coast walkers. At the last sighting, one of them had been seen catching a bus in Reeth. So, who is the guy waiting for? Is it to pick up what's left of his dysfunctional team to take them back home to London?

We don't see or hear any more of him or any of the Detectives after this, and none of them turn up at Robin Hood's Bay. There had been suspicions throughout the journey that their party hadn't been playing a straight bat with their walking. They were frequently not seen along the various sections of the trail. But often arrived ahead of everyone else looking spick and span as they sat at the bar of some village inn at the next stopping place on route.

Passing the White Swan, we find it open and call in for some refreshments. Wainwright once came here and signed the Visitors' Book. After ordering our drinks, we ask the proprietor if we can look at it. She brings it to us, and we soon spot his comment.

Wainwright had complained in his original guidebook that when planning the Coast-to-Coast walk during the early 1970s, he had tried to get a meal here, and all the surly landlord could offer him was a bag of crisps. Twenty years later, when he returned to the inn whilst filming his walk for television, the menu had changed so much for the better, that a walker who had been in there earlier that day, commented that Wainwright should visit the place now, and he actually had.

Leaving the inn, we cross a bridge over the main railway line to Scotland. The day is warm and in glorious bright sunshine we meander down more country lanes.

Eventually we arrive at a busy main road. If followed, the road leads into the nearby town of Northallerton. After walking along it for a while, we turn off onto a track going across country. The trail takes us past the back of a farm building and soon afterwards we come out onto a quiet lane. Walking a short distance along it, we leave it to amble down past yet another farm.

The farm is one of many places today to feature an Honesty box. The first of these we encountered late yesterday afternoon in the village of Bolton-on-Swale. Put there by trusting rural entrepreneurs, they provide a treasure chest of food and drink items for the weary walker, and rely on their honesty to pay for it. Walkers leave their payment in a jar and help themselves to any change.

Sad to say, that if such a box was ever to be provided in my birthplace of Hull, then not only would its contents and the money be likely to disappear, but sadly, the box as well.

Today could indeed be called the day of the honesty boxes. Several of the farms and cottages we pass by seem to have a variety of wares for sale. These range from bottles of chilled soft drinks to bananas. I'm enjoying financing the local economy, a piece of fruit here, a flapjack there. These small rewards help us to keep going, putting a little more energy into our tanks when we're flagging.

Leaving the farm behind, we follow an endless lane until it eventually brings us out at a crossroads. From here, we almost immediately head down yet another long farm trod and walk towards an enormous chicken shed.

The sound of clucking and cackling birds grows louder with every step. From a distance, we at first mistake it for a factory farm. But as we get closer, we can see that the huge wooden structure has raised side panels positioned all the way along the bottom of its walls, and they are all open. These allow the chickens the freedom to roam the surrounding field, and as we draw near, thousands of hens can be seen spilling out onto the grass. Most of them appear content to stay close to the shed and don't wander off too far.

Beyond the chicken hut, we pass through the garden of what appears to be a run-down cottage. Pauline climbs over a stile up ahead of me and suddenly lets out a scream. There is a large plastic rat stuck close to where she has placed her hand.

Years later, the much-improved cottage would enter into the spirit of the Coast-to-Coast walk and provide the mother of all honesty boxes for passing walkers.

Unlike other humble offerings along the way, this 'Iron Ranger' is gigantic, a six-foot-high refrigerator plugged directly into the mains. On its door, a sign proudly displays the words 'Emma's Fridge'. Inside, it's packed with a vast array of goodies, ranging from ice-cold energy drinks to a wide variety of things to eat or chew. On a hot summer's day, it's a veritable oasis and comes as a great relief to walkers. If I were awarding prizes for the best honesty box on the Coast-to-Coast trail, this one would be the clear winner.

Soon after the cottage, we come to a railway line.

After first checking for trains, we gingerly cross the tracks and then climb over an ancient ladder stile on the other side.

Taking our backpacks off, like a scene from the Railway Children, the three of us sit side-by-side on the top step of the roomy stile and watch for the next train to pass. We don't have long to wait, as a rumbling sound can soon be heard in the distance. Sadly, we're disappointed, when instead of waving at carriages full of passengers; it's a freight train heading for the industrial Northeast. Apart from the driver, there's no one else to wave at.

Leaving the railway line behind, the route continues across a cornfield, where a clear path is deeply etched amidst the recently cut stalks. In the distance, we can now see the blue remembered hills of Cleveland. The same hills I walked over as a student on the Lyke Wake Walk nearly twenty years ago. When we finally arrive at them, we'll virtually be in our home territory of North Yorkshire. It feels good to have more of an idea of what lies ahead.

Walking down a narrow country lane, we pass by an open field where standing side-by-side are two scarecrows. They're so well-made that they look almost human. Pauline stands between them with her arms around each of their waists while I photograph her. Noticing that the scarecrow's have been autographed by other walkers, we write our names on them. Later, we hear from the Dutch Girls that

A Walk to the Sea

they knew we were ahead of them because they had spotted our signatures. The scarecrows become a feature for passing Coast-to-Coast walkers.

We're getting closer to the Cleveland Hills and can now see an assortment of television antenna and drum-like satellite dishes on the top of Beacon Hill, the first of them.

Entering another cornfield, in the middle of it we pass by the ruins of Broken Hill farm. The farm cottage is now just a pile of red bricks, but you can't help wondering about the lives that were lived here. Who were the people who once resided in this farmhouse and awoke every morning to glorious views of those stunning hills?

Beyond the pile of bricks, the path leads us down through another farm. This one is inhabited, but some of the farm buildings look suspiciously as though they have recently been built using bricks from Broken Hill farm.

A peacock struts nonchalantly by, and we can hear the sound of traffic on the nearby dual carriageway. The noise of speeding vehicles increases, growing louder as we make our way down the farm road towards it.

With a roar like thunder, the road suddenly pops us out on the side of the busy A19. Lorries and cars shoot by us at 70 mph on both sides of the carriageway. It looks like it will be quite a challenge to get across this wide major road.

Before we attempt it, we spot a sign that points to a nearby petrol station which houses a shop. Despite feeling tired, we hobble across to see what goodies they have to offer. Unless we detour into Osmotherley, which is dramatically uphill and a further two miles away, there'll be no more shops for several days.

We're now less than a mile off our destination of Ingleby Cross and today's walking is nearly done. Once we get across the busy A19, we'll be able to go on autopilot all the way down into the village.

After purchasing a few items, we leave the shop and take our lives in our hands as we attempt to cross the numerous lanes of the busy road. The dual carriageway needs tackling in two stages. Spotting a gap in the traffic, we race across the lanes to the central barrier. Waiting for a moment for another space between the vehicles, we rush for the safety of the grass verge. From here, we saunter our way down into the village.

The Blue Bell at Ingleby Cross must has stood here for several centuries and will have once been an old coaching inn. Short, but muscular, the inn's landlord appears to be a retired jockey. And as though catering for his stable lads, the camping facilities are just as rough and ready.

We're the first walkers in today, and are directed to pitch our tent on a large patch of grass at the rear of the pub. We choose a good spot next to a picnic table, making it easy for packing and unpacking our backpacks. The Cleveland Hills are now within touching distance and offer much promise for what lies ahead.

I'm excited. This is the first time I've been back here since my student days, almost two decades ago.

As it's still early afternoon, I selfishly suggest to Pauline that once the tent's pitched, she and I should leave it and climb the road up through the afforested side of the Cleveland Hills to find Mount Grace Priory, an old monk's retreat that Wainwright once visited.

After getting our breath back, leaving Leon and our sacks behind in the tent, we begin the climb up the steep forest road to where the Priory lies hidden.

I had imagined that the old monastery would just be a pile of stones, a dilapidated ruin you can look around for free, like Shap Abbey. But after arriving in the place, we discover that you're actually supposed to pay to see these ruins. Luckily, we've entered the Priory from the rear and so didn't have to pass the pay desk situated at the front entrance. Nevertheless, I daren't go too far in, in case we're pounced on for our admittance fees. These might be as high as eight pounds each, money we can use to treat ourselves to a meal in the pub this evening. Pauline, however, is unperturbed by the risk of possibly having to pay, and she gets full value as she wanders about looking into every nook and cranny.

By the time we arrive back at the Bluebell Inn, the grass at the rear of the place is filled with tents. The Romans have left theirs and are once again appreciating the benefits of being camped at a watering hole. The Dutch Girls have also come in, along with the mother and son. But the family with the dog have continued on into Osmotherley, where there is a more spacious commercial campsite that offers spotlessly clean showers and toilets.

An unfamiliar tent has been pitched and two new walkers have joined us. These guys are Air Force pilots, and we're impressed when they tell us that this is their fifth crossing of the Coast-to-Coast walk, and this time they're attempting it in reverse, east to west.

We are, however, slightly less impressed, considering all the sweat and strain that has gone into our walk across England over the past eleven days, when they claim that in their jet planes, they can fly the whole length of the Coast-to-Coast route in a matter of minutes.

Nevertheless, we're now camped in the foothills of the North York Moors, and keeping our nerve, three more hard days, and we too, like the air force pilots before us, will be able to say that we've walked all the way across England, from one coast to the other.

Chapter 35 - The Start of the Trouble

This is the day of the walk, that more than any other, I've really been looking forward to. A chance to retrace my footsteps over the Cleveland Hills. The last time I was here was nearly two decades ago, when I was just a boy.

Today, we have a hard twenty miles to cover, so we take down the tent and set off early. As we follow the road up from the Blue Bell Inn towards the nearby-afforested hillside, the climbing begins almost immediately. At eight o'clock in the morning, it's a strenuous nightmare. Although we've only been walking for just a matter of minutes, the back of my tee-shirt, with my pack pressed firmly against it, has already caused it to once again become wet with sweat.

On reaching the forest road, banks of conifer trees crowd in on either side of us and the road climbs dramatically upwards. It contours first left and then right and then up and further right, then up again and further right. Yet we still can't see the final tree line through which we should be able to glimpse the horizon.

Thick rows of conifers still lie between us and the top of the ridge. As soon as one tree line is reached, another takes its place. What is worrying is that we're getting further and further away from the point on the horizon where the satellite dishes and television antennas are situated.

I have a clear memory of these being located near the trig point. The concrete obelisk declaring the highest part of the land on the top of Beacon Hill. The place where our traverse of the Cleveland hills begins.

Despite now having lighter backpacks, the ascent at times feels very close to vertical. Just like on the first day of the walk, when we climbed Dent, we're once again being pulled backwards by gravity.

With the smell of pine in the air and sweat dripping off me, there is another turn of the forest road, and yet we still seem to be some way off the top of the hill. Drastic action is required.

I suggest to Pauline that instead of us continuing to follow the road, which is getting further and further away from the place on the horizon where we want to be, we should try taking a shortcut.

By heading straight up through the trees, we could make a beeline for the top of the ridge. Tired out herself, Pauline readily agrees to give it a go.

Turning off the road, the three of us enter the confines of the trees. Almost immediately, we discover that the earth we're standing on is far worse than the road. Made up of knee-deep loose soil and fern leaves, the ground slopes dramatically upwards. In the semi-darkness, as we attempt to move forward, we trip over tree roots and fallen branches. Our boots

A Walk to the Sea

dig deep into the moist, fern covered soil, but we can barely stand upright and have to cling onto the closely compacted trees that block out the light. Despite being just yards away from the forest road, this is a dark, forbidding place.

After spending just five minutes trying to make our way upwards through the dense terrain, we have to admit defeat and give up. Now totally dishevelled and covered in twice as much sweat as before, we retrace our steps and emerge from the trees. We've wasted both time and energy and will have to continue our trudge along the forest road.

A few months later, I would read in our local paper that someone had discovered a woman's body hidden amongst these trees, very close to the area where we'd been climbing. A man had apparently murdered his wife, and armed with a spade, came here and buried her. It must have seemed like the perfect place to hide a corpse, and after experiencing the denseness of the plantation, it makes you wonder just how on earth they ever found it.

After yet another turn of the road, it begins at last to head directly up towards the skyline and the top of the ridge.

Finally arriving at the end of the forest road, a sign points the way to the village of Osmotherley and a wide track branches off to our left in the direction we need to be going. Turning down it, the track appears to be just below what we believe to be the final tree line, and we can see the sky above it. But as we make our way along it, the track's becoming waterlogged, and we're having to jump from one piece of solid earth to another to avoid our boots getting wet in one of the many rutted pools.

The track does seem vaguely familiar to how I remember it from my student days, when I made my way along it to reach the trig point on Beacon Hill to start the Lyke Wake Walk.

But we're now beginning to notice expanses of reeds growing up through the muddy track. Surely, it should look more used than this. Is our guidebook out of date and has this path been discarded?

Throughout the walk, the three of us have had to learn to behave like North American Indians and develop our pathfinding skills. Our now experienced eyes are forever scanning the ground, looking for signs of compressed grass and boot marks. These help to confirm that we're on a well-trodden path and therefore more likely to still be on route.

This track is overgrown and there are few signs to suggest that it's recently been trod. What about the feet of all the generations of Coast-to-Coast and Lyke Wake walkers who must have come this way? There is little evidence of their presence. Has the route changed since our guidebook was written? Or has the recent wet weather turned the path back into a wilderness, hiding any signs of passage? Surely, we can't have made a mistake as we're definitely going in the right direction.

Despite alarm bells sounding in our heads, we press on. The thought of all the energy we've spent coming down the track makes us reluctant to turn around. Persevering, we continue on, but I'm noticing that the horizon and the tree line above us are getting further and further away. This isn't looking good.

The decision whether to go back or to carry on is suddenly taken out of our hands as a solid clump of trees blocks the path. We finally have to admit that we've somehow gone wrong.

Stopping to consider, logic suggests that there is a higher path somewhere up above us. Despite not seeing one, we must be on the wrong track.

Should we once again attempt to climb up through the trees and the bracken, to reach it from where we are?

Staring up, the ascent through the undergrowth looks foreboding and we finally have to admit defeat. Turning around, we tediously begin the journey back, hopping, skipping, and jumping our way to the forest road.

Wet and dishevelled, we're relieved at least that we're standing back on the main route. It's taken fifteen minutes for us to arrive here. This means that there and back, we've wasted half an hour, adding both extra time and mileage to our journey on what is already a very long day.

Where did we go wrong? I once again approach the signpost that points the way to Osmotherley. As I do so, looking sideways, I can now see the almost hidden entrance to a higher-level track. It had been camouflaged by tree branches and the undergrowth, which hangs heavy with last night's rain. We'd turned off onto the other track about five yards too early. Taking a deep breath, we begin to wearily make our way along the correct path.

The terrain is instantly so much better, there's little water, it's easier underfoot and there are now clear signs of walker's boot marks.

I hate going astray, wasting both time and effort walking in the wrong direction, and then having to retrace our footsteps. I'm convinced that it unsettles your body's metabolism. When it has happened during the walk, it always seems to take quite a while afterwards for us to shake it off and get back into our normal stride.

Following a rough but gently rising path, we arrive at the Television Booster Station. A silent building to which are attached a whole array of transmitting drums and dishes. These catch the signals from satellites in outer space. Beyond it we leave the main route for a moment, and passing through the trees to our left, discover the world spread out below us.

From our lofty position on the hillside, we're looking at a view, which stretches all the way back to the Pennines, halfway across England. As we stand and stare out over the land we've travelled, it's hard to believe that we've really walked so far. And yet this is only one half of the country.

Returning to the main path, we walk on a few yards further and come to a broken-down wall, which now has barbed wire along the top of it. On the other side of the wall, standing silently in the corner of a field, is an obelisk. Placed here before the war by the Ordnance-Survey, this is the trig point designating the highest place on Beacon Hill, the first of the Cleveland Hills. But it's so much more than that, it's the original starting point for the Lyke Wake Walk.

This is the stone I touched almost twenty years ago as an innocent setting off on a grueling 40-mile trek across the North York Moors.

Standing there in its silence, it gives no hint of the anguish that it has caused for so many over the years. There is no sign of the hundred thousand or more walkers, who, over the decades, must have passed this stone with so much excitement and hope in their hearts. There is also no evidence of the bodies of all those Lyke Wake Walkers (captured in old, faded photographs) who once laid prostrate around it, lying there utterly spent after taking on the walk in reverse.

I touched this stone back then, before the ordeal of attempting a forty-mile crossing of the North York Moors within 24 hours. The last time I saw it was as a student at midnight on a June evening in 1975.

Today it stands there looking so innocent, as it quietly casts a shadow behind the broken-down wall. In its silence, it denies all knowledge of the pain and suffering that it caused for so many walkers over the years. For some, like myself, it has been the start of the trouble, a cruel introduction to long-distance walking. For others, it may well have put them off walking for life.

I stand and stare at the stone, at this solid block of cast concrete, and wonder how half a lifetime ago I so casually strode through the gap in the broken-down wall to touch it. Does it know that I've returned? Does it recognize me? Perhaps it will be a silent witness to my homecoming.

Walking on, just beyond the trig point, a glorious panorama of the switchback of the Cleveland Hills suddenly stretches out magnificently before us. I feel like shouting,

"Hi, I'm back!"

Before we start, we once more move to the edge of the hill to take a final look out over the land we've spent the last week and a half crossing.

Up here on the Cleveland Hills the Pennines seem such a distance away. Have we really walked all this way across England? Three more days, and we'll be finished, back in our old routine. I don't know if that's good or bad.

Chapter 36 - Our Path is Blocked by a Cello

Steadily making our way along a broad moorland track down Beacon Hill, it gives us the opportunity to get our breath back after our recent climb. It's another fact about this walk, for every up there is always a down. As we descend, we're surrounded by purple heather, and the views towards Middlesbrough are spectacular. Because the walking is so much easier now, we fairly zip down the hill.

Arriving at a narrow moorland road at the bottom, we come to Coalmire, an area of afforestation. Here, amongst the trees, a few years later, a roughly inscribed memorial stone would be erected. The stone would honour the memory of Bill Cowley, the instigator of the Lyke Wake Walk. Sadly, it would soon lay dejected in the long grass and only be acknowledged by those who knew.

Entering the wood, we stroll along a shady path which twists and turns its way through the compacted trees. There are several tempting false trails we could follow, but experience has taught us to stick to the main path. Nevertheless, it seems to be taking an age to find our way out of the afforestation. But eventually, coming to a stile, we can at last leave the trees.

Climbing over it, we enter a pleasant green pasture where sheep are lazily grazing. Sitting on a grassy embankment eating their lunch and having a rest are the Dutch Girls and the mother and son. They've done barely three miles, and today's journey to the Lion is twenty, with the first twelve over the Cleveland Hills being particularly hard. We wonder at them stopping so early but say nothing.

Leaving the meadow, we wade across a shallow beck. I instantly recognize it as the place where my boots let in water all those years ago on the Lyke Wake Walk. Beyond it, we follow a narrow country lane and, passing a farm, notice that the land is ominously beginning to rise.

At an old red telephone box, we begin to steadily climb up towards the second of the Cleveland Hills, Live Moor. A rising dirt track leads us to the foot of what looks almost like a stairway. Steps have been crudely cut into the earth as it climbs its way up through a dense forest. Ascending it should bring us out onto the lower slopes of the next hill. In single file, we scale each of the hacked-out steps. With the steepness of the rocky staircase, we stop every ten yards or so to get our breath back.

Halfway up, we arrive at a landing, a narrow ledge that, for a moment, gives respite from the climb. As I stand leaning on an old wooden gate, I notice that the year 1966 is carved into it. I wonder just what it commemorates. After a short rest, we continue our ascent of the second part of the stairway. On reaching the top of the steps, we clamber over another stile and

A Walk to the Sea

leave the trees behind.

We're now on open ground. It's easy walking on a flagstone path that steadily rises to the crest of the moor. Nevertheless, it's still uphill, and we take a minute's rest every so often before eventually arriving at a pile of rocks which appears to declare the top of the climb.

This crude cairn signifies that we're at the highest point on the moor. Looking back, we have quickly gained height and the views all around us are sensational. We can see the North Sea and the whole of the coastline from the oil terminals at Middlesbrough down towards the pointed headland near Scarborough.

We now have a well-defined track over open moor to follow. Travelling a little way down it, a stone pillar, which has some large initials carved into it, blocks our path. This is apparently the monogram of the original landowner, showing where the boundary of his land lay.

In the distance, we can see the dilapidated remains of a disused glider station. It stands looking dejected on the edge of the next Cleveland hill, Carlton Bank.

Positioned at the end of a long abandoned, overgrown moorland runway, I wonder just how permission was ever given for such an eyesore as this to be built in the North York Moors National Park.

I can only assume that it was because there was a precedent for it, as vintage motor cars used to race up and down the hillside during the nineteen-twenties and thirties.

As we follow a narrow track along the edge of the escarpment, we spy something strange on the path up ahead of us. A man is lugging a huge cello on his back. Following him are the members of his orchestra, who are also carrying musical instrument cases.

We discover later that this outfit is called 'Extreme Music' and that they give impromptu performances out in the middle of nowhere. It was probably this lot we heard performing at midnight down by the river Swale.

Whilst it certainly is a novelty, the problem is that at this moment we are all walking along a narrow path with a sheer drop off the cliff edge to our left and a bank of raised rutted heather moorland to our right. The musicians are strolling along in single file, in a fairly compact group. Because of the slow speed the man at the front carrying the cello is going, we soon catch up with them. They're blocking the path and it will be difficult to get past them.

With great tenacity, we one by one pick off various members of the orchestra. But having so far passed the woodwind section and a couple of violinists, the cello player seems oblivious to the number of walkers stacking up behind him. I guess that his walking pace is being dictated by the incumbrance of the instrument on his back. But on this narrow track, with his huge cello spread across his shoulders, there's no way we can get past him and there don't appear to be any passing places coming up. Not looking back, the man is either ignorant of our plight or, with the weight of his musical instrument, has his own problems to deal with, and is simply not caring.

We still have a long hard day in front of us and can't afford to waste time by joining his entourage. The only thing we can do to get past him is to leave the path and try to gallop ahead over the high rutted heather.

Giving Pauline and Leon a signal, we begin our run. But as we do so, the man, who had seemed oblivious of our presence, instead of slowing his pace and allowing us to pass, suddenly puts on speed. Like entrants in the Wacky Races, we run side-by-side. and only by increasing our pace even further are we able to gallop past him.

This isn't the first set of unusual walkers we've come across on our journey. We met two nurses in the Lakes, one of whom had a huge solid glass cider flagon strapped to her back. Passing walkers were encouraged to drop their spare change into the bottle and most grinned sadistically as they did so. The girl was collecting money for a charity. When we passed by her, she was carrying nearly half a bottle load of loose change on her back, which consisted mostly of one and two pence pieces. So large was the glass bottle that, with all the leather strapping required to support it, she looked like a Sherpa in the Himalayas. The weight of all those coins must have been unbearable, but she didn't seem to notice and cheerfully accepted any donations she was given.

A trig point shows that we're now at the top of Carlton Bank. At 1500ft it's the highest place so far on the Cleveland Hills. There is a vast blue heaven above us, and we can see for miles over the whole of the Cleveland plain. There in the distance, standing all alone, is the Matterhorn shaped Roseberry Topping, the Cleveland hill that got away. We can also spot ships queuing up to harbour at the oil terminals at Middlesbrough.

Before we begin our descent, I stand with my arms outstretched between the trig point and an ancient boundary stone while Pauline photographs me. In my mind, with my long hair and wearing my hippie bandana, I imagine that I'm emulating the iconic image of Jim Morrison, legendary singer of the rock band, The Doors. I'm re-enacting his 'No one here gets out alive' pose. The people around me probably just see a scruffy, sweat stained walker leaning on two columns of rock out of sheer fatigue.

As fantastic as they are, the curse of the Cleveland Hills appears to be that each time you labour and strain to gain a significant height, you then have to lose it all again, before you can begin the climb up onto the next hill.

A Walk to the Sea

Slowly and carefully, we pick our way down Carlton Bank. At the bottom, we arrive at a location where there was once a series of boundary markers known as the Lord Stones. These bore the monograms of the local landowners and showed where the boundaries of their land lay. As we reach there, I also recognize it as the place on the Lyke Wake Walk, where 20 years ago our backup team waited to serve us with hot drinks and Club biscuits.

It's also the place where I was finding it difficult to believe that we had only just covered five miles and was seriously contemplating giving up. Today, with eleven days of solid walking under our belts, I'm feeling only slightly tired, and fifteen minutes' rest should enable us to recharge our batteries.

It's rumoured amongst walkers that there is still food and drink to be had at this place. Whilst twenty years ago my student backup coach waited here to feed us, it's now said that there is a café hidden somewhere between the hills. As we stand there, nothing can be seen. But making our way towards some parked cars, we find the original Lord Stones Cafe and its toilet facilities. A place where, in later years, we would get dried out after a downpour on the Cleveland Hills.

Staggering, sweating and dishevelled up to the café entrance, we unshackle ourselves from our backpacks and gain appreciative glances from some of the car driving customers who've come out here for the day. Going inside, we're amazed to find that we're able to order chip sandwiches and mugs of coffee. Feasting and resting at the Lord Stones will give us the chance to get our strength back and put some more energy in the tank. But we'll leave it feeling a little heavier from the delicious food we've consumed.

For walkers, the original Lord Stones café, run by John Simpson, was the finest eating-place along the Coast-to-Coast route. It was a friendly oasis in the metaphorical desert of the Cleveland Hills, and you'd arrive at it just when you were feeling like taking your first break of the day. Here you could buy sandwiches, hot meals, cakes, coffee, tea, soft drinks and even pints of beer out in the middle of nowhere, and at reasonable prices.

There is still a restaurant there today, but it's more upmarket, and both the ownership and the philosophy appear to have changed. So somehow, despite their friendliness, it's not quite the same. But it's still good to have somewhere out here where you can refresh yourself.

Moving on after our rest at the Lord Stones, it takes time to get our feet going again. The walk up the path to the Falconer Seat, which sits on the end of the ridge of the next hill, is quite strenuous. Several times on the way up we have to revert to standing with our hands on our hips, sucking in the air, as we look back at the view of Carlton Bank.

A Walk to the Sea

Eventually, drenched in sweat, we drag ourselves along the final twenty yards of the climb and heave ourselves down onto the wide, stone built memorial seat.

A sign reads that it was put here to commemorate Alec Falconer, a local rambler who campaigned for the opening up of another National Trail, the Cleveland Way. From our high viewpoint, laid out below us, we can see the whole patchwork of the Cleveland plain.

A couple of years later, Pauline and I would sit on this seat at two o'clock in the morning alongside fellow walkers Robin, and Andy. We had met them on the Pennine Way, and during that trek I'd told them about my experiences on the Lyke Wake Walk. They were so intrigued by it that they had wanted to experience it for themselves.

Setting off at midnight, by the time we arrived at the Falconer Seat, all four of us were feeling tired, and like normal people, should have been at home asleep in bed. As we squeezed together on the stone seat, we felt snug and warm and, one by one, dropped off to sleep. It must have taken some tremendous will power for Andy to wake us all up to leave it.

With our breath returned, we vacate the seat and continue along the Switchback of hills. Once again, after walking along a ridge, we go steeply down, only to almost immediately climb back up again.

The next hill I can see no point in climbing. We've

dropped down as low as we can go, only to have to begin the strenuous effort of having to climb all the way back up again. Other than yet another great view, the hill seems to have nothing of any significance on the top.

After tentatively climbing back down again, we follow a steeply rising path as it leads us towards the final climb on this switchback of hills, the ascent up onto Hasty Bank via the Wainstones. These are a high rocky outcrop made up of huge boulders. Legend has it that a Danish Chieftain was killed somewhere around here. And the name, the Wainstones, comes from a Saxon word, meaning that it is a place to wail or lament.

Steadily climbing up on a stony path towards them, we pass through a narrow passageway between high rocky edifices and then clamber up onto the outcrop to reach its summit.

I'm standing once again on the top of the Wainstones after an absence of almost twenty years. The views all around us are sensational, just as they have been on all the Cleveland Hills.

Walking over the tops of the giant boulders to the edge of the outcrop, I find the two distinctive, front facing slabs of rock, with a gap between them, that I last stood astride at dawn in June 1975.

I remember standing there like a primitive Ancient Briton as the sun slowly began to rise up on the horizon, its warming rays taking the chill away from my body.

Returning to the top of the outcrop, I casually scour the surfaces of the boulders looking for my initials, the RM, which I carved on one of them back on that distant day. I don't really expect to find them, but to my utter amazement, there they are.

Rather than being erased, both wind and time appear to have hollowed out the letters even further. The distinctive R and M with a short line underneath them that I chiselled out in my own hand all those years ago. They are unmistakable. What a find, proof that I was once here. Pauline and Leon are impressed, and like so many other travellers who have passed through the Wainstones over the centuries; they add their initials. It's a strange thing, but we've visited these rocks often over the years, and sometimes my initials are there staring me in the face, and at other times, despite looking in the same place, they can't be found.

As we sit on the huge slabs of rock, relaxing with our backpacks off, getting our breath to return, a young Welsh guy and his very pretty girlfriend, who have also been backpacking the Coast-to-Coast walk, appear down below us. As he passes along the narrow passageway ascending through the Wainstones, his massive, colourful backpack looks so stretched and bloated that he appears to have a floral armchair on his back. His girlfriend follows behind him carrying nothing. But I'm sure that most guys would have gladly carried that weight all day, just to be able to share a tent with her on an evening.

Moving on. The edge of the high moor is now immaculately paved in a long line of old stone slabs. These are rumoured to have come from the floors of derelict cotton mills. They have worn in well and make for pleasant walking. How the Lake District National Park could learn from this. Back in the Lakes, we seem to have been stepping on perpetual rocks and scree, bad on the feet and so easy to slip on and turn an ankle. The Park's method for protecting eroded paths would appear to be to throw more scree down and use the boots of generations of walkers to tramp-it-in.

From our moorland plateau, we can now see the second half of today's journey, Urra Moor. It's rising up on the other side of a dissecting road and is covered in purple heather.

Our final Cleveland hill suddenly descends in a rocky slope, and we carefully pick our way down it towards the road at Hasty Bank. About halfway, the hill plateaus out, and we arrive at a seat bearing a plaque dedicated to a walker who died close by here on the Lyke Wake Walk. Feeling exhausted ourselves, we sit and rest for a while in reverence on Robbie's Seat. Perhaps, if we're lucky, this is what we might all become in the end, some intriguing name, on the back of a wooden bench. An indication that we once passed this way.

Chapter 37 - The Lion on Blakey Ridge

Standing by the roadside at Clay Bank Top, we watch the passing traffic as we slowly get our breath back. Despite still having a little energy left in our tanks, we really have had enough for the day, and this would be the ideal place to stop.

It's just two thirty in the afternoon. But we've completed twelve miles of hill walking, of continuously going up and down, and the hills have taken their toll. Unfortunately, unless we tramp a couple of miles further down the road into the village of Great Broughton, there is now nowhere close by to camp.

There was once a farm along here, where a jolly farmer would let you pitch your tent amongst his chickens and rough pasture. I remember watching him rubbing his hands together with both glee and disbelief every time another walker turned up and paid a fiver to camp there. Sadly, the man must have died, as camping at the farm is no more.

As we can no longer stay there, our only options are for us to follow the road down into Great Broughton to find a campsite. This will mean having to walk back in the morning, adding four miles in total to our journey. Or, we can carry on to the Lion Inn on Blakey Ridge, which is nearly another nine miles away. Alternatively, we could wild camp on the moors.

We make the choice to reach the Lion. There seems little sense in walking four miles for nothing, so we might as well grasp the nettle and cover a further eight and a half miles today. We also know from our guidebook that after an initial steep climb up onto the moor, the path gradually levels out, and the day finishes with a tramp of six miles along the flat track bed of an old railway line. Once on this, we should be able to switch to autopilot and follow it all the way to the Lion Inn on Blakey Ridge.

Pauline issues our rations and the three of us stand and suck on some cheap toffees. We're hoping that they will give us a little more energy for what lies ahead.

Crossing the road, we go through a gate and immediately begin the climb up onto the moor. Walking on a rising stone slab path, we stop often, but quickly gain height. After about twenty minutes of climbing, we arrive on the edge of Urra Moor, where we rest for a moment next to a wooden fingerpost that points the way to the Cleveland Hills.

Standing there staring back at them, the hills really do look like a Switchback ride. The continuous rising and falling of them can clearly be seen. For some minutes, we stand gasping for breath after our climb. It's been hard, but we've been quick to get here and the walking from now on should be relatively easy.

As we're about to move off, Pauline spots a tent pitched about a hundred yards away amongst the purple heather. Someone must have settled for the wild camping option.

Suddenly, in front of it, a fleshy nude figure appears, rolling about on the heath. Is it some form of flagellation, a sort of masochistic ritual, like a monk wearing a hair shirt? Does the man wish to pay a penance by scratching himself all over in the undergrowth? Alternatively, does he simply want a wash after his journey, and as there's not a tap handy, he's taking a dew-bath, using the moisture collected on the heather to freshen himself up. Hoping that it's the latter, we leave him to his ablutions.

Stepping out on a clear narrow path, the strip of dried earth we're walking on stands out almost white as it snakes its way across the moorland heather.

Our journey takes us past a very distinctive looking bowl-shaped rock which lies close to the edge of the path. Possibly, both human hand, and intemperate weather, have ground it out over the centuries into the shape it is today. Either way, it looks as though it's been here for hundreds of years, and the stone bowl must fill with water each time it rains. I wonder how many weary travellers have knelt down here to drink or wash from it.

The clear path continues as it makes an easy, steady climb towards the top of Urra Moor. The trig point designating the highest place on it comes into view. Ahead, we can now see the raised bank of the disused ironstone railway line as it contours its way around the moor.

After first dipping down into a waterlogged section of heather, we climb up the embankment and onto the track-bed of the former Rosedale Railway. Despite the rails being taken up during the 1930s, you can still see the outline of the wooden sleepers clearly etched into the cinder track.

The walking is even easier now. Passing by an old wooden notice board, written on it in large, chalked letters, is the word 'Blow'. This is either a command for steam engines to blow their whistle, or a sign that we're nearing Bloworth Crossing, a former junction on the moorland railway.

Going through a wide gate which blocks the track, we find ourselves at the crossing. Apart from the fact that we're walking on an embankment, there is little evidence that there was once a pulse of life here. The crossing keeper's cottage, where the Junction Master and his family lived, once stood by the side of the track. The crews of steam engines must have passed the time of day from their cab with the family. Now there is no sign of their existence.

Leaving Bloworth Crossing behind, we continue on along the track as it contours first left and then right. We're now walking high above the top of the moorland valley of Farndale, and the views are superb. After a while, we pass through another gate,

A Walk to the Sea

which seems to be miles away from the junction at Bloworth Crossing. On and on we go, with the track swinging first left and then right. The novelty of playing trains is fast wearing off. Our feet are becoming sore from walking on the cinder track, and there is still no sign of the Lion Inn.

Passing by a pile of fading white lime, I remember it as being the landmark signalling to Lyke Wake walkers that it was nearly time for them to leave the track and turn off for Esklets and Rosedale moor. Now it stands forlorn, gradually being covered by the heather. If only it could talk, it would speak of the hundred thousand or more anguished Lyke Wake walkers who must have once passed by it.

The railway embankment sits like a raised narrow causeway across the moor. Despite our aching feet, we feel safe and dry up here amidst the wet boggy moorland that surrounds us.

The sun has gone in and the wind has got up, it's making a strange sound, howling like a banshee. As the cloud shadows chase across the heather, it seems such an isolated spot. We've met no one else so far on the track, but now a dog-collared parson and his companion pass by us. He cuts an eerie figure in this out-of-the-way place, with his round brimmed, clerical hat and his long black cape blowing high up in the air with the strong breeze. Turning around to look back down the track a few minutes later, the two of them can no longer be seen. Did they really exist,

I wonder, or have we just experienced a moment in time and seen a ghost?

Passing by several large heavy blocks of chiselled stone, which lay discarded amidst a pool of water on the side of the track, I instantly recognize them from my Lyke Wake walk nearly twenty years ago.

This is the place where the steam engines would have taken on water. When I first passed by here in 1975, there was still some of the old railway paraphernalia left. A chain which once lifted the heavy stone block covering the hole in a water trough still dangled from a metal pole. I remember it making an eerie clanking sound as it swung in the breeze.

We've endured turn after turn of the railway track, but as yet there's no sign of the inn. Walking on a few yards further, we pass through a cutting. As we do so, there on the horizon, we finally catch our first glimpse of the Lion Inn on Blakey Ridge. It's still a distance away and around another bend, but at least it's now in sight. Putting our heads down in the strong wind, we speed on towards it.

At last, a path leads off the railway track, heading directly for the Lion, and we follow it. After passing by an old cock-fighting pit, we finally arrive at the inn. Making enquiries at the bar, we're directed to put our tent up on a wind-swept moorland ridge next to the car park.

Finding a place relatively free from sheep droppings presents quite a challenge, and we have to settle for using rocks to cover any evidence of those close to our tent. But at least we've arrived here before the Romans, and the Dutch Girls, and have had a choice of pitch.

Tonight, we've decided to treat ourselves to a bar meal. This will save us from having to deal with our dirty pots, as the only water available is in the inn's toilets.

The Lion lives up to all of our expectations in terms of food, drink, hospitality, and surroundings. Halfway through the evening, the Extreme Challenge musicians turn up and give a performance. Chatting with fellow walkers later, everybody is confident that they will complete the walk.

Perhaps, because of my penurious past, I can't help thinking that places such as the Lion are excellent if you're not on a budget. But if you have limited funds, then while all those around you are drinking, ordering meals and making merry, it could just seem like a cold, draughty place on the moors, where each time the Inn door opens, you experience a sudden chill.

Returning to our tent in the pitch black, an orange light flickers on and off on a distant moorland ridge. It's the beacon on the top of the Bilsdale Mast, yet another television transmitter station on the North York Moors. The light warns passing aircraft of the antenna's presence. One day we'll climb that far-off hill to reach it.

Ray Moody

Pauline at the Howitzer above Grasmere

Chapter 38 - Glaisdale Rigg is a Joy to Tread

We leave the Lion amidst a thick early morning mist. Walking along the edge of a lonely moorland road, cars and vans race down it through a grey veil towards us. We're careful to avoid stepping onto the tarmac. The occasional dead sheep lying on the side of the road provides ample evidence of what might happen if we do.

At a tall standing stone bearing the name Old Margery, we leave the road. Following a rough track, we cut off across the moor. The track at first dips down and then eventually climbs out of the heather onto an isolated moorland road. We emerge almost opposite another very distinctive-looking standing stone, which is known affectionately as Fat Betty, or the White Cross.

These stones or crosses were once way markers for travellers journeying over the moor. Wayfarers with a little money to spare would often place the odd coin on top of them for those less fortunate than themselves. Like all of those philanthropists before her, Pauline leaves her loose change for any needy modern-day walkers.

Leaving Fat Betty, we initially head off down the road towards Rosedale. But we soon turn off it onto a narrow tarmac pathway. It makes for easy walking as it heads in a straight line across the moor.

On reaching a large wooden gate, we leave the tarmac and follow a rough track through the heather. It brings us out on the top of a valley.

We're walking high above the valley of Great Fryup Dale. What a strange name. I wonder if they do a decent breakfast down there.

Arriving at our next landmark, a shooting hut known locally as Trough House, we take a few moments to have a closer look at it. The well-maintained building is locked, so passing walkers couldn't shelter inside if the weather were to turn nasty.

Departing from there, the early morning mist has now lifted, and we have impressive views down the valley. Small pieces of coal begin to appear on the rutted heather track beneath our feet, and the surface is becoming waterlogged. The path turns with the valley and continues to run along its rim. The moor rises, and we follow a narrow track through the thick heather.

Wainwright tells us that at the top of the rising moor there should be a road somewhere off to our right. We can't yet see it, but as a car travels down it, we gain some idea of where our present rough track will lead us off to meet it. With the path levelling out, we finally leave the moor via a well-built wooden stile and find ourselves standing on another lonely moorland road.

The tarmac makes for pleasant walking and the

views all around us are stupendous. Rigg after rigg, or fold after fold of moorland ridge, can be seen going off into the distance. We're walking on the top of the North York Moors, and I'm reminded, as I discovered twenty years ago, that it's always done under a big sky. Fluffy white clouds float high above us in a vast blue heaven.

In the distance, another old standing stone appears, which marks the entrance to Glaisdale Rigg. We plod on down the road towards it.

Glaisdale Rigg is a former toll road to Whitby, which Wainwright suggests will be a pleasure to walk on. Turning off onto this wide, ancient, moorland highway, we agree with him. Going steadily downhill, we seem to be walking much more quickly now. Perhaps it's because we know that the end of the walk is within sight and tomorrow we'll be finished. After a few miles, a dry-stone wall blocks our way, signalling that it is time to leave the Rigg. We turn off it and head down into the village of Glaisdale.

As we walk through its deserted streets, Glaisdale appears to be yet another quiet commuter village. On entering its grocery store, the teenage assistant looks at us suspiciously. She seems nervous. Is it my bandana or my dishevelled appearance? The girl serves us quickly, uttering few words. Young and naïve, I believe we're being mistaken for vagabonds off the moor, not three people who've just walked nearly 200 miles (if you add on our mistakes) across England.

How different this place is from the family-run store in Moor Row, where we were so readily acknowledged as being walkers out on an adventure. They were so pleased for us to sign their visitor's book.

Leaving the store, we make our way through what seems increasingly like an almost deserted village. I guess that most of the inhabitants are out at work or school for the day, as there isn't even a dog wandering about. As we leave the village, we stop to visit an ancient packhorse bridge, which lies just beyond Glaisdale's railway line.

The journey now takes us into an old, dark wood. Initially, we walk above a river, but the path soon moves away from it. The wood dips down, becoming muddy, and we traverse a series of aged stepping-stones. These must have been laid centuries ago, to keep travellers out of the mire. Passing by a large outcrop of rock, our guidebook suggests that a hermit once lived here.

The wood is quiet, but a railway line at one-point crosses over the nearby river. Through the foliage, we see flashes of a train as it speeds by on route for Whitby. The path rises again, but the way out of the trees still seems a long time in coming. A car passes by up ahead, letting us know that we're at last nearing the road.

A Walk to the Sea

Leaving the wood, we emerge out onto a country lane. Walking down it, we soon arrive in the village of Egton Bridge. Our feet are aching a little, and the road walking is now being done under a hot sun. Crossing over a bridge, we leave the village and follow an old toll road that runs alongside the grounds of an ancient country estate.

After a mile of walking down it, we arrive at the main road leading into the steam railway village of Grosmont. A sign says that a field close by provides basic camping. But talk on the walk has been about a farm in the hamlet of Littlebeck, where it's claimed that the camping is both competitively priced and the place has friendly owners. There are also strong rumours of walkers receiving a mug of tea or coffee and a slice of homemade cake on arrival. I love cake, so it's like holding a carrot on a string in front of a donkey. It entails walking six miles further today, but a shorter final day's walk tomorrow. It also means that we'll climb the one-in-three road out of Grosmont today, rather than have to face the ascent first thing in the morning. To enable us to recuperate before the climb, we plan to take a short break and have something to eat in the buffet on Grosmont's Victorian railway station.

Originally opened in 1836, both the station and the Whitby to Pickering railway line were closed for passenger services in 1965. Fortunately, it was mothballed, and from 1967 onwards, a group of volunteers began to slowly find the finances and the manpower to bring it back to life. Today, it's a successful preserved railway that is still mostly run by volunteers. The stations and platforms along the track look exactly as they did when the line closed during the 1960s.

Following the road down into the village, we soon find ourselves standing on the station platform. On entering the buffet, we discover that the place looks like a scene from the classic British movie, 'Brief Encounter'. Ordering tea and egg sandwiches on the way in, it's only when we sit down to eat them that we realise we're surrounded by characters from the 1940s. They could be the actual cast of the television comedy series Dad's Army. Indeed, Captain Mainwaring appears to be sitting directly opposite us.

Have we entered a time warp; I wonder? People mill around the doorway of the buffet, looking like they're part of wartime Britain. Everyone is wearing period clothing and carrying gas masks. Later, we discover that it's a special WWII re-enactment weekend run every year by the North York Moors Railway.

After our meal, we enjoy the thrill of watching steam engines puffing in and out of the station. Leaving the platform, we arrive back on Grosmont high street, and almost immediately begin walking uphill as we start to climb out of the village.

A Walk to the Sea

At the far end of the high street, we follow the road as it turns into a country lane. The real climbing, up a one-in-three hill, now begins.

It's hard work. It feels as though we're walking in slow motion, as it seems to be taking an age to pass by fields and farmhouses. The continuous climb out of Grosmont is proving to be horrendous. The sun beats down on our heads, and perspiration once again flows like a river down my back. We're making our way up a tarmacked road that keeps on rising. Just as we did during the first day of the walk on the 'small' hill of Dent, and as we've done throughout our journey when we've been ascending, we fix points up ahead and then head for them. A bush here, a tree there. We stop at each of these places to rest for a moment before fixing another stopping point for us to aim for. We've used this method effectively during the walk, and it's always proved successful.

The sound of a car rumbling over a cattle-grid up ahead signals that we must be nearing the top of the road. On reaching it, the purple heather of the North York moors suddenly opens up all around us, and the views in front are spectacular. We can see the sea on the far horizon, and down below us, traffic speeds along the busy Scarborough to Whitby Road. In the distance, over to our right, we can also discern the soon to be removed trio of huge white golf balls, which make up the Fylingdales Early Warning System.

At a signpost, we leave the tarmac and, climbing onto the moor, walk towards a distinctive Howe or burial mound. Arriving there, we make a beeline across the heather as we head for the busy Whitby Road.

On reaching it, we wait for a lull in the almost continuous traffic before being able to cross to the other side. Now facing the on-coming cars, we walk along the edge of the road for a while before leaving it to climb over a stile.

We now follow a wide path across ancient moorland, through which a series of electricity pylons are spread out at equal distances. At the end of the moor, we join a pleasant country lane that soon leads us down into the hamlet of Littlebeck.

Purposely going off route, we climb up a narrow side road past a Methodist Chapel. After half a mile, we find ourselves standing outside the cottage at Intake Farm.

Pauline knocks on the door, and we stand and watch a group of feral kittens as they play with an old, discarded shoe. I cross my fingers and hope that the rumours about the cake are true. We're about to find out.

The door of the cottage opens, and a very pleasant farmer's wife greets us, ushering us into her abode. "Would we like a shower?" she says, as we enter.

She then leads us into a farmhouse kitchen, where a long wooden dining table serves both as somewhere to eat, and as an office desk.

The table is covered in books, papers, local church magazines, mugs, teapots, a cake tin, etc.

"Tea or coffee?" she asks,

Then I hear the magic words.

"Would you like a piece of cake?"

So, it's true!

I need no further urging and I'm cut a huge slice. The farmer's wife seems genuinely friendly, and when her husband comes in, he proves equally so. What a find it is for us to spend our last night of camping here.

Grisedale Tarn

Ray Moody

On those spectacular North York Moors

Chapter 39 – Deliverance

The final day of the walk has arrived. There's a sadness about it, mixed with thoughts of soon being able to get out of crumpled clothing, of ridding ourselves of this permanent weight on our backs and not having to spend another night cramped in the tent.

Despite the pleasant setting on the trim lawn, I didn't sleep at all last night and lay waiting for the dawn. I was far too excited thinking that we might soon have completed the Coast-to-Coast walk. Wedged together like three sardines, I kept reminding myself to never again buy a ridge tent or a double sleeping bag. Fortunately, the night wasn't long, and the sun rose early.

I've had no pillow throughout our journey and latterly have had to lay my head on the padded part of my backpack waist strap. Earlier on, I did have the relative luxury of the clean clothes bag to rest my head on, but as this got smaller and my wet clothes bag got larger, I've had to revert to my backpack belt.

Something else we've therefore learnt on this walk is the necessity of carrying one of those 'squashy' camping pillows if you want to get a good night's sleep. They squeeze up into a tiny pack and weigh practically nothing. All the European walkers seem to have them. Those guys really know how to equip themselves.

After two weeks of walking across England, we're now on the cusp of being able to say that we too have completed the Coast-to-Coast walk.

Along the way, we've heard tales of people who got this close and failed at the last gasp. A leg went, or they sprained an ankle. One man we met, who was on his second attempt, claimed that his knee had collapsed just twenty miles from the end of his first effort. I think I would have dragged myself in.

Leaving the farm, we retrace our steps back into the hamlet of Littlebeck, and then follow a path that makes its way down through yet another old Rupert Bear type wood.

As we head towards the centre of it, the heat of the sun, and the steady descent, cause my back to pour with even more sweat than usual. Twisting and turning our way through the trees and bushes, the humidity is almost unbearable. But we finally arrive at the waterfall of Falling Foss, and just beyond it, find the Hermitage.

Whilst the waterfall is spectacular, the Hermitage is unique. A twelve-foot-high, hewed out boulder, three hundred years ago, a hermit once lived here.

Entering the huge rock through a narrow doorway, we sit on a stone seat that protrudes all the way around the inside wall. It would have taken a decade or more for the hermit to chisel it out. Thinking about it, the sound of his constant chipping must have resonated throughout the wood for years.

A Walk to the Sea

It's dark and dank inside the boulder, but there's a small hole in the ceiling with soot blackened around it, where smoke once escaped from the Hermit's fire. There is also evidence that the opening to the great rock once had a stable door over which the recluse would have stood and stared out across at the waterfall of Falling Foss.

Pauline goes back outside and climbs up behind the huge rock. On the top, she finds a stone seat on which the hermit must have sat on warm days.

Sometime later, I took a large party of students for a walk through this wood. When we arrived at the Hermitage, few of them appeared to be fascinated by the fact that a man once stood here and spent so many years of his life hacking his way into this huge rock to make himself a home.

Leaving the Hermitage, we pass by the old Woodcutter's cottage. It lies empty and semi-derelict and seems such a lonely place in the middle of the wood.

A few years after this, a family would take up residency there and open it up for refreshments, giving the wood a pulse of life at its centre. The paths through the trees are unkempt and muddy, but they would also later be much improved.

Just beyond a bridge, we make our way across a stream and begin to climb out of the trees. The environment is changing from that of a dark, dank wood to a lusher green one.

Following along numerous rising paths, we eventually arrive at a car park. In the wood, we felt quite remote, but it's not yet ten o'clock in the morning and there are already three or four cars parked here, so it must be a popular tourist attraction.

Leaving the car park, we turn off down a quiet country lane. On passing an isolated farm cottage, through the windows we can see several Second World War British army trench coats hung up. Pauline imagines this is a sign that the cottage once provided a home for an army deserter.

The farm marks the turning off point for the crossing of yet another moor. On the distant horizon, cars travel down the busy Whitby Road. We head off over the heather towards it. Halfway across the moor, we reach a very distinctive- looking tree. It stands on its own, all alone in the middle of a wasteland of peat. Despite the poor soil conditions, it appears to have grown and survived. The tree is instantly recognizable to all those who have done the Coast-to-Coast walk. Like so many others before us, we stand beneath it and photograph ourselves.

Continuing on across the moor, the peat is becoming waterlogged, and we're having to hop, skip, and jump our way to the road. Despite our athleticism, we arrive there with our boots full of bog water and have to empty them out on the roadside.

But having now got the bit between our teeth, our legs are gaining momentum, as though knowing that

A Walk to the Sea

we're getting closer to achieving our goal. Walking alongside the busy Whitby Road, a constant stream of traffic speeds past us, and we must keep to the safety of the grass verge.

Crossing the road, we climb a stile and then begin the journey over our final moor. It's a long moor with a well-trodden narrow track heading straight through the heather. Made by the boots of earlier walkers, the path occasionally disappears as it enters wide areas of boggy peat. Once again, we have to literally hop, skip, and jump over these waterlogged morasses. Halfway across, we spot Whitby Abbey, and then the cyan blue of the North Sea rises dramatically up on the horizon to greet us.

Reaching the end of the moor, we have difficulty in finding the correct path off it, and for a moment, flounder about. Then suddenly we come upon a daunting scene.

Scattered all around us are the fresh remains of a recently savaged sheep. It's unrecognizable. Bones, flesh, and woolly hair are strewn about everywhere. We grow wary and look for the wild animal that must have carried out this attack. Is it still here, licking its lips in the undergrowth? There's practically nothing left of the sheep, and we wonder what kind of ferocious beast could have done this. Is it just a coincidence that we're so close to Whitby?

Pauline does her best scouting work and picks up the trail again. We follow a path that leads to a stile.

Climbing over it, we continue on down a long, narrow, overgrown passageway.

The ground beneath our feet is muddy and uneven, and nettles come at us from both sides. It's almost as bad as the tortuous corridor near Reeth, but not quite. In my shorts, I once again try to twist this way and that to avoid the inevitable nettle stings. But no matter which way I turn, I'm stung and stung again. Despite ineffectively rubbing my legs with what I assume to be a dock leaf, I'll have to live with the irritation until it wears off.

At the end of the long passage, we come out onto a quiet country lane and follow it as it leads us down into the small settlement of High Hawsker.

Quickly passing through the village, we leave it on a busy coastal road. A hundred yards along it we enter a vast caravan park and commence walking down through it. There's no doubt now we're swiftly making a beeline for the North Sea, which once again is looming up on the horizon.

There are several signs to follow as we pass through the rows of caravans. Travel stained walkers are kept well-away from the plush mobile homes. Any false movements made by us are quickly corrected by unseen voices shouting directions from behind net curtained windows.

"It's that way!"

The caravan park begins to slope dramatically down towards the cliff top. The boundary of the park finishes at some wild grassland. Following a rough track through it, we suddenly find ourselves standing on the cliff high above the North Sea.

There is a sheer drop down to the crashing waves below us and the coastline of rugged cliffs curve away off into the distance. The scene is so spectacular that I'm elated.

"You can't buy this lass," I say to Pauline. "It's Yorkshire!"

This is our native Yorkshire and I'm so proud of these sea cliffs; they really do look so magnificent.

For the second time on our long journey, seagulls wail in the sky high above us. But now the walking is being done on the other side of England. There are just three miles left to go to the end of the walk and, sadly, to the finish of our great adventure. Surely, we will make it, even if we have to drag ourselves in on one leg.

A rollercoaster of undulating cliff path begins. But we're walking much more slowly, wanting to get to Robin Hood's Bay, but knowing now that we almost inevitably will.

Savouring these final moments of the walk, this has been an adventure that perhaps with the winning post being so close at hand, we don't really want it to end.

The three of us are in silent mode as, in our heads, we relive our long trek across England and contemplate that our journey is nearly over. We'll soon be entering the real world again.

But the walk has a final sting in its tail. The cliff suddenly drops dramatically down in a precipitous slope at a place where the sea has badly eroded it away. Is this the last obstacle on the walk, will it all be flat after this, will it all be gravy?

We cautiously descend, hopefully, for the ultimate time, and on tired legs wearily climb all the way back up again to reach the cliff top.

Continuing along the path, people pass by us, chattering amongst themselves, not knowing or caring about what we've just done or achieved. They have no knowledge of what we've endured. Of the fourteen days of carrying heavy backpacks or the nights spent confined together in a cramped tent fighting for a share of the sleeping bag. Not to mention sweating our way through most days and getting soaked to the skin naturally by rain on others.

Sadly, now that we're almost back in civilization, I have a dilemma. When passing people on the cliff top should I continue to maintain the courtesy of the hills, where all the way across England we've said, "Hello!" to every walker we've met. Or do I revert to city mode and ignore everyone.

Here it causes a dilemma, whilst out in the wild, people greet each other naturally. But now, saying hello to passersby is often only met with blank stares.

'What's he saying hello to us for, we don't know him!'

A Walk to the Sea

I'm finding this a problem, but Pauline seems to be able to pitch it just right. When she says hello to anyone, she usually gets a positive response, even from dog walkers or day-trippers. Perhaps because of the state of me, all I'm getting are strange looks. So, I encourage her to walk up ahead, to save me from the embarrassment of not receiving any replies to my friendly hellos.

As we've made our way across England, I've spoken to total strangers who we've met for a fleeting moment in some out-of-the-way place on the moors or fells. They understand the code, the courtesy of saying hello when you meet. These walkers might have been from the higher or lower echelons of society, but out there in the wild, we're all vulnerable, and so we're all equal. Sadly, once close to civilization, most people aren't walkers, just people enjoying their day out. So perhaps they don't understand the code. But wouldn't it be a better world if we all just said hello to everyone we meet?

Was that sudden drop the final descent on our journey? The path is now contouring on the same level. Up ahead, a white-painted coastguard lookout station has come into view on what appears to be the corner of a bay.

This must be it then, the turn into Robin Hood's Bay. The high cliff top path is curving inland, and the bay is gradually opening up below us. The corner is soon turned, and in-between the hawthorn and bramble hedges guarding the cliff edge and the sheer drop down to the sea, we catch glimpses of the red roofs of the fishing village of Robin Hood's Bay. Through a gap in the hedge, Pauline spots the slipway that leads down into the North Sea and the end of the walk.

On the horizon across the bay at Ravenscar, I can also make out the television mast that signals the end of the Lyke Wake Walk, the thing that is probably responsible for all of this, the start of the trouble.

We now know that we will get there and adopt a casualness about our walking as we stroll in along the last vestiges of the cliff top path.

Going through a gate, we finally leave the cliffs behind and pass by the first cottage in Bay Town. A suburban street is reached, and it brings us out opposite the site of the old railway station. We're now, without a doubt, back on terra firma.

Following the main road, it leads us to the top of Robin Hood's Bay's infamous long winding narrow thoroughfare, a quaint cobbled street that slopes its way perilously down to the North Sea.

The street is crowded with holidaymakers. As we make our way down it, people stare at us and at our soiled clothing. They don't realize it, but they're looking at three individuals who have spent the last 14 nights squashed together under canvas, and a man who hasn't had access to a razor for many days.

My clothes have been slept in and sweated in, and

A Walk to the Sea

yet I'm wearing the best of what I have left. My sagging socks have long since given up the ghost and I've once again had to dry the wet on my tee-shirt using the overnight heat of my sleeping bag.

Anyway, I've discovered that putting a clean tee-shirt on every day has been a complete waste of time. With my backpack on, at the first sign of any daily exertion, the back of it almost immediately becomes wet with perspiration.

As we make our way down the inclining street and pass through the crowds, the 'Ice-cream Guzzlers' as Wainwright so politely called them, part. As he also accurately forecast, I feel proud, a man amongst men, and despite the gender bias, Pauline probably feels the same.

The slope down to the sea twists and turns for one final time, and the Bay Hotel looms up to our left. Drinkers sit outside it like the spectators at a race.

True romantics, we've been hoping that the tide will be in so that we can walk down the slipway straight into the frothy foam. Sadly, it's out, but there is seawater left in the little gullies and rock pools. We leave the slipway, and with the constant wailing of seagulls in our ears, make our way across the foreshore in search of the sea.

And finally, there it is, the North Sea, stretching to infinity, just as the Master Fell-Wanderer said that it would. With the last of our energy, we immerse our boots in the first lapping waves. The foaming water flows over the top of them. As it does so, our hands reach into our pockets to root out the pebble that two weeks ago we each picked up off the sand at St Bees.

Then, with all three of us suitably armed, we nod to each other and then, in unison, let our pebbles fly. As they drop down into the North Sea, we turn and look at each other. Now we too can say that we've walked across England, from one side to the other, Coast-to-Coast.

Standing in the queue waiting for the bus to Scarborough, a Coast-to-Coast walker, who we met during the final days of the walk, passes by. Smiling, he nods his head towards us.

"See you out there on the trail," he says. Then, with a knowing wink of his eye, is gone.

We beam with pride. This confirms it then, we've been accepted as fellow long-distance walkers.

Chapter 40 – Aftermath

Pauline and I have now done the Coast-to-Coast walk a further twelve times since our first adventure. Over the years we've also completed many other long-distance walks, including the Pennine Way, the West Highland Way, the Cleveland Way, the Cumbrian Way, the Great Glen Way, the Dales Way and various bespoke walks in the Lake District. But it was on that first great walk that we learnt such a lot about long-distance walking.

The most important thing we learnt was the hard lesson of carrying too much, and the need to keep the weight in your sack down to a minimum. The final realization for me was the day we crawled into the campsite at Ennerdale Bridge, and I unshackled myself from my backpack. It fell off me like a huge boulder. As it hit the ground, I'd swear that the earth actually shook.

When we later took a day out at Kirkby Stephen and I caught the train home, I carried almost a full backpack of unnecessary items with me. It really showed the need to be selective about what you carry on a walk if you want to be able to enjoy it.

We do allow ourselves one or two 'luxuries', such as my pocket radio, for lying in the tent listening to the world late at night. But you don't want to wake up every morning with the dread of having to behave like a Packhorse and feel as though you're being saddled up as you strap on a far too heavy backpack.

Now, when I'm filling my sack, I consider whether something is really necessary. Apart from camping gear, I carry a reasonable number of tee-shirts, a pair of shorts, jogging pants, a hat, and several pairs of underwear and socks. Mind, I have noticed on our adventures that people don't always want to be seen with us. But that's the beauty of long-distance walking. You can look like 'whatever' and nobody out there seems to notice or even care.

Some years after we completed our first Coast-to-Coast walk, we backpacked the Pennine Way, just to be able to use another guidebook written by Alfred Wainwright. On that trip, we met a young couple, Robin and Andy, and I remember the look on Andy's face when he lifted my backpack and weighed it in his hand, comparing it with his own.

"How do you do that?" he said.

We learnt it from experience gained on the Coast-to-Coast walk.

Another thing we quickly learnt was the need to wear waterproof boots if you don't want to have the constant worry of your feet getting wet, giving you a blister. Today, most of the walking boots you can buy are waterproof. But on our first trip, wearing cheap boots, our socks were often soaking at the end of the day, even when it wasn't raining.

We therefore learnt the need to carry plenty of pairs of socks to replace those that do get wet. Sadly, we discovered that even waterproof boots can let water in, as it often comes in from the top. But I just couldn't contemplate wearing a pair of those ridiculous gaiter things.

Tent wise, it should be as light and roomy as you can afford, certainly no heavier than 2.4 kilos. And never buy a ridge tent or one of those crazy bivvy bags if you want to be able to sit up and relax after a hard day's walking.

Despite the wet days, the blisters, and the constant weight of our backpacks, we enjoyed our first Coast-to-Coast walk. So much so that the following summer, we had an itch to experience the whole adventure all over again.

We're not the only ones who have completed the Coast-to-Coast walk more than once. I know of others who have done it often over the years. If you enjoy a movie, do you just watch it once and never bother viewing it again simply because you've already seen it? Especially if like the Coast-to-Coast walk, it's a particularly good movie.

Every walk we've done has always been different. Whilst most of the route has largely remained the same, the people we've met, and our experiences along the way, have never been the same twice. One or two of the walks might have been familiar, but our recent twelfth crossing was just as exciting as our first.

Every Coast-to-Coast walk will depend on who

you meet and your adventures out there along the trail.

But not wanting to become sheep, we did leave the Coast-to-Coast alone for a while as we trekked most of the other major long-distance walks in Northern Britain. And we got a shock some years later when we decided to do it again.

It was the middle of July and must have been the day after the schools had broken up for the summer holidays. The seafront at St Bees was packed with Coast-to-Coast walkers and their families and friends who'd come along to see them off. When we climbed up St Bees Head, it was like being in some sort of cavalcade, a long procession of walkers and their entourages. One woman was even shoving a child in a pushchair over the cliff top in a final show of encouragement for her spouse.

The walk over St Bees Head was just one big parade, and we wondered whether it would be like this all the way to Robin Hood's Bay. Had the Coast-to-Coast walk become so popularized and even tawdry over the years we'd been away? But once we got beyond the lighthouse, the walkers thinned out, and we never saw most of them again. It was amazing.

In recent times, we've noticed several commercially organised parties doing the walk. Eight to twelve strangers coming together under the charge of a walk leader. The participants in these groups often have a wide variety of ages and backgrounds. Different personalities and abilities walking together under a neutral leadership.

Some of them might have signed up because they lack the confidence to attempt the walk on their own, but don't want to be denied the chance of doing it. Some may have joined up to enjoy the company of others, as I have enjoyed the experience with Pauline. Whatever the reason, I think it's great for the opportunity it provides.

The Coast-to-Coast Packhorse Service was our saviour on our first walk. And it has been so on many other occasions when we've needed a hand with our backpacks. The service has now existed for over twenty-five years, and for many walkers it has certainly been their best friend on route, just as their strapline so proudly boasts.

There is nothing quite like the sheer joy of being able to get your heavy backpack carried when, for whatever reason, you need to. The reliability of the service, and the trust you can put in it, cannot be overstated. It can make the difference between success and failure on the Coast-to-Coast walk and prove to be the best value for money you'll spend on your journey across England.

When we first used the Packhorse Service over twenty-five years ago, it was much more basic. Walkers would have to pick their backpacks up from, and leave them off for collection, at a limited number of specific places on route. Sometimes, if you were lucky, it might be at the campsite where you were staying. But most often it wasn't, and you'd have to do unnecessary mileage to find the pickup-point to retrieve your sack. The following morning, if you wanted it carried again, you would have to travel the same extra distance to leave it there ready for collection.

Backpacks were also at one time left in a series of lockers, which had especially been set up along the trail. One, for example, was situated at the rear of the car park of the Traveller's Rest, on the way into Grasmere. But the pickup point might just as likely be the lobby of some well-heeled hotel or a dusty barn.

It was only when Simon and Lindsay Jones took over the business that they streamlined the whole service. They initiated the concept of picking up and dropping off your sack at the place where you were actually staying, whether this was a bed-and-breakfast establishment or a campsite. They also established a small fleet of vehicles, booking of accommodation, and provided a passenger transport service for walkers. Doing this enabled us, and thousands of other walkers, to both enjoy and successfully complete the Coast-to-Coast walk.

The Packhorse is now in new hands, but it continues to provide an effective service, with even more innovations and improvements being introduced.

In recent years, there seems to have been more Backpackers wild camping on the Coast-to-Coast walk.

I love the idea of wild camping, of finding some lonely idyllic spot to pitch the tent, a place with wonderful views across a wide-open landscape. I can appreciate sitting in the tent miles away from anywhere watching the sun slowly going down, and in the morning waking up to the same sensational vista. It does indeed seem wonderful. But at the same time, I can also feel vulnerable, particularly when the vista disappears in the dusk and there's some strange sound outside the tent which you can't quite account for, as some wild animal starts to roam about in the dead of night.

Places can also look so different in the dark, especially if you need the loo. Pauline and I both have very vivid imaginations. We can quite easily imagine UFOs landing after midnight and finding us out there in the middle of nowhere, with no one around to notice, whisking us off to goodness knows what planet. We had the same misgivings and felt just as susceptible in the pitch black on the Cleveland Hills, when Pauline and I later did our night-time crossings on the Lyke Wake Walk.

Another idiosyncrasy I have about wild camping, is that when you're out in the countryside and the ground you're sleeping on is bumpy or furrowed, then I can quite easily conceive that I'm resting on the buried remains of some long dead Ancient Briton. This I certainly felt like I was doing when we wild camped at the old Roman site of Chew Green on the Pennine Way.

An experienced wild camper we met on the Coast-to-Coast walk suggested that to enable you to decide whether you'd like it or not, you should try it out somewhere familiar first, such as in your home territory. He also claimed that a malt loaf was the best food to take with you. But for me, it would mean having to carry a tub of butter to spread on it.

Personally, rather than isolating myself on some remote moorland ridge and waking up on a morning feeling somewhat unwashed and slightly dazed, I like meeting up with fellow walkers at the various campsites along the trail, and enjoy the camaraderie that can develop.

When it comes to route finding on the Coast-to-Coast walk, Alfred Wainwright's guidebook, together with the way marking, has served us well over the years, and generally helped us to stay on track. The paradox seems to be that other than the basic maps and instructions in your guidebook, the only time you really do need a full-scale map on the walk is when you've gone off-route and are lost. It's therefore good to have them along as backup and fortunately, you can now buy a book of maps covering the whole journey.

A Walk to the Sea

On our first trip, being on a budget, we couldn't afford to purchase OS maps to cover the whole of the walk and had to occasionally rely totally on the instructions in our guidebook. So, when we came to any tricky bits, or were unsure, such as when crossing over the Pennines or finding our way to Kidsty Pike, we always tried to keep other walkers in sight. Sometimes this worked well, and at other times it didn't, such as when the party in front decided to stop for lunch. Using this method, we would also occasionally be led astray.

The trouble is that when you get into another walker's slipstream and let them do the route finding; you stop concentrating yourself on the directions. Then, when there is a problem, and you consult your guidebook, you find that you're out of context and so much more likely to make a mistake.

I've also found that admitting to yourself that you have gone off route is a hard thing to do, especially when you might have to accept that you've just walked for twenty minutes in the wrong direction. But we've discovered that the sooner you take a deep breath and head back to your last known sighting of the correct path, the better.

When you're out on the fells and have a long day ahead of you, even walking half a mile off route requires you to retrace your footsteps, which adds up to you having walked an extra mile. It also means that you've probably added twenty minutes to your overall journey time.

On our first Coast-to-Coast walk, Pauline and I had a real dread of getting lost on the high fells of Lakeland and the Pennines. These places seemed like the wilderness to us. Sometimes the fear that we might have gone off route would come over us, and we'd be silently praying that we'd soon see a footprint, a recognizable landmark, or some fellow walkers to confirm that we were still safely on the trail.

After we'd completed the Coast-to-Coast walk several times the correct way, west to east, just as the Master Fell-wanderer so rightly ordered, we decided to try an east to west crossing. In some ways, the walk seemed easier, except for the climb up to Kidsty Pike, which was horrendous. We were also much more isolated from fellow walkers, as ninety percent of them were doing the walk the proper way.

However, on our final day, when we came down off St Bees Head, it was a lovely warm summer afternoon and holidaymakers from the local caravan park thronged the seafront. The tide was in and covered the beach, so people were sitting in deckchairs, and on towels, all along the promenade. There was a merry chatter of children's voices and the constant wailing of seagulls high above our heads as we made our way down it.

Descending a concrete slipway to reach the sea, we waited for the tide to wet our boots and complete

A Walk to the Sea

the walk. Unlike at Robin Hood's Bay, where we'd usually been ignored by the crowds, as the waves washed over our boots and our pebbles flew far out into the Irish Sea, a cheer went up from the surrounding holidaymakers. Some of them even clapped. We had received recognition from them because they appreciated that we had just walked across England.

A paradox of doing the Coast-to-Coast walk is the expense. Walking for your vacation sounds inexpensive, but when you add up the cost of food, drink, accommodation, and travel to St Bees and back home again, especially if you're Toast-to-Toasting, then it can be quite expensive. Certainly, a lot more than what you'd pay for a cheap package holiday abroad.

To keep costs down, some walkers, when planning the walk, will look at the mileage between the various stages and consider, for example, that it's only nine miles between Rosthwaite and Grasmere, so it's far too early to stop, and they will plan to continue on to Patterdale.

But the truth is, that once you've left Borrowdale, climbed up past Eagle Crag and over Greenup Edge before tediously making your way down through the boggy peat and rocks to Grasmere, then even if you're young and fit, your body will tell you that it feels as though it has already done sufficient work for the day.

It's quite possible to continue on, to climb up Great Tongue, pass Grisedale Tarn and then endure the long, slow descent down to Patterdale. But you're unlikely to enjoy it, certainly not as much as you would if you started this section of the walk fresh the following day.

However, if you're on a budget or time is short, this may well be the way you have to go. But the fewer days you take to complete the walk, the more likely you are to turn it into a trudge.

We've discovered that leaving St Bees on a weekend means that you're likely to be setting off with other walkers who you'll keep meeting up with along the trail. Sometimes you'll catch up with them and walk at the same pace, and at other times you may maintain a distance between you as you wish to be on your own. But when the weather turns nasty on Kidsty Pike, or when crossing over the Pennines, then it is nice to see your fellow walkers ahead, both for company, and for confirming that you're still on route. And if you're feeling unsure or vulnerable, then you can temporarily join one of the walking parties you keep coming across.

When we're out on the Coast-to-Coast walk, we give names to the various parties of walkers we keep meeting up with along the way. This is so that we can refer to them when we see them again on the trail. We usually base the names on the characteristics of the different walkers, and have been known to say,

A Walk to the Sea

"Look, there's the Hats!" or the Romans, or the Sticks, or the Dutch people, or the Green Shorts, or One Man and his dog.

The Dutch Girls told us that they named one group the 'Blister Family' and another the 'Yellow Mats'. I shudder to think what people have called us!

Some of the friendliest walkers we've met on the Coast-to-Coast have been visitors to Britain. It was a German guy who showed me how to fit a gas canister to one of the old-style camping stoves. He came over when he saw my gas hissing out as I tried to change the canister. I'd had the same trouble fitting one at other campsites, but nobody British ever offered to help.

The Coast-to-Coast walk is indeed a strenuous undertaking, some people don't make it. But I have been surprised by how many pensioners attempt it.

On our first walk, two guys in their early seventies, both displaying an array of souvenir mounts of places they'd be to on their walking sticks, backpacked with us most of the way.

A brave brother and sister I communicated with were so keen to get started on the Coast-to-Coast walk that they didn't want to wait for the following summer to do it. So, they backpacked it in November. With the evenings drawing in early, they were faced with very short days and spent long, dark nights freezing in their tent. Most of the facilities along the route were closed, including all of the commercial campsites. But one or two of the camping places were kind to them. Laylands Farm, near Bolton-on-Swale, brought them out some hot water bottles and St Peter, at the campsite in Reeth, gave them the use of a caravan for the night at no extra charge. They survived the experience and completed the walk, but whether they enjoyed it is debatable.

Having taken so much stuff with us on our first Coast-to-Coast walk, which had particularly spoilt day one, I was determined to enjoy every inch of the terrain on our second trip.

Looking around me at the views as I made my way up St Bees Head, I held onto a short wooden rail. Suddenly, I felt a sharp pain in one of my fingers. Examining it, I saw that a long splinter of wood had shot up under my nail. I had to spend the next few miles walking over the cliff top with my head down, not seeing anything as I tried to get it out.

On another trip, we camped for the night at a farm in Shap. Despite it being August, we were so cold in our sleeping bags that something had to be done. I came up with a brainwave which I don't mind sharing with you. I took our two drinking water bottles (a couple of plastic screw-top soft drink bottles) to the farmhouse washroom and filled them with water from the hot tap. Then, with the tops securely fastened, we put them into the bottom of our sleeping bags and soon got warm.

A Walk to the Sea

On our first Coast-to-Coast walk, when we met two air force pilots at the Blue Bell Inn in Ingleby Cross, and they told us that they had done the walk four times, we wondered whether they were quite right in the head and stared at them in total disbelief.

There we were, desperate to make it just once across this country to Robin Hood's Bay, and these guys were actually on their fifth crossing. Surely nobody would want to do this walk more than once? I mean, why would they?

But when you've dipped your feet in the sea at Robin Hood's Bay, thrown the pebble you picked up off the beach at St Bees, had your pint in the Bay Hotel and returned home. Then, perhaps a week, a fortnight, a month or even a year or two later, the idea might just enter your head. Well, why not a second crossing, you enjoyed it the first time!

You may even try to justify it to yourself by suggesting an east to west crossing this time. Or try to appease the thought by looking for an alternative walk. After all, you don't want to become a sheep.

So, you will walk the West Highland Way, the Dales Way, the Cleveland Way, the Cumbrian Way, the Great Glen Way and all sorts of bespoke walks in the Lakes. And in a moment of madness, you may even succumb to walking the Pennine Way. But somehow, for some, that itch just won't go away.

There is something about the Coast-to-Coast that other walks don't seem to provide. It gives you the opportunity to get off the planet for two weeks and to disappear from the real world.

Small perks at the end of a day's journey become luxuries. An iced bun, a banana or the ultimate of a bag of hot potato chips, things we take for granted in our everyday lives, suddenly take on greater significance. It provides the chance to be yourself, to be whatever you want to be for a fortnight. Wear a bandanna, or a silly hat, or a tee-shirt with some outrageous slogan on it.

Of course, when the walk begins, and the mileage and blisters kick in and when you're cussing your way up the 'small hill' of Dent, the romanticism of the Coast-to-Coast walk may pale a little. But the mileage will finish, the hills will flatten, and the blisters will heal. If I had been rich enough not to have to work, I would have made an annual two-week crossing of England part of my normal life.

I believe that you begin to understand the reasons why you do the Coast-to-Coast walk a few days after you've arrived back home. When the pain of sore feet and ladened backs, and the memories of rain-soaked days and other discomforts have faded. And you once again come face-to-face with the real world.

Sadly, Alfred Wainwright was so correct when he said that you should enjoy your walking while there is still time. And I guess that means while you can still manage it. It's only when you get older that you start to realise the number of metaphorical Coast-to-

A Walk to the Sea

Coast walks still possible to you are becoming fewer with each passing year.

We've met people on the walk who waited for retirement before attempting it. Maybe only then did they have enough free time available. But for everyone, walks like this will eventually become no longer feasible, and perhaps the best we'll be able to do are just snatches of them.

Coming down Great Tongue, near Grasmere, on the Coast-to-Coast walk a few years ago, we came across two eighty-year-olds, who were slowly making their way up. As we passed by them, we spoke, and they told us that once a week they use their bus passes to come into the Lakes from Lancashire to climb a fell. This allows them just enough time to get so far up and back down again before catching the bus home. They may no longer be able to manage the whole fell, but can still relive memories from their younger days.

These weren't the oldest people we've met out there in the wild. On another walk, the West Highland Way, after leaving the Bridge of Ochy, we had to climb over some high fells at the edge of Rannoch Moor before coming down into Glencoe. There were still patches of snow on the tops and Pauline and I were feeling rather apprehensive, as we were up there all alone. Eventually, the rough path began to descend and as it turned a corner, we came across an old couple who were nonchalantly sitting on a boulder in the middle of nowhere, eating their sandwiches. They both looked about ninety and, chatting away to each other, seemed totally unconcerned or fazed by their austere surroundings. Passing by them, we felt quite guilty for having been worried.

Walking with Pauline over hill and dale for over twenty-five years, I only recently discovered that her innate fear of thunder and lightning had always made her apprehensive about the possibility of it happening while we were out there on the trail.

This fear had been reinforced early on in our walks when we were caught out in an electric storm on the Pennine Way and were miles from anywhere.

The lightening that day had bounced off the ground all around us, and there was simply nowhere to hide as we made our way through a series of soaking wet peat groughs. The storms continued throughout the whole of that walk, and we often came across sheep who'd been struck by lightning and were lying rigid in the fields. On one occasion, with the lightning flashing, we even had to shelter in an old barn with a long dead animal at our feet. Pauline, therefore, deserves much praise for overcoming her demons and walking with me.

The Coast-to-Coast is a wonderful walk, which has provided us with so many great, companionable adventures over the years. It has allowed us in these modern times to escape from the real world and get

A Walk to the Sea

away from it all for a while. It has given us the freedom to be out there, caring about nothing but walking safely from one place to another.

On these adventures, I've dressed how I've wanted, worn a hippie hat and a bandana in my sixties, and unlike on the city streets, nobody appears to notice or even care. Indeed, the walk has provided me with a taste of something I last felt as a teenager during those halcyon days of youth, when anything seems possible.

We therefore owe a debt to Alfred Wainwright for allowing us to share his 'Great Adventure'.

If you decide to do the walk, the range of emotions you will experience while out there will be many, so enjoy. Remember that you will be following in Wainwright's footsteps, our footsteps, and those of thousands of other walkers, every step of the way.

Printed in Great Britain
by Amazon